Language, Society and Power

'*Language, Society and* ... ...es ... o-date view ... .n clear explanations and examples. Teachers of A-Level English Langua⁻ ... ...ide range of stimulating approaches to language issues.'
    John Keen, *University of Manch ster and P ... ... NEAB A-Level English Language*

'The book represents a fresh and sound approach to key topics in sociolinguistics ... clearly focused on the interplay between language, society and power. It is written in a lively, easy-to-read style and it contains a wealth of well-chosen topical examples ... of the kind that st ... readily relate to.'
    Charlotte Hoffmann, *University of Sheffield*

This is the book for anyone who has ever wondered how language influences thought, how language impacts on our daily life, and how power is negotiated, achieved and perpetuated through language.

Written in a lively and accessible way, with examples drawn from everyday life, *Language, Society and Power* looks at language use in politics and the media; differences in language use according to gender, ethnicity, age and class; how language affects and constructs our identities; and the significance of our attitudes towards language use and our notions of correctness.

Language, Society and Power brings together a wide range of topics showing the links between them and explaining fundamental theories about connections between language, thought and power.

Features include:

- exercises to encourage students to investigate ideas for themselves
- end of chapter summaries
- a glossary of key terms

A highly interdisciplinary textbook which shows the centrality of language across the humanities, *Language, Society and Power* is an essential introductory text for students of English language and linguistics from A-level upwards, and of great relevance to students of media, communication, cultural studies, sociology and psychology.

The book grew out of a very popular course taught for many years by the authors in the English Language and Linguistics Programme at Roehampton Institute London. Shân Wareing recently moved to the University of Wales College, Newport where she is Head of Learning Development. Previous publications include *Patterns in Language* (1998) by Shân Wareing and Joanna Thornborrow, *Beginning Syntax* (1993) by Linda Thomas, and *Child Language* (2nd edn 1999) by Jean Stilwell Peccei.

Language, Society and Power

An introduction

Edited by Linda Thomas
and Shân Wareing

LONDON AND NEW YORK

First published 1999
by Routledge
11 New Fetter Lane, London EC4P 4EE

Simultaneously published in the USA
and Canada
by Routledge
29 West 35th Street, New York,
NY 10001

*Routledge is an imprint of the
Taylor & Francis Group*

© 1999 Linda Thomas, Shân Wareing, Jean
Stilwell Peccei, Joanna Thornborrow, Ishtla
Singh, Jason Jones

Typeset in Times and Futura by
J&L Composition Ltd, Filey, North Yorkshire
Printed and bound in Great Britain by
TJ International Ltd, Padstow, Cornwall

*British Library Cataloguing in
Publication Data*
A catalogue record for this book is
available from the British Library

*Library of Congress Cataloging in
Publication Data*
Language, society and power/Linda Thomas
... [et al].].
    p. cm.
  1. Sociolinguistics.   2. English language–
Social aspects.   I. Thomas, Linda.
P40.L2998   1999   98-51931
306.4–dc21   CIP

ISBN 0–415–18744–3 (hbk)
ISBN 0–415–18745–1 (pbk)

For Debbie and Jen

Contents

3 Language and politics 31
Jason Jones and Shân Wareing

4 Language and the media 49
Joanna Thornborrow

5 Language and gender 65
Shân Wareing

9 Language and identity 135
Joanna Thornborrow

10 The standard English debate 151
Linda Thomas

Figures

Newspapers

During the course of our discussions, reference is made to and data are taken from British and American newspapers and magazines. A list of these publications is given below:

Dail Mail	UK national daily newspaper
Daily Star	UK national daily newspaper
The Daily Telegraph	UK national daily newspaper
Evening Standard	London daily newspaper
Glasgow Herald	Scottish daily newspaper
The Guardian	UK national daily newspaper
The Guardian Weekend	Supplement to Saturday's edition of *The Guardian*
The Independent	UK national daily newspaper
National Enquirer	US weekly tabloid news magazine
News of the World	UK national Sunday newspaper
The Observer	UK national Sunday newspaper
Observer Review	Supplement to *The Observer*
The Psychologist	Monthly members magazine for the British Psychological Society
The Sunday Telegraph	UK national Sunday newspaper
The Sunday Times	UK national Sunday newspaper
THES (The Times Higher Education Supplement)	UK national weekly newspaper
Time Out	London weekly magazine
The Times	UK national daily newspaper
The Times Weekend	Supplement to Saturday's edition of *The Times*
USA Today	US national daily newspaper
Washington Post	Washington DC daily newspaper

Contributors

Jason Jones is Lecturer in English Literature and Linguistics at Roehampton Institute, London. His main research interests are in dialectology and dialectal erosion and change, specialising in the dialects of the southwest of England.

Jean Stilwell Peccei's teaching specialities are language acquisition and psycholinguistics. She is the author of two books in the Routledge Learning Workbooks Series: *Child Language* (2nd edn, 1999) and *Pragmatics* (forthcoming).

Ishtla Singh is Lecturer in English Language and Linguistics at Roehampton Institute, London. Particular areas of interest include historical linguistics, pidgins and creoles and issues of language planning in creole-speaking territories.

Joanna Thornborrow is Senior Lecturer in English Language and Linguistics at Roehampton Institute, London. Her research interests are in discourse analysis and stylistics, with a particular focus on language in the media and institutional talk. She is co-author with Shân Wareing of *Patterns in Language: an introduction to language and literary style* (1998).

Linda Thomas is Principal Lecturer in English Language and Linguistics at Roehampton Institute, London. Her main interests are in sociolinguistics, variation in English grammar, and the teaching of English language in the national curriculum and in Initial Teacher Training. She is author of *Beginning Syntax* (1993).

Shân Wareing is Head of Learning Development at University of Wales College, Newport, having worked at Roehampton Institute London with the rest of the team as a lecturer in English Language and Linguistics and in Education Development. She is co-author with Joanna Thornborrow of *Patterns in Language: an introduction to language and literary style* (1998).

Preface

This book is based on a course of the same name that runs in the English Language and Linguistics Programme at Roehampton Institute London, and on which all the authors have taught. It began life as *Language, Power, Politics and Sexuality*, a short (five week) introduction to language issues for students studying literature. Over the years the course has grown as interest in language study has grown, and it is now an introductory course for students studying language and linguistics, whilst continuing in popularity with students of literature. Many of the students taking the course are combining their studies with subjects such as sociology, media studies, women's studies, education, and history, where they find the issues raised are also relevant.

In preparing this book, we have assumed no prior knowledge of linguistics. We hope that students taking courses on the social and political dimensions of language use will find this a useful foundation text. Students of disciplines that include the study of language use, discourse and ideology, power relations, education, the rights of minority groups and equal opportunities, should also find this a helpful text. Learners of English may find this a useful route to a better understanding of language use. Since we see language use as being central to many, or most, human activities, we hope that students studying apparently unrelated disciplines may also find it helpful to have a book which covers the range of issues we deal with here. And we have tried to make the text appropriate and interesting for the general reader.

The ideas covered in this book have been explored and developed with groups of students since the early 1980s. They are presented here as eleven topics, currently covered in a modular course on a week-by-week basis. Although they may look it, the topics are not discrete, but have overlapping themes and common threads which we have tried to bring out. Nor are they exclusive. As you read you may well think of other areas of language use which are worthy of investigation or consideration, such as the relationship between language and health, or language and the law. Issues like these are not omitted because we think that they are unimportant, but because in a book of this length there is not space to cover everything. We hope what we have covered will assist your thinking about the relationship between language and the different dimensions of the societies in which we live.

The authors have taught the course from which this book was generated as a team. We felt that as a group we shared common values both about the topics we taught and our approach to teaching, and that this provided us with a solid foundation for writing this book also as a team. We distributed the topics amongst the six of us, according to our areas of special interest, and met regularly to review the drafts of our chapters and to discuss revisions. Our aim was to produce a coherent text that still reflected the ideas and writing styles of individual team members. To some extent, the different 'voices' of the authors should still be apparent.

Amongst other decisions we had to make as a team of authors, we had to decide on how we would use pronouns such as *I*, *we* and *you*. We could, for example, have decided to write impersonally, and avoid using personal pronouns as much as possible, which is quite common in academic writing. We had to decide if we should refer to ourselves in the chapters as *I* (the individual writing the chapter) or *we* (the team of writers). We also had to decide whether we should use *you* to address our readers. The conventional, impersonal academic style is often criticised by people with an interest in the social and political functions of language because, as is discussed in Chapter 3, it can be used to make ideas seem less accessible than they need be, and to increase the apparent status of the writers by making them seem 'cleverer' than the readers. In the end, we felt the most honest and sensible thing to do would be to use *we* to refer to the team of authors, to acknowledge the input we have all had in each others' thinking and writing, but to use *I* if we write about our personal experiences. We have addressed you the readers as *you*. Chapter 3 considers the political implication of pronoun use in more detail.

Each chapter of this book deals with a different area of language, although there are connections between many of the chapter topics. We designed the book so that it can be read from cover to cover as a continuous text, but also so that individual chapters can stand alone and be read in their own right. We divided chapters into subsections, partly to indicate the structure clearly with subtitles, partly to help you find the sections you need to read if you don't need to read the whole chapter.

The first chapter considers the question 'what is language?', and raises some of the underlying questions and ideas you should bear in mind throughout the book. The next three chapters (Chapters 2 to 4) all concentrate on the ideological properties of language, and how language can be used to affect people's hopes, fears, voting patterns and consumer decisions. Chapter 2 is concerned with the connections between language, thought and representation. It considers the extent to which language can be said to shape our view of the world, whether it is possible to have a worldview before learning language, or to separate worldview from language. Chapter 3 moves on from the conclusions of Chapter 2 to consider whether, and how, language can be used in politics, and in other fields, to persuade people of a point of view, and how language can make some attitudes appear 'normal' and 'natural', while making others seem 'illogical' or just 'wrong'. Chapter 4 considers how language is used, and to what effects, in newspapers, television and other media, in news reporting, advertising, and entertainment.

Each of the subsequent three chapters (Chapters 5 to 7) deals with language use as it is connected with particular subgroups of people within the population. The terms or 'labels' that can be or are applied to members of those groups, and the effect of those labels, are considered. The chapters also look at how members of those groups use language in distinctive ways. Chapter 5 is concerned with language and gender, Chapter 6 deals with language and ethnicity and Chapter 7 deals with language and age. Chapter 8 considers how a further set of subgroup divisions affect language use, focusing on social class.

The final three chapters (Chapters 9 to 11) are concerned with attitudes towards language, and the relationship between language and identity. Chapter 9 deals with language and social identity, Chapter 10 deals with the debates around standard English, and Chapter 11 provides a conclusion to the whole book, giving an overview of attitudes towards language.

Throughout the book we will be concentrating on the English language, although we will occasionally use another language to illustrate a particular point. The main varieties of English we'll be looking at will be British and American English.

There is a glossary of terms with brief explanations at the back of the book. Words which appear in the glossary are printed in bold the first time they occur in a chapter. You will also find at the end of each chapter recommended further reading which you can follow up if you want to learn more about a topic. If you want to check whether a topic is covered in this book, and where, the index at the back gives page numbers.

We have included activities throughout the text. Some will ask you to reflect on your own use of, or feelings about, language. Some will ask you to talk to other people, to elicit their language use or thoughts on certain issues. Some will require you to collect data from other sources around you, such as the newspapers or television. Some you will be able to do alone, and some need group discussion. One of the main reasons we have included activities is that we believe that the ideas we are discussing in this book really come alive when you begin to look for them in the language which goes on around you. We have seen students' attitudes change from mild interest, or even a lack of interest, to absolute fascination when they have started to investigate language use for themselves.

If the ideas we have presented here are ones you have come across before, we hope we have presented them in such a way as to provoke further thought, or make connections you hadn't previously made. If you haven't thought about some of the ideas we raise here before, we hope that you also find them exciting and spend the rest of your life listening to what people say, reading newspapers, and watching television commercials, differently.

Acknowledgements

We would like to thank the following people for their contributions: Deborah Cameron and Jennifer Coates who designed the original course, who have given us advice on writing over the years, and to whom this book is dedicated. We hope that both the current course and this text accurately represent their original aims and ideals. We are also indebted to the students who have taken Roehampton Institute's 'Language, Society and Power' course, in its various manifestations, for their interest and excitement, for the opportunity to test our ideas, for the feedback they have given us and the data they have found for us. We would in particular like to thank two of these students, Su and Louise, who read and commented on the draft manuscript. We also thank Routledge's anonymous readers, who gave us useful and encouraging advice; Jennifer Coates for editing advice; Doris Stilwell and Sabina Chorley, who helped us find some of the newspaper data; Louisa Semlyen and Miranda Filbee, our editors at Routledge, for all their work on our behalf; Patrick Thomas and Martin Chorley for not minding too much the work we did at the weekends. The team would like to thank Jean Stilwell Peccei for preparing the glossary.

The authors and publisher would like to thank the following for permission to reproduce copyright material: Lines from *Miss Smilla's Feeling for Snow* first published by Munksgaard/Rosinante in 1992, and in Great Britain by Harvill in 1993. Copyright © Peter Høeg and Munksgaard, 1992, and in the English translation © Farrar, Straus & Giroux Inc. and The Harvill Press, 1993. Reproduced by permission of The Harvill Press. Excerpts, 'The guide', 'A massive car bomb...' and 'the newspaper claimed', from *The Guardian* reproduced by permission of the Guardian Media Group plc. Excerpts from *Language, Thought and Reality: selected writing of Benjamin Lee Whorf*, edited by John B. Carroll, reproduced by permission of the editor and the MIT Press. Extracts from articles by John Rae and Victor Lewis Smith from the *Evening Standard* are reproduced by permission of the *Evening Standard*. Extracts from articles by Peter McKay, Maggie O'Riordan and Linda Lee Potter from *The Daily Mail* are reproduced by permission of *The Daily Mail*/Solo Syndication Ltd. Quote from the article 'Yorkshire Water makes a pud of the English Language' published 31 January 1997 in *The Daily Telegraph* is reproduced by permission of the Telegraph Group Limited. © Telegraph Group Limited, London, 1997. Extracts from articles by David Walker and Emma Cook from *The Independent* and the *Independent on Sunday* respectively are reproduced by permission of authors and *The Independent/Independent on Sunday*. The extract from Beryl Goldsmith's article in *The Sunday Telegraph* (26 January, 1997) is reproduced by permission of the author.

While the authors and publisher have made every effort to contact copyright holders of the material used in this volume, they would be happy to hear from anyone they were unable to contact.

Chapter 1

What is language and what does it do?

Shân Wareing

1.1 Introduction

This chapter provides a context for the topics discussed in the rest of the book, by explaining our approach to the study of language, and positioning this approach in relation to other ways of thinking about language. First, the chapter considers why language is a phenomenon worthy of study; using an example of a letter to a newspaper, the ways in which language, society and power might be related are considered. Second, the chapter considers the nature of language, and how its forms (i.e. its manifestations as spoken or written words, or as signs in sign language) and functions (i.e. what people use language for) may be described and categorised. The chapter then explores some of the **variations** found in language systems, and the social meanings which are attributed to different languages, **dialects** and **accents**. Fourth, the concept of power is introduced, with a definition and discussion of where in society power is located. The chapter concludes with a discussion of 'political correctness', focusing as an example on the debates on the terminology associated with disability.

1.2 Why study language?

People find the subject of language interesting and worth studying for many different reasons. Language can, for example, be used as a way of finding out more about:

- how our brains work, from investigating how children learn language, or how damage to our brains results in certain kind of language disorders (psycholinguistics);
- how to learn and to teach different languages (applied linguistics);
- the relationship between meaning, language and perception (philosophy);
- the role of language in different cultures (anthropology);
- the styles of language used in literature (stylistics);
- the different **varieties** of language people use, and why there are linguistic differences between different groups (sociolinguistics);
- how to make computers more sophisticated (artificial intelligence).

Many of these areas overlap, and the topics discussed in this book employ ideas and methods from more than one area listed above.

Frequently, people who are not linguists are interested in language too. To test the truth of this statement, you only have to look at the letters pages of newspapers and count the number of letters printed per week which are on language-related issues. The following letter appeared in *The Daily Telegraph* (7 September, 1997). It refers to an earlier letter published in the same newspaper, which appears to have been a complaint about the language used in Ofsted reports on schools and pupils. (Ofsted is the organisation responsible for monitoring standards in schools in the UK: OFfice of STandards in EDucation.)

Ofstedspeak

Lucinda Bredin's concern about the language of Ofsted reports (Review, August 24) is justified. The mysterious world of Ofstedspeak can be difficult to penetrate.

The word "satisfactory" which smacks of mediocrity, is discouraged by Ofsted. The word "sound" is encouraged instead.

The bright and shining ones at Ofsted have also given the thumbs down [to] the word "ability".[1] Inspectors are asked not to refer to pupils' different levels of ability. They must instead write about levels of attainment, meaning what pupils can do in relation to what might be expected of them.

That happily relieves everyone of having to say of any child that he or she lacks ability. Poor attainment may be the result of poor teaching, or inappropriate curriculum or, come to that, Government policy.

As the second wave of inspections takes place, reports will be written in a different language from before. In particular, where a first wave report has said that pupils are performing well in relation to their ability, that will be out of order in a second wave report.

There is real danger that Ofsted language will become so arcane as to be unintelligible to ordinary citizens.

Peter Dawson
Ofsted registered inspector
Derby

This letter actually picks up on many of the issues to do with language which we will be dealing with in this book. First of all, there is the concept of whether what we call things does matter, and whether it is a worthy topic of debate. The fact this letter was written at all suggests that is does matter, and that it is a topic worth debating.

A second language issue raised by this letter is the use of jargon; jargon can seem impenetrable to anyone outside a small group of 'those in the know', as Peter Dawson, the letter writer, states in his first and final sentences. If you are not familiar with the **discourse** of the British school education system, you will probably feel that the word *Ofsted* itself fits into this category.

Third, *Ofstedspeak* as a term is interesting in its own right. It has been coined by analogy with **Newspeak**, the form of English invented by George Orwell in his novel *Nineteen Eighty-Four*. This illustrates another point about language: human beings use language creatively and make up new words which can nevertheless be understood by others who are familiar with the culture in which the new word was developed. If you have read *Nineteen Eighty-Four*, you may perceive a reference to Orwell's dystopian nightmare in the title of the letter. You might feel reminded of the potentially sinister use of language to meet the political goals of those in power, suggested by parallel between the term *Ofstedspeak* and *Newspeak*; this is a fourth issue about language raised by this letter.

A fifth point, related to the fourth, is the relationship between language and reality. When we assess someone, do we actually measure their ability, or only their attainment (i.e. do we measure what they are inherently capable of, or only what they achieved on a particular day under particular circumstances)? Peter Dawson obviously thinks that we can actually test ability, and the use of the word *attainment* is a fudge, an attempt to use **euphemism** to cover up an unpleasant truth with a 'prettier' word. On the other hand, I prefer the word *attainment* because I agree with Ofsted that only attainment can be measured, and that ability cannot be measured. If the letter writer and I were to continue this debate, we would be arguing not just about words but our view of education and our beliefs about the nature of human beings. Words can signal strongly our attitudes to fundamental things; debates that may appear to be about words can actually be about values and worldview.

It is not only which word more accurately reflects my worldview, or Peter Dawson's worldview, which matters here. Which word is chosen may also affect people's perception of the world, and of themselves (a sixth language issue raised by the letter). A pupil who does badly at school because of poor teaching, or an inappropriate curriculum, or government policy, may want to return to learning later in life. Whether or not they do so may well be influenced by whether they thought their previous lack of success in education was due to low ability (and therefore they may feel that they are never likely to improve) or just to low attainment (in which case, under different circumstances, they may feel they would do much better).

Finally, the letter also illustrates the important matter of who gets to decide how language is used. 'The bright and shining ones at Ofsted' have made a decision about how reports will be written (i.e. using the word *sound* rather than *satisfactory* and the word *attainment* rather than *ability*). Peter Dawson disagrees with this usage and has written to a national paper to complain about it. However, as a registered inspector for Ofsted, he is likely to have to use these terms, despite his objections, if he wishes to stay in his job. Moreover, the children whose performances are going to be categorised either under the term *attainment* or under the term *ability* do not have any say at all in the discussion about which term is used.

These aspects of language, and in particular the last mentioned (the extent to which language reflects and creates our perception of the world, and who makes decisions about what is appropriate language use) are major concerns of this book.

ACTIVITY 1.1

Below are two suggestions for straightforward 'fieldwork' tasks you could carry out if you are interested in finding out more about attitudes to language held in the society around you.

1 Check the letters page of two or more newspapers for a period of time such as two weeks or a month. How many letters about language use appear? Are there common themes in the comments the letter writers make? Do you agree with the arguments they put forward?
2 Keep a mental or a written note of the references people make to language use. Particularly record any comments people make that are regretful or angry about changing language use. Do you agree with the sentiments expressed? If so, why? If not, why not?

1.3 What is language?

Having discussed what you can expect from this book, let's take a closer look at some of the main themes and ideas we'll be dealing with. The first of these is what language actually is. There are several different ways of thinking about language; which way you think about it depends on which aspect of language you are interested in.

1.3.1 Language: a system

One of the obvious ways of thinking about language is as a systematic way of combining smaller units into larger units for the purpose of communication. For example, we combine the sounds of our language (**phonemes**) to form words (**lexical items**) according to the 'rules' of the language(s) we speak. Those lexical items can be combined to make grammatical structures, again according to the **syntactic** 'rules' of our language(s). Language is essentially a rule-governed system of this kind, but there are other ways of thinking about how language works and what we do with it, and it is those which we are concentrating on in this book.

For example, we usually assume that we use language to say what we mean. However, the processes by which we create 'meaning' are actually very complicated indeed, so we're going to start with what's called a 'model' of meaning. A model is a way of thinking that will help us get started on an idea but which may soon prove to be too simple to be really accurate, at which point we will have make it more complicated!

One model for explaining meaning is to assume that every group of sounds or letters which make up a word has a one-to-one relationship with a meaning. And for every meaning you can think of, there is a corresponding group of sounds (a spoken word) and letters (a written word).

When describing this way of thinking about language, traffic lights are often used as a comparison. For the meaning *stop* we have a red traffic light. For the meaning *go* we use a green traffic light. In the UK, red and amber lights showing together mean that you should stop, but that the next signal to follow will be green for *go*. An amber light on its own tells you to *stop*, and that the next light to show will be the red one on its own. The fact that the lights can only show in certain sequences and combinations is a bit like the syntax which governs word order in sentences, and permits the sequence:

today I went swimming

but not the following sequence (an asterisk* before a phrase denotes that the expression is not one which speakers of that language will accept as well-formed):

*went today swimming I

There are several limitations linked to thinking about language as a system like traffic lights. First, there would only be one signal (group of letters or sounds) for every meaning. If this were the case, Peter Dawson would not be able to disagree with Ofsted about the use of *satisfactory* versus *sound* (where clearly there is some overlap in meaning). Second, there would be a limited number of meanings and signals available. Admittedly we could use a green and amber combination, but what would it mean? You would know if you had been informed already, but what would you do if you were driving along and suddenly came to a traffic light showing amber and green? You might well assume that the lights had malfunctioned, rather than that a new message was being communicated.

1.3.2 Language: the potential to create new meanings

One of the reasons why language is actually a far more complicated entity than traffic lights is that we can use it to create new meanings. Here are some expressions which illustrate language being used creatively to express new meanings:

> *Over-processed hair*
> Doreen had an absolute *mare*
> *unleaving*
> *Mcjobs*
> *Sweatshirting*

These are all expressions which I can remember hearing or seeing for the first time, but which I did not have any trouble understanding.[2]

Some of these expressions may be ones you've heard before or use yourself. Some of them may strike you as outdated already. It's difficult to think of examples of language being used creatively, because successful new uses get adopted very quickly and become just a normal part of everyday language. However, what you can probably still see is that words can be used in new ways to

---

ACTIVITY 1.2

3   List any expressions you recently heard or started to use for the first time. Can you remember how you felt about using them for the first time? If you are interested in pursuing this area further, ask people of a variety of ages if they are aware of new expressions coming into use. You could compile a list of expressions based on their answers and, if you have the time available, use the list as the basis of a larger survey to find out how many people are already using these expressions, and whether there's a pattern to who uses them and who doesn't.

---

mean new things, and can be instantly understood by people who have never come across that word before. This ability is one of the things that sets human language apart from the kind of communication that goes on, for example, between birds, which can only convey a limited range of messages.

1.3.3 Language: multiple functions

Another important dimension of language is the very different purposes we use language for all the time. In the course of a day you will probably use language referentially, affectively, aesthetically, and phatically. Below are some examples to illustrate these different ways of using language.

You use language referentially when you say 'put that bunch of flowers on the table'. Your instruction is referential because it gives information about what you want placed (the flowers) and where you want them placed (on the table). This aspect of language, its ability to communicate information, is very important. Examples of contexts where this aspect of language is very obvious are: pilots discussing flight paths with air traffic control; recipes; assembly instructions with self-assembly furniture; school textbooks; directions on how to get to a friend's house. In all these cases, accurate, non-ambiguous information will be sought as a priority.

However, the transmission of information is certainly not the only reason we use language, and there are many linguistic choices we make every day which are not a consequence of information transmission at all. For example, you could use any of the utterances (a) to (e) below and convey the same factual information. But by selecting one as appropriate and not another, you would be exploiting the affective aspect of language and showing yourself to be sensitive to the power or social relationship between you and the person you are addressing.

(a) Put that bunch of flowers on the table.
(b) Please put that bunch of flowers on the table.
(c) I wonder if you'd mind putting that bunch of flowers on the table.
(d) If you wouldn't mind awfully, do you think you might put that bunch of flowers on the table.
(e) For goodness' sake, just put that ****ing bunch of flowers on the table!

On the other hand, as you arranged the flowers, you might say utterance (f) or (g):

(f) Flowers like flames from bright fields ...
(g) Rose rows; canoe canoe?

In this case you wouldn't be trying to give anyone information either. You would be exploiting the ability of language to give us pleasure by its sounds and rhythms and by play with meanings: its aesthetic properties.

If later in the day someone came in and said 'Oh lovely flowers' and you said 'thanks', you would both be exploiting the phatic properties of language. This is the everyday usage of language as 'social lubrication'. No important information is being exchanged, but you are both indicating that you are willing to talk to one another, are pleased to see one another, and so on.

In this book, we're largely concerned with the first two functions of language: its referential function and its affective impact. These two functions are the ones most clearly associated with power. The referential function is the one associated with what objects and ideas are called and how events are described (i.e. how we represent the world around us and the effects of those **representations** on the way we think, as the letter above about the language of Ofsted reports highlighted). The affective function of language is concerned with who is 'allowed' to say what to whom, which is deeply tied up with power and social status. For example, saying 'I think it's time you washed your hair' would be an acceptable comment from a parent to a young child, but would not usually be acceptable from an employee to their boss!

1.3.4 Language diversity

Let's focus on another aspect of language now: the aspect of who speaks what language, and what variety of that language they speak.

If you travel to France, you probably expect to be spoken to in French. Language boundaries and national boundaries do often coincide, but of course the picture is a lot more complicated than that. In lots of places which are not England or France, English or French is spoken (for example, in India, Canada, and in many African countries). Moreover, in each different country, different versions of English or French are spoken. Indian English is different in some of its grammatical structures from British English, for example.

Languages do not only vary between countries, however. They also vary within countries. Schools in large cities are often attended by children who speak many different languages. And not only are many different languages spoken within primarily English-speaking countries like Britain and the US: there is also a great deal of variation within English itself. Chapter 10 looks at variation within English in more detail.

People often have very strong attitudes towards different languages and different varieties of language. Consider this letter from *The Guardian* (20 September, 1997), written after the people of Scotland and Wales had voted on whether to have separate elected governing bodies from the main UK government:

> Having survived the nail-biting Wales referendum results on TV, I hope and pray that as soon as their assembly is set up, it will be made illegal to speak the unintelligent [sic][3] gibberish called Welsh outside Wales.
>
> Malcolm Everett
> Brighton
> East Sussex

It is not clear from the letter how seriously the writer intended his point to be taken. *Gibberish*, however, is a strong word to use about other people's language and suggests how deeply prejudices can go against language, against other cultures and ultimately, against other people. Clearly, no language is *gibberish* to those who speak it, and equally, no language, including English, makes sense to a non-speaker.

Who speaks which language (or which variety of a particular language) and the attitudes of people towards that language (or language variety), are further issues inherently connected to the concepts of power and society. An important area we'll be dealing with in this book is the link between the language a person uses, their idea of their own identity, and the conclusions other people may make about their identity (see Chapter 9).

To conclude this part of the chapter: language is a system, or rather a set of systems (a system of sounds, a system of grammar, a system of meaning); variations in usage are often systematic as well. Within these systems, there is scope for creativity and invention. How an individual uses the systems available to them varies according to who the speaker is, how they perceive themselves, and what identity they want to project. Language use also varies according to the situation, whether it's public or private, formal or informal, who is being addressed, and who might be able to overhear. Integral to these choices we make about language use is the dimension of power, and that will be discussed next.

1.4 Power and society

Power is quite an abstract concept, but an infinitely important influence on our lives. Moore and Hendry (1982) describe it as:

> ... the force in society that gets things done, and by studying it, we can identify who controls what, and for whose benefit.
>
> (1982: 127)

One way we see power at work in society is through politics. By means of our vote, in a democracy, we give politicians the right to make laws on our behalf. If we break those laws, society has the power to punish us. 'Political power' controls many aspects of our lives: how much we pay in taxes, what our health care and education is like, how fast we can drive, what kinds of drugs are available to us and many other areas and activities. This power is enforced through individuals such as police officers, judges and prison officers, whose jobs give them the right to affect other people's lives. Other people who have power as a consequence of their roles include teachers, parents and employers. We can classify this kind of power as 'personal power'. Finally, some social groups have more or less power than others. The poor, the disabled, ethnic minorities and women are all groups which may find themselves having lower social status, fewer economic resources, and being discriminated against. Typically, the people with most 'social group power' are white, wealthy and male. This is not to say that all white middle class men are more powerful than all people from other social groups, but white people, wealthy people, and men are disproportionately represented in positions of power.

ACTIVITY 1.3

---

4   This is a topic for debate, if you are studying in a group: how is your life influenced by political, personal and social group power?

An obvious question to raise at this point is 'how are power and language related?' Power is often demonstrated through language; it is also actually achieved or 'done' through language. For example, political power exists by means of language, through speeches, debates, through the rules of who may speak and how debates are to be conducted. Laws are written and discussed in language, and individuals give orders through language.

It isn't just in the public sphere that power is 'done' through language. For example, parents often talk to small children in a way which makes quite clear the power relationship between parent and child (see Chapter 7 for more on this). The way the parent talks to the child is partly what creates the power dynamic between them, reinforcing the other power differences (parents have more physical, legal and economic power than their young children, for example). As people grow up and enter young adulthood (or even middle age!), they sometimes find that their parents still use some of the same features of language as they did when their offspring were very young, recreating and affirming the original power relationship.

Moreover, we learn about the world, about how to behave and what to value, through language. Language often serves the interests of dominant social groups, usually because these are the groups who have the most control over it: politicians and lawyers, owners of international media conglomerates, and other influential, high-profile figures. Consequently, the oppression of those with less power, and less access to the media and the production of written records, can seem 'natural', 'normal' or even invisible. Consider the expression 'Christopher Columbus discovered America', which has been a common way to describe the voyage of 1492. This represents the event from the perspective of the colonial powers of Europe. To the indigenous people of America, the arrival of Christopher Columbus was not the 'discovery' of their country but the beginning of a long-lasting, far-reaching process of loss of independence. However, until recently, only the version of events which presented the perspective of the more powerful group was to be found in history books. Thus language reflected the 'truth' of the more dominant group, and largely hid the 'truth' of the less dominant group. The use of the word *discovered* in this context might seem 'natural' to you, until you consider its implications and the power dynamics at work.

In this book, we are interested in opening up the interaction of language and power for scrutiny. Sometimes you may have a sense of powerlessness in a conversation which makes you resentful. Sometimes you may look at an advertisement which tacitly assumes a set of values which you strongly reject, and yet is successfully selling a product worldwide. What are the linguistic mechanisms at work? Is it possible for individuals to choose to use language differently and, by so doing, create a different kind of society?

This question is at the heart of campaigns to change the language used to refer to minority groups. Language reform has been around for a long time: it was very influential in the eighteenth century, for example. In the 1980s, campaigns to change language use attracted considerable media attention and the term 'political correctness' (or PC) was and still is used to describe such campaigns. The term 'PC' has an interesting history. According to Cameron (1995), although it was probably first used in a straightforward way, in the sense of political actions which the speaker approved of, it increasingly took on an ironic sense and was used amongst people active on the political left as a self-mocking joke to describe the extreme and unrelenting standards of behaviour of some of their fellow activists. In this sense it was directed at those who were overly pious or 'holier-than-thou'. While 'politically correct' was used in this ironic sense, to be politically 'incorrect' was to mean 'something like "I am committed to leftist causes, but not humourless or doctrinaire about it"' (Cameron, 1995: 122). The term 'political correctness' was then appropriated by the political right as a slur against *all* left wing activity. This, as Cameron points out, leaves those on the political left in a difficult position. How, for instance, do they answer the question 'Are you politically correct?' when they're not sure if the answer 'Yes' means 'Yes I'm left wing' or 'Yes, I'm bigoted/extreme/doctrinaire/joyless'. This appropriation of meaning is what Cameron calls a 'triumph of linguistic intervention' and its success is apparent in that the negative **connotations** of 'political correctness' are so well established that it is now virtually impossible to use the term in any positive sense. So anything you label as 'PC' takes on the negativity of the label, obscuring the real issues about whether the thing itself is worthwhile or not. The term 'political correctness' is thus a good illustration of the way words can 'slide around', having slightly different meanings for different people, and being a 'site of struggle' (in this case, a struggle over who controls the meaning and thus whether 'political correctness' is a good thing or a bad thing, a joke, a serious threat or a worthwhile cause). It is ironic that having been a 'site of struggle' over meaning itself, the term 'political correctness' can be used against proposals for language reform, on the basis that such proposals are interference with language and its meaning. Such attacks have resulted in sets of joke coinages such as 'vertically challenged' (short), 'chronologically challenged' (old), and 'follically challenged' (bald), which effectively undermine serious attempts at language reform and deflect attention away from the underlying issues. (For more on political correctness, see Cameron, 1995; Dunant, 1994).

An example of an area where language reform has been applied is that of disability. Words such as *handicapped*, *cripple*, *lame* and *spastic* were criticised. Replacements included terms such as *disabled* and *mobility-impaired*. It is worth giving some attention to these changes, and the arguments which underpin them.

The least controversial argument for language reform is that the first set of terms is offensive to those with disabilities, and the second set is more polite. Using the second set rather than the first will therefore make disabled people feel more respected members of society. Slightly more radical is the argument that language use affects perceptions (see Chapter 2 for further discussion on this topic), and that the use of negative terms like *handicapped* encourages the perception that disabled people are dependent and incapable, rather than that it is the material environment which is lacking in facilities and is disabling. Changing the terms used should therefore change the perceptions of people (both those with and those without disabilities), and this in turn should influence transport, housing and employment policies and practice, increasing access for disabled people to services and opportunities.

A third argument frequently raised relating to language reform, is one which does not fully endorse campaigning for linguistic change. According to this argument, language change can be superficial and cosmetic, and may have no impact on the real material conditions of people's lives. Do disabled people really enjoy better lives as a result of linguistic reform, or is the fuss about language actually at the expense of campaigning for ramps, elevators and audio systems? If society is prejudiced, will its attitudes really be changed by new terminology, or will the pejorative sense associated with the old term in fact transfer to the new term? It is true that this may be the case, but it is possible for those campaigning for language reform to argue that they want both linguistic change *and* material changes: they don't have to settle for just one or the other.

1.5 Summary

This chapter outlined why the topics of language, society and power might be worth studying, and why in this book we are assuming the three topics are related. Several ways of thinking about, or 'modelling', language were offered and some of the kinds of variations in language you might encounter were commented on. The chapter looked briefly at what 'power' is, and identified how language, power and society might be related.

The study of language is worthwhile, we believe, because is it such an important part of all our lives. We also believe that by studying it we can learn a great deal about how society is structured, how society functions, and what are the most widespread, but sometimes invisible, assumptions about different groups of people.

Some people find that this knowledge is valuable because it contributes to their understanding of themselves and their relationships with others. Knowledge about language, society and power may enable people to make choices in their language use which make them feel better about themselves. People can also find knowledge about the areas discussed in this book valuable because it can be used to challenge what they perceive as unfairness in society. Whatever your reasons for reading this book, we hope you find it interesting and useful.

Notes

1   The use of square brackets in this sentence indicates that the original text has been altered in some way, and that what is contained within the square brackets is the addition of the present author. In this case, the text was shortened slightly, by removing some words from either side of the word *to*.

2   *over-processed hair* describes hair that has been damaged by heat and chemicals (e.g. it's been dyed, permed, tonged and sprayed).
    'I had an absolute *mare*' means 'I had a very bad time'. *Mare* is a short form of 'nightmare'.
    unleaving is a word invented by the poet Gerard Manley Hopkins from the poem 'Spring and Fall'. It appears to refer to the fall of leaves from trees.

Mcjobs is a sarcastic reference to low-paid, low-skilled jobs without career prospects. It was invented by analogy with the burger company McDonalds' advertising strategy of making up words with *Mc* in font of the them (e.g. *Mcburger*). *Sweatshirting* is a word I encountered as a heading in a mail order catalogue (*Racing Green*, Autumn 1997) for the pages with sweatshirts and jogging bottoms on them.

3   The use of the Latin term *sic* indicates that what may appear to be a mistake made in this publication was in fact a correct transcription of the original. In this case, the letter writer may have confused the words *unintelligible* (language which cannot be understood) with *unintelligent* (not clever). He may have made a mistake in writing his letter, the newspaper may have made a mistake in their reproduction of his letter, or he may have deliberately chosen *unintelligent* to cast a slur on the Welsh people.

Suggestions for further reading

Andersson, Lars-Gunnar and Trudgill, Peter (1992) *Bad Language*, Harmondsworth: Penguin.
    This is a small accessible book written for the general reader which aims to start you thinking about language issues.
Dunant, Sarah (ed.) (1994) *The War of the Words*, London: Virago.
    A collection of essays directed at the general reader, including 'The culture war and the politics of higher education in America', 'Sex and the single student: the story of date rape' and 'Liberté, Égalité and Fraternité: PC and the French'.
Montgomery, Martin (1996) *An Introduction to Language and Society* (2nd edition), London: Routledge.
    An introductory text which covers a wide range of social and linguistic issues.

Chapter 2

_____

Language, thought and representation

Ishtla Singh

2.1 Introduction

> Out of the right fob hung a great silver chain, with a wonderful kind of
> engine at the bottom... which appeared to be a globe, half silver, and half
> of some transparent metal: for on the transparent side we saw certain
> strange figures circularly drawn, and thought we could touch them, till we
> found our fingers stopped by that lucid substance. He put this engine to our
> ears, which made an incessant noise like that of a water-mill and we con-
> jecture it is... the god that he worships... because he assures us... that he
> seldom did any thing without consulting it...
>
> (Swift, 1726 [1994]: 28)

On first reading *Gulliver's Travels*, this extract seemed puzzling to me. Why
were the Lilliputians describing everyday objects in such a strange manner?
Surely they must have known what a watch was and would have had a word for
it? I realised, on reading this, that cultures are different from one another and
what is perceived as ordinary in one (like a watch) is not necessarily understood
in the same way in a different culture. This extract also illustrates that these differences of experience and perception may be encoded in language (by the non-
existence of the word *watch* in the language of the Lilliputians, in this instance).
This relationship (between experience, perception and language) will be discussed in this chapter as a starting point for the specific topics that you will
explore later in this book. We will begin by defining language as a system of **representation** and will then consider the extent to which it informs our thoughts
and analytical processes.

2.2 Saussure's theories of the Sign

It is common to think of language as a way of describing and giving information
about the world around us. If you own a wristwatch, you can call it a *watch* and
be sure that other speakers of English will know you are referring to the gadget
on your wrist. There appears to be a transparent relationship between the word
watch and the object, your watch. In this chapter we are going to probe the relationship between words and what they represent more closely, and consider the
ways in which the language we use might affect the way we think.

To complicate things, however, we aren't going to talk about objects but about concepts. By concept we mean the perception you have in your mind of something. This might be the idea of your watch, or the idea of a tree which you can call into your head while sitting in an enclosed room, or your idea of something which doesn't exist in a concrete form: a unicorn, tomorrow or frustration. We have to assume, for the purposes of discussing theories about language, that we can't actually 'get at' reality, but only at the way you interpret your senses and form a concept in your head as a result. This concept, we will be arguing, is affected by the language that is available to you.

To complicate things still further, we aren't going to talk about 'words'. This is because we want to make a clear distinction between the written form or sounds we use to represent a concept (which we will call a label) and the concept itself.

The ideas we are presenting in Figure 2.1 are a partial summary of those held by Ferdinand de Saussure (1857–1913), who formulated theories on (i) the idea of language as a system and (ii) the nature of the linguistic sign.

2.2.1 *Langue* and *parole*

Saussure proposed a theory of language which assumes that by the time we are mature, we all have a perfect and complete template of our language in our heads, and he referred to this template as **langue**. *Langue* is:

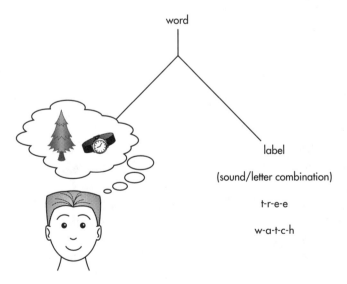

Figure 2.1 Words represent labels and concepts

our [innate] knowledge of the systematic correspondences between sound and meaning that make up our language (including the knowledge of what utterances are possible in our language, and what utterances are not).

(Andersen, 1988: 24)

For example, if you are an English speaker, you know that the sound/letter combination *tree* is possible in your language, but that *xng* is not. You also know that *tree* has a meaning for English speakers, but that *xng* does not. However, *xng* is meaningful in one of the Bantu languages, where it means 'to run'. Your instinctive understanding of the meaningfulness of *tree* is the same as a Bantu speaker's understanding of *xng*.

Your innate knowledge of your native language extends beyond this level. For example, you also know that your language allows certain structures and excludes others. As an English speaker, you belong to a global **speech community** which consists of all the people in the world who understand English, and have a template of how it works in their heads. Consequently, you know that

I planted a tree yesterday

and

Alex the tree pinched me as I went past

are grammatical sentences in English (even if the second one is unlikely in the world as we know it) but that

*a I yesterday tree planted

is not a grammatical English sentence.

We should add here that it can be difficult to decide exactly where a speech community begins and ends. For example, if you are an English speaker from Dallas, Texas, you will probably use language in ways similar to other inhabitants of Dallas, while differing in your use of English in significant ways from an English speaker from Calcutta, India, or from Norfolk, England. In this way we can say that there are smaller speech communities within the larger global one. In Chapters 6 and 9 we will look at examples of people using English in different ways who could therefore be said to belong to different speech communities. If *langue* is the perfect knowledge of a language that we have in our heads, in practice, according to Saussure, we sometimes deviate from this template. **Parole** refers to the way in which we actually use language, including the errors we make when confused, or mispronunciations because we tried to talk with our mouths full. If someone were staggering home drunk one night and stumbled into a tree, they might say something like:

tha' bloody shree hit me!

Now, your *langue* tells you that the tree couldn't possibly have hit you, and also that the typical pronunciation is not *shree*. However, inebriation can distort pronunciation and perceptions. Thus, the way in which language is used on this occasion (the *parole*) does not reflect what a member of the community of English speakers knows about the label *tree* and what is represented by it (the *langue*).

2.2.2 The linguistic sign

Langue, as was explained above, is the term used to describe the innate knowledge of the systematic pairings of labels and meanings which form a language. Saussure's theory is that these pairings produce a system of **signs**. Each sign has two parts to it, a **signifier**, which we have been calling a 'label', and a **signified**, which is what we have called 'a concept'. The actual sign is not one or both of these elements; the sign is the association that binds them together (see Figure 2.2).

Saussure states that, once the correspondence between the signifier and signified has been established, it tends to appear natural and invisible to speakers of that language:

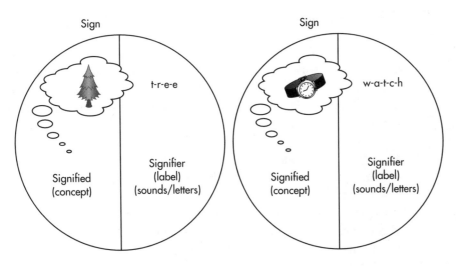

Figure 2.2 Signs are made of signifiers and signifieds

> Just as it is impossible to take a pair of scissors and cut one side of paper without at the same time cutting the other, so it is impossible in a language to separate sound from thought, or thought from sound.
>
> (Saussure, in Harris, 1988: 29)

If we accept this theory, it has very important consequences. Amongst other things, it implies that the way we use language can affect the way we think, because of the indivisible link between our concept of something and the language we use to represent it. In other words, language affects our perception of reality.

However, although the link between the label (signifier) and the concept in our minds (signified) can *seem* natural, obvious, and indivisible to us as speakers of that language, this is in fact far from being the case. If there were really an unbreakable link between the sounds/letters of *tree* and the concept of a tree which you have in your head, then people all over the world would also have to use *tree* for their concepts of leafy, bark-covered objects. Clearly they don't; French people, for example, call the same concept *arbre*, while Germans call it *Baum*. Although for English speakers there is a very strong link between *tree* and what we perceive to be a tree, for speakers of other languages, the link will be equally strong between their perception of the object and the particular sounds/letters they use for referring to it.

Saussure referred to this phenomenon as the **arbitrariness of the sign**, by which he meant that there is no reason why we can't call a tree an *arbre* or, for that matter, an *ostrich* or an *umbrella*. There is actually a pun here for some

ACTIVITY 2.1

1   You will need other people for this activity. Take two familiar objects and agree that you will reverse their names (for example, you will call dogs *tulips*, and you will refer to tulips as *dogs*). Now ask each other questions, including the reassigned names, which the other person must answer. For example,

QUESTION: Have you ever been bitten by a tulip?
ANSWER: Yes, but not badly. I didn't need a tetanus injection.

When you have exhausted the questions you can think to ask, discuss whether you found the activity difficult, and whether you can imagine a world where all the names where swapped overnight.

English speakers. The French and English words *arbre* and *tree* combined produce the word *arbitrary* (for those who pronounce it *arbitree*), reminding us that there is no reason why anything we name should not have a different name, as it probably does in a different language. If all the members of the English speech community agreed that from now on that all objects with leaves and bark should be called *ostriches*, there would be no reason why communication shouldn't continue to work perfectly well.

2.2.3 The arbitrary division of reality

Saussure also argued that what is treated as a separate concept in a language, worthy of its own letter/sound combination, is also arbitrary: 'different languages cut up reality in different ways' (Andersen, 1988: 27). For example, we could investigate two different languages and find that Language A uses three different words to refer to *still water*, *rain* and *floodwater*, but that Language B only has one word which is used for all three kinds of water. Language B might, on the other hand, have a word for *sandstorm*, unlike Language A. The reason behind such a difference might lie in the ways in which the two communities live. Speakers of Language A might belong to a settled community in a fertile valley which experiences water in various forms, while speakers of Language B might be desert nomads, who have no need to distinguish between different types of water but for whom sandstorms are common.

Another aspect of Saussure's theory is his claim that signs depend on one another for their meaning. Take the example of Language B above. If the circumstances of the speakers of Language B changed, they might find that it would be useful to distinguish rain from other kinds of water and adopt the word from Language A (in the same way that English adopted the word *yoghurt* from Turkish). The consequence would be that the original word used for *water* in Language B would have to shift slightly in meaning, because it would no longer include the concept of rain water, since this now has its own sign.

The idea that signs depend on one another for their meaning, and that by adding a sign, or by removing one, the others have to shift their meaning, is an important one. The introduction of the title *Ms,* discussed in Chapter 5, is a good example of this theory in practice.

To summarise Saussure's theories, he proposed that we divide up the world into arbitrary concepts, and we assign arbitrary labels (sound/letter combinations) to those concepts. The union of concept and label he called a sign. He argued that signs depend for their value on the other signs in the language system: they 'shift around' to make room for one another. For native speakers, it is very hard to perceive the division between the label and the concept; despite the arbitrariness, we perceive them as 'natural' and the arbitrariness is invisible to us. We perceive language as a transparent tool for talking about reality. This is what, we shall argue, makes it possible for language to have such a powerful effect on our perception of reality. In the next section, we will look in more detail at the claim that the language we use can affect our view of the world.

2.3 The Sapir–Whorf Hypothesis

While Saussure was interested in language as a system, other scholars were interested in the linguistic and philosophical differences between cultures, and the impact language has on our perception of reality. The work of anthropologist, Edward Sapir (1884–1939), and his student, Benjamin Lee Whorf (1897–1941), in this area has come to be known as the Sapir–Whorf Hypothesis. It has two parts: the theory of linguistic relativity and the theory of linguistic determinism.

The theory of linguistic relativity states that different cultures interpret the world in different ways, and that languages encode these differences (this corresponds to Saussure's theory that we divide up the world in arbitrary ways). Some cultures will perceive all water as being the same, while others will see important differences between different kinds of water (such as rain, flood water and still water, as we saw in the example above). The difference in perception will be apparent in the languages, because speakers have to articulate the way they see the world, and will develop differences in their languages accordingly. The term *relativity* refers to the idea that there is no absolute or 'natural' way to label the world. We label the world according to our perception of it and that perception is relative: it varies from culture to culture.

The Sapir–Whorf Hypothesis also incorporates another theory, the theory of linguistic determinism. This states that not only does our perception of the world influence our language, but that the language we use profoundly affects how we think. Language can be said to provide a framework for our thoughts and, according to the theory of linguistic determinism, it is very difficult to think outside that framework. Sapir stated that: 'We see and hear and otherwise experience very largely as we do because the language habits of our community predispose certain choices of interpretation' (quoted in Lucy, 1992: 22). Once a linguistic system is in place, according to this theory, it influences the way in which members of that speech community talk about and interpret their world.

One of Whorf's most famous explorations of linguistic relativity and linguistic determinism is his 1939 paper 'The Relation of Habitual Thought and Behaviour to Language' (reprinted in Carroll, 1956: 134–59). Whorf focused particularly on grammatical features, including the **tenses** of **verbs**, which might be thought of as the 'unnoticed "background" to speakers' thinking about the world' (Cameron, 1992: 136).

Whorf compared the Hopi language, an indigenous language in the south of the United States, with a group of languages he referred to as Standard Average European (SAE) which included English, French, German and other related European languages. As a result of his research, he claimed that 'the grammar of Hopi bore a relation to Hopi culture, and the grammar of European tongues to our own Western or European culture' (in Carroll, 1956: 138). One of the linguistic differences that Whorf highlighted in his Hopi–SAE comparison was ways of talking about concepts such as time and space.

European languages distinguish between physical and abstract entities. Physical entities are anything we experience through sensory faculties such as sight and touch. They have substance and exist in what in what we perceive to be three-dimensional space. Abstract entities, on the other hand, are not tangible: they do not have substance and space in the sense that physical matter has them.

In European cultures, we seem to treat our experience of physical matter as primary and use it to shape the ways we think and talk about the abstract. We objectify the abstract by talking about it in physical terms. Therefore an abstract concept such as an argument can be talked about as if it were a physical entity; we 'put' an argument or point of view, we 'move a debate forward', 'grasp' a point or 'squash' a suggestion. We frequently talk about abstractions in terms that bestow them with substance and space, as sometimes demonstrated by the physical gestures that accompany or even replace expressions such as 'that went right over my head'.

Hopi does not represent abstract concepts using physical **metaphors** in the same way, and this can be demonstrated from the way it is possible to talk about time in Hopi. According to Whorf, all people have an awareness of time, 'the basic sense of becoming later and later' (in Carroll, 1956: 139).

In European languages, we can mark our verbs to indicate whether we are talking about the present, the past or the future, as shown in the following examples:

	pronoun	verb	pronoun	verb
future	he	will have	she	will dance
present	he	has	she	dances
past	he	had	she	danced

The use of this system could be said to reflect and reinforce our belief that time is basically ordered into three separate periods. For us, the past is over and done with (and is therefore at the most consigned to memory), the present is happening now, and the future is yet to be and can only be imagined. On the whole therefore, SAE cultures seem to have interpreted and linguistically represented the abstract concept of time in physical terms, as something that can be divided into discrete units that progress in a linear fashion. We can draw time as a line that starts in the past, passes though 'now' and goes into the future:

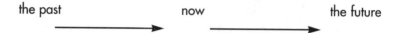

the past   now   the future

This is not the case in Hopi. Even though the Hopi too have a sense of time as a 'becoming later and later', they view its passage as a duration of stages rather than as a row of discrete units. Thinking of the human cycle may make this clearer. The human life cycle can be said to start at one stage, say the embryonic, and then progress through to different phases such as baby, infant, pre-adolescent, adolescent, young adult and mature adult. Each of these stages can be more or less clearly defined but they are not really discrete, because each flows into the other. At each point, the individual is still the same person, even though aspects of their appearance and certain characteristics may have changed.

The Hopi conceive of the passage of time in much the same way. Thus an expression such as *ten days*, which reflects a belief that each day is a different entity, is not possible in Hopi, where 'the return of the day [is] felt as the return of the same person, a little older but with all the impresses of yesterday' (Whorf, in Carroll, 1956: 151). This concept of time explains why Hopi verbs have no tenses like those in European languages. Whorf gives no examples, but states that the verbs instead denote 'different degrees of duration' (ibid.: 144).

Thus, SAE languages and the Hopi language differ in certain fundamental aspects, a development that seems to stem essentially from different worldviews. The two types of culture have evolved in different circumstances and with different influences, and so it should come as no surprise that their experiences of 'reality' have diverged. It is also unsurprising that each worldview would have informed other aspects of culture in addition to the linguistic, since 'language, culture and behaviour... have grown up together, constantly influencing each other' (Whorf, in Carroll, 1956: 156).

Whorf states that European cultures are preoccupied with time-keeping; we wear watches, keep calendars, take a great deal of interest in historical chronology and worry about 'saving', 'wasting' and 'running out of' time. The Hopi on the other hand are very different in their outlook. Their understanding of time as a duration means that certain cultural elements that SAE speakers perceive as essential are, to them, irrelevant. Speakers of European languages like keeping records as a means of preserving the past before it disappears. However, this is not important for the Hopi people because 'everything that ever happened still is, but in a necessarily different form' (Whorf, in Carroll, 1956: 153).

Sapir once claimed that once 'the language habits of the group' have been fixed, its speakers are at their 'mercy' (Sapir in Lucy, 1992: 22), which suggests that we are passive victims of our language. However, all the actual Sapir–Whorf Hypothesis states is that perceptions are encoded in language systems and can be reinforced through *constant and unquestioned use* by their speakers. As Cameron (1992: 136) points out, Sapir himself stated that as our awareness grows, 'we must learn to fight the implications of language', that is, to question our language and the way we use it.

ACTIVITY 2.2

2   We do not actually have to go outside the English-speaking community to find examples of linguistic relativity. For example, think of the way abortion is talked about. The following terms are all used in debates about abortion: divide them up as far as possible into those more likely to be used by people who oppose abortion and those who think it should be available. Add any additional terms you can think of which might be used, and decide if they belong more on one side or the other.

> Pro-life; unborn children; fertilised eggs; scientific meddling; pro-choice; embryo abuse; the treatment of genetic diseases; human vivisection; lethal discrimination against the unborn; the pre-embryo; a potential person; spare eggs; preventing the birth of a disabled child; murder; selective pregnancy reduction; the pursuit of designer babies; the anti-choice movement.
>
> (taken from D. Rowan, 'Eggs and Baking'
> *The Guardian Weekend* 22 April, 1990)

We have divided the terms into two lists below, but some terms (such as *fertilised eggs*) might appear in both.

pro-life	pro-choice
unborn children	fertilised eggs; spare eggs
scientific meddling	the treatment of genetic diseases
embryo abuse	the pre-embryo
human vivisection	a potential person
lethal discrimination against the unborn	selective pregnancy reduction
murder	the anti-choice movement
the pursuit of designer babies	preventing the birth of a disabled child

If you have strong feelings about the availability of abortion, you may find the terms in one of the lists upsetting or offensive. This example demonstrates how it is possible to question or challenge perception and talk about the world in different ways.

2.4 One language: many worlds

The most effective way of illustrating the creation and acceptance of distinct realities by speakers of one language is to look at examples of where it can and actually does occur. One area where the process can be observed is racist terminology. Take for example a racist term such as *Paki*.[1] Assume that you were born into a community where all Asians,[1] regardless of where they were born or what language they spoke, were referred to by this term. You would probably hear it in utterances where this group were being vilified, so you would form a negative stereotype (or perception: the signified, in Saussure's terms) of such people, and the term *Paki* would be its signifier. When you heard the word being used, and when you started to use it yourself, you wouldn't stop to think, 'now, what's the concept behind that word?', because the word is a complete linguistic sign: the thought and the term are one and the same. Furthermore, since *Paki* would be the only word available to you and your community to talk about Asians, it is the only one you would use, and every time you did (most likely in a denigrating way), you would reinforce the negative thoughts behind it. Therefore, because your language only gave you that one linguistic sign to denote Asians, you would always think of them in terms of it. In addition, because you were not consciously aware that *Paki* arose from your group's negative experiences and consequent perceptions of Asians, and because you never heard of them being talked of in any other way, you would believe that the negative meaning of *Paki* is objective, factual truth.

Another example can be seen in the language of the nuclear arms industry. A. M. Karpf, writing in *The Guardian* on 20 October 1988, calls this language 'Nukespeak', which she defines as 'a specialised vocabulary which isn't neutral... but ideologically loaded in favour of the nuclear culture'. This means that this **discourse** is the result of, and promotes, an **ideology** that nuclear armaments are not frightening or dangerous but beneficial and harmless. This discourse is created in a variety of ways. Nuclear weapons are given labels that have positive **connotations** (such as *cruise*), that are opaque (such as *MIRV*: an acronym for Multiple Independently Targeted Re-entry Vehicle) or have mythical and majestic connotations (*Polaris, Poseidon, Titan*). Some labels carry connotations of innocence or harmlessness. The Hiroshima bomb, for example, was called *Little Boy* and the neutron bomb was nicknamed *cookie cutter*. Such terminology is insidious because the application of labels with positive and/or harmless connotations makes such things seem normal and less scary. Continued use of such labels, combined with a deliberate elimination of any that suggest unpleasantness, danger or death (Karpf points out that 'Nukespeak' avoids all mention of death), makes it difficult to talk about the nuclear industry in anything other than positive terms. To illustrate this, Karpf cites American researcher Carol Cohn, who explored the development of American nuclear strategies and their implementation at an American University Center for Defense Technology. To carry out her research, Cohn adopted 'Nukespeak' but found that 'the better she became at using this discourse, the more impossible it became for her to express her own ideas and values.' Cohn states:

> the more conversations I participated in, the less frightened I was of nuclear war. How can learning a language have such a powerful effect? ... I could not use the language to express my concerns, because it was conceptually impossible. This language does not allow certain questions to be asked, certain values to be expressed.

'Nukespeak', therefore, makes the world of nuclear warfare seem safe and familiar. Its exclusive use in some settings reinforces a positive attitude to nuclear perception and makes it difficult to entertain any other: 'if we do learn and speak it, we not only severely limit what we can say, but we also invite the transformation ... of our own thinking' (Cohn). Such transformation is worrying because it is not conscious; we are not always aware that our worldviews are being manipulated or directed. We may accept usages such as those of 'Nukespeak' (which, for example, gain widespread currency through use by the media) because like Cohn, we are forced to: 'she found that when she spoke English rather than [Nukespeak], the men responded to her as if she were ignorant' (Karpf). Once acceptance of such discourse occurs, it can become what we consider '**common sense**' or 'truth', and therefore remain unchallenged.

However, as Cohn demonstrates by voicing her concerns, we do not have to be totally passive recipients of the ideas encoded in our language; we can (and do) question and contest them as our awareness of the issues involved grows.

ACTIVITY 2.3

3 Consider the following phrases and determine what ideology is encoded in them. What groups would be likely to use each and in what contexts? terrorist, freedom fighter, nuclear deterrent, eco-warrior, nuclear offensive, nuclear capability.

2.5 Summary

In this chapter we presented Saussure's theories of the sign: that concepts and labels are essentially arbitrary, but are linked to form signs; that the value of signs comes from other signs in the language system; and that, to speakers, signs appear a natural and transparent way of representing reality. The Sapir–Whorf Hypothesis states that cultures have different values and their language usages reflect their different perceptions of reality (the theory of linguistic relativity). It also states that continuous usage of a particular language, or a discourse within that language, reinforces the perceptions encoded in the language so they become firmly entrenched and difficult to question. However, as our understanding that language (in representing certain hidden ideologies) can manipulate and direct our perceptions increases, so too does our ability to challenge usages and the perspectives behind them. These are the key ideas which will be explored in more detail in the following chapters.

Notes

1   In the UK the term 'Asian' is used to refer to people whose ethnic background is from the Indian subcontinent: e.g. India, Bangladesh, Pakistan. In the US this term is used more extensively to include people whose ethnic background is from a wider geographical area incorporating, for example, China, Indonesia, Japan, Korea, Vietnam. *Paki* is a racist abuse term in the UK directed at anyone whose ethnic background appears to be from the Indian subcontinent.

Suggestions for further reading

Montgomery, Martin (1996) *An Introduction to Language and Society*, 2nd ed., London: Routledge.
   Chapter 10 of this introductory text discusses the issue of language and representation, clearly illustrated with data from news reporting.
Fairclough, Norman (1989) *Language and Power*, London: Longman.
   An introductory text to the area of language use and power, Chapter 4 provides a clear discussion of how ideology becomes entrenched in discourse and accepted as 'common sense'.

Chapter 3

Language and politics

Jason Jones and Shân Wareing

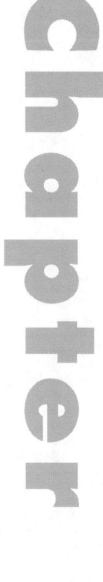

3.1 Introduction

In this chapter we are concerned with how language can be used to achieve political ends. The chapter starts with a discussion of what politics is, and how it is possible to see many of our ordinary choices and decisions as having some political consequences. We will then consider the implications to political language of the arguments made in the previous chapter, which showed how language both reflects and affects our perception of the world. We will discuss the ways in which language can be used to create and reinforce certain value systems, focusing on the role of **discourse** in shaping the beliefs which affect people's behaviour, motivations, desires and fears, and in establishing certain **ideologies** as '**common sense**'.

After this, we will consider some of the linguistic strategies people use to avoid making direct and honest statements, based on the arguments of George Orwell. Common **rhetorical** devices will be covered in the next stage of the chapter. Politicians have to find ways of making an impact on the public, and they often exploit the rhetorical aspects of language to achieve this.

First of all, let's consider what is meant by the term 'politics'.

3.2 What is meant by 'politics'?

George Orwell claimed that 'in our age there is no keeping out of politics. All issues are political issues' (1946: 154). Politics is concerned with power: the power to make decisions, to control resources, to control other people's behaviour and often to control their values. Even the most everyday decisions can be seen in a political light. In the supermarket, some brands of coffee are marketed on the basis of fair wages having been paid to the workers in the developing countries where the coffee was produced. Every time you buy coffee, you choose between these brands and brands which are often both cheaper and advertised more prominently, but which don't make this statement about fair wages. When you choose, you make a small contribution to the continued existence either of a company that claims to pay workers fairly, or one that doesn't make this claim. You make political decisions when you decide whether or not to buy recycled paper goods, organically grown vegetables or genetically modified food. When food is imported from countries with political regimes or particular policies opposed by people in your country, you will be lobbied not to buy goods such as wine or apples from those countries, as was the case with the boycott on South African produce during the apartheid era. There is no avoiding political decisions, even in the most domestic, everyday areas. In this chapter, we will largely use the language of 'career' politicians who govern countries to illustrate our ideas about political language. However, as we have argued, politics stretches far wider than this narrow definition, and political language is in use all the time, all around us.

<hr>

ACTIVITY 3.1

<hr>

1   Consider the uses of the word 'politics' in the expressions below. If you had to explain what these expressions meant, perhaps to a speaker from another culture, how would you rephrase them? Avoid using the word 'politics' in your rephrasing.

   (a)   They made careers for themselves in politics
   (b)   Sexual politics
   (c)   Don't get involved in office politics
   (d)   The personal is political
   (e)   Philosophy, Politics and Economics
   (f)   Environmental politics

<hr>

From your answers to this activity, it will be probably be clear that politics can refer to a wide range of activities. Your answers might have included: (a) the process of deciding national policy; (b) gender equality; (c) the jockeying for position which goes on in small, tightly knit groups, often achieved by the process of leaking and withholding information; (d) the way people negotiate roles in their private lives (also related to gender); (e) the history of political systems; (f) a whole range of activities do with transport, housing and consumption. There is indeed no keeping out of politics!

3.3 Politics and ideology

Politics is inevitably connected to power. The acquisition of power, and the enforcement of your own political beliefs can be achieved in a number of ways;

one of the obvious methods is through physical coercion. Many events in history, regarded as significant, involve the imposition, by force, of the rule of one group of people onto another group. This is what, in essence, most wars are about. Under dictatorial regimes, and military rule, those in power often control people by using force. In democracies, physical force is still used legally, for example to restrain people accused of criminal activity.

Other kinds of coercion are implemented in a democracy through the legal system. For example, there are laws about where you can park your car, about not destroying other people's mail, about where and when you can drink alcohol. If you break these laws, you can be fined, or even arrested and imprisoned. These are all examples of political ends achieved by coercion.

However, it is often much more effective to persuade people to act voluntarily in the way you want, that is, to 'exercise power through the manufacture of consent . . . or at least acquiescence towards it' (Fairclough, 1989: 4), instead of having to continually arrest them for wrongdoing. To secure power, it makes sense to persuade everyone else that what you want is also what they want. By encouraging your citizens to embrace your goals of their own accord, any cost-conscious ruler is able to save money on armed forces and police officers. To achieve this, an ideology needs to be established: one which makes the beliefs which you want people to hold appear to be 'common sense'. This makes it difficult for them to question the dominant ideology.

The concept of ideology was first introduced by followers of Karl Marx, notably Louis Althusser. Althusser wondered how the vast majority of people had been persuaded to act against their own best interests, since they worked long hours at laborious tasks and lived in poverty, while a very small number of people made enormous amounts of money from their labour, and enjoyed lives of luxury. In order to explain why the impoverished majority didn't just refuse to work in this system and overthrow the rich minority, Althusser reasoned that the poor had been persuaded that this state of affairs was 'natural', and nothing could be done to change it. This is the context which 'ideology' was originally used in.

Nowadays 'ideology' tends to be used more widely, to refer to any set of beliefs which, to the people who hold them, appear to be logical and 'natural'. 'Ideology' is not necessarily a pejorative term, because it can be argued that absolutely everything we know and think is in fact an ideology. As was proposed in the previous chapter, it is possible to regard our understanding of reality as entirely mediated by language and the system of **signs** available to us. That system of signs, according to this argument, is in fact not an unbiased reflection of the world, but a product of the ideologies of our culture.

People can question the ideologies of their culture, but it is often difficult. It can be a challenging intellectual task, but it can also result in social stigma.

People who question the dominant ideology often appear not to make sense; what they say won't sound logical to anyone who holds that ideology. In extreme cases, people who ask such questions may even appear mad. So while it is possible to question the dominant ideology, there is often a price to be paid for doing so.

3.3.1 Implicature

Political discourse relies very heavily on the principle, discussed in the previous chapter, that people's perceptions of certain issues or concepts can be influenced by language. As has been said before, one of the goals of a politician must be to persuade their audience of the validity of the politician's basic claims. The use of **implicature** is one of the means by which this can be achieved. Implicature allows the audience to make assumptions about the existence of information not made explicit in what is actually said. It is information that might be deduced. It can help to manufacture 'common sense' by communicating the speaker's opinions without spelling them out. Because of this, it is harder for the audience to identify and (if they wish to) reject views communicated in this way. Implicature can be used to persuade people to take something for granted which is actually open to debate. The following statements contain implicatures:

- We will save the NHS (British Labour Party manifesto, 1997)
- Put country before party this election (British Referendum Party election pamphlet, 1997)
- Invest in a future we can *all* enjoy (British Labour Party election pamphlet, 1997; original emphasis)
- Make the difference (British Liberal Democrat Party manifesto, 1997)
- The green alternative for a better quality of life (British Green Party manifesto, 1997)

We will save the NHS implies that the NHS (British National Health Service, funded by public money) needs saving, i.e. that the present government is damaging the NHS. *Put country before party this election* implies that voters might have placed loyalty to a political party before the welfare of the country in previous elections. The slogan *Invest in a future we can all enjoy* implies that not everyone has enjoyed the past, or would enjoy the future if things continued as they are. *Make the difference* and *a better quality of life* imply that everyone agrees that there is room for improvement in the current political system, and establish this point of view as 'common sense'.

These examples all show political language attempting to shape ideology by using implicature to suggest that we (the politician and the audience) already agree in our worldview that things could be better than they are at the moment.

3.3.2 Language as thought control: Newspeak and political correctness

The discussion above suggested that it might be possible to use language to manufacture an ideology which would steer the way people think. However, we will now consider a more extreme line of argument: that language can be used to control the way people think.

If we accept that the kind of language we use to **represent** something can alter the way in which it is perceived by people, then you might wonder whether, by controlling the discourse, one can control how another person thinks. This is the premise which Orwell's novel *Nineteen Eighty-Four* (first published in 1949) explores. A totalitarian society of the future has Ingsoc (English Socialism) as the dominant political system. The system is enforced by the mandatory use by all citizens of a language called **Newspeak**, a radically revised version of the English language from which many meanings available to us today have been removed. In an appendix to *Nineteen Eighty-Four* entitled 'The principle of Newspeak', Orwell explains that 'the purpose of Newspeak was not only to provide a medium of expression for the world-view and mental habits proper to the devotees of Ingsoc, but to make all other modes of thought impossible' ([1949] 1984: 231). The principles of Newspeak are therefore grounded in the Sapir–Whorf Hypothesis: that language determines our perception of the world (see Chapter 2). Orwell wrote:

> It was intended that when Newspeak had been adopted once and for all and Oldspeak forgotten, a heretical thought – that is, a thought diverging from the principles of Ingsoc – should be literally unthinkable, at least so far as thought is dependent on words. Its vocabulary was so constructed as to give exact and often very subtle expression to every meaning that a Party member could properly wish to express, while excluding all other meanings and also the possibility of arriving at them by indirect methods. This was done partly by the invention of new words, but chiefly by eliminating undesirable words and stripping such words as remained of unorthodox meanings, and so far as possible of all secondary meanings whatever. To give a single example. The word *free* still existed in Newspeak, but it could only be used in such statements as "This dog is free from lice" or "This field is free from weeds". It could not be used in its old sense of "politically free" or "intellectually free", since political and intellectual freedom no longer existed even as concepts, and were therefore of necessity nameless.... A person growing up with Newspeak as his sole language would

no more know that *equal* had once had the secondary meaning of "politically equal", or that *free* had once meant "intellectually free", for instance, than a person who had never heard of chess would be aware of the secondary meanings attached to *queen* and *rook*.

([1949] 1984: 231)

Of course, this is only a fictional situation. You might well question the viability of not only enforcing the exclusive use of a language such as Newspeak, but also of preventing people from thinking of certain concepts simply by taking away the words and meanings that encode these concepts. In fact, Orwell himself stated that he did not believe thought to be entirely 'dependent on words'.

The principles of linguistic determinism on which the fictional Newspeak is founded could be argued to underlie aspects of moves towards 'political correctness'. Newspeak, admittedly, was the product of a malign dictatorship in Orwell's novel, while 'political correctness' could be viewed as a benign attempt to improve the world. However, the two interventions into language use, one fictional, one real, may share certain assumptions, as we will explore.

The origins of the term and concept of 'political correctness' (PC) are interesting and complicated (see Cameron, 1994; 1995). The term is used as an insult, as a joke, and in sincerity by people who believe its importance. When used by the latter group, it is underpinned by the assumption that the terms used to represent minority groups matter. Examples of 'PC' terms which have had an impact on language use include *visually impaired*, *blended family* (to refer to a household incorporating children from several relationships), and ethnicity terms which include reference to a person's country of origin, such as *African-American*. Non-'PC' terms are considered by some not only to be offensive, but to create/reinforce a perception of minority groups as unequal to the majority, which in turn may have a detrimental effect on the way we organise our society.

'PC' language use could be argued to be particularly significant in the relation to disability, since many changes could be made to the way most organisations operate which might have a positive effect on the lives of many people with disabilities. For example, some people make a distinction between impairment and disability, using impairment to refer to a condition (such as loss of vision or a limb), and disability to refer to activities which are difficult or impossible to undertake (for example, reading small print or climbing stairs). This is intended to draw attention to the fact that someone's inability to read a book or reach the top floor of a shop is as much a consequence of lack of facilities, as of their impairment. Larger print might allow the visually impaired person to complete a book; an elevator would allow a mobility-impaired person to reach the top floor. The language change is part of a deliberate attempt to improve facilities for disabled people by drawing organisations' attention to the difference between impairment and disability.

It should be noted that some people who would not support the argument that changing language changes perceptions, and ultimately can change the way buildings are designed and books printed, nevertheless would support 'politically correct' language usage to talk about minority groups. They argue this on the grounds that it is important to use appropriate and inoffensive terms, in order to be respectful to disabled people.

Although 'political correctness' is not trying to control people's thoughts in the way that Orwell's Ingsoc did through Newspeak, it nevertheless represents an attempt to alter people's perceptions of certain '**signifieds**' (concepts) by replacing old '**signifiers**' (labels) with new ones. One reason why many people objected to 'political correctness' was that it appeared to have an agenda concerned with changing the way people thought.

So far in this chapter, we have considered the use of language to influence people's view of the world, using the examples of George Orwell's invented language, 'Newspeak', and of 'political correctness'. You may think that any deliberate intervention into language use which attempts to influence the way people think is wrong. However, it may be worth considering whether intervention for a good reason (such as to improve the lives of disadvantaged people) can be justified, while the intervention for a bad reason (such as to limit people's lives) cannot. Of course, what constitutes a 'good' or a 'bad' reason is a question for political debate, which takes us back to politics again.

3.4 The language of deception

There is a well-worn joke:

> QUESTION: How can you tell whether a politician's lying?
> ANSWER: You can see their lips move.

Even if you do not think politicians lie regularly, you may agree with George Orwell that political language is 'largely the defense of the indefensible'. Orwell perceived the majority of politicians to be corrupt confidence swindlers and he particularly disliked the kind of language politicians adopted, describing it as follows:

> political language has to consist largely of **euphemism**, question-begging and sheer cloudy vagueness.... Political language – and with variations this is true of all political parties, from Conservatives to Anarchists – is

designed to make lies sound truthful and murder respectable, and to give an appearance of solidity to pure wind.

(1946: 157)

Orwell suggested a number of rules for language use which he argued should be followed by politicians and, indeed, all speakers and writers in the interests of clear, honest, understandable communication:

(1)   Never use a **metaphor**, **simile** or other figure of speech which you are used to seeing in print.
(2)   Never use a long word where a short one will do.
(3)   If it is possible to cut a word out, always cut it out.
(4)   Never use the **passive** where you can use the **active**.
(5)   Never use a foreign phrase, a scientific word or a jargon word if you can think of an everyday English equivalent.
(6)   Break any of these rules sooner than say anything outright barbarous.

(1946: 156)

Let us consider the implications of these 'rules' one at a time. Rule 1 states:

(1)   Never use a metaphor, simile or other figure of speech which you are used to seeing in print.

This is a warning against the use of what might be called 'pre-constructed phrases', in which commonly made associations and assumptions are reiterated, not challenged. In section 3.3, we argued that repeating certain phrases contributes towards making the ideas contained in them seem 'common sense': it is part of the process of constructing an ideology. Orwell isn't complaining about using well-worn phrases for this particular reason. He is against it for almost the opposite reason: that over-used phrases sound as if they mean something but often mean nothing. They show intellectual laziness on the part of the speaker and because they are often examples of 'sheer cloudy vagueness', they don't help the listener to understand the concepts being discussed either. In either case, the use of well-worn phrases stops people thinking clearly.

Consider the phrase *a strong economy*, for example. It is a figure of speech, in this case a metaphor (discussed in section 3.4.1 below). The economy is not strong in a literal sense: it cannot lift heavy weights, for example. This phrase may mean to you low inflation and steady and sustainable improvement in the amount of business conducted by manufacturers and service providers. It is certainly a frequently used phrase, and could be argued to both be rather vague in meaning, as in Orwell's argument, and have an ideological function, since people may react to the idea of a strong economy without thinking about precisely what the phrase means.

(2)   Never use a long word where a short one will do.

In English, long words tend to sound more formal and dignified than short words, although there may be very little difference in meaning between a long and a short word. Consider:

help	assistance
end	conclusion
work with	collaborate with
break	adjournment
last	preceding

It is very common for a person who wishes to assert their authority and superiority to use longer words to impress, to intimidate or perhaps to mystify and confuse their audience. Politicians, academics, lawyers and doctors are often guilty of this, although many would also defend their choice of words by saying they were appropriate for the context.

(3)   If it is possible to cut a word out, always cut it out.

Another technique which makes what is said sound superficially more impressive and intimidating, and has the effect of making it harder to understand, is the use of additional, unnecessary words.

(4)   Never use the passive where you can use the active.

This is a point about grammar. Using an active sentence construction is usually more direct and informative. Using a passive construction often sounds more formal, more convoluted, often gives slightly less information and can be harder to understand.

Active:	Jay cut the grass
Passive:	The grass has been cut (by Jay)

In the active, the person responsible for the main action, called the **agent**, in this case Jay, comes first in the sentence. In the passive, the agent comes later in the sentence and can actually be left out altogether. *The grass has been cut* is a perfectly acceptable sentence, but does not tell you who has cut the grass.

Passive sentences sometimes have *by* in them (as in *by Jay*) which can make them easier to spot.

> (5) Never use a foreign phrase, a scientific word or a jargon word if you can think of an everyday English equivalent.

People use foreign phrases, scientific words, and jargon for many reasons, some good, some bad. However, to communicate information clearly to a wide audience, everyday terms are often most effective. The choice of a term which is prestigious but which many people will not understand is often used for affective rather than informative reasons (see Chapter 1). That is to say, the speaker intends to impress the hearer with how sophisticated they are, or how much they know.

It is true that sometimes a very precise word is needed. For example, if you were being operated on, you would want exactly the right amounts of the right anaesthetic to be given to you, and you would want the surgeon to use the right equipment. On such an occasion, you might be very glad to know that specialist terms were available to allow communication to be as fast and as clear as possible. Jargon is appropriate when it allows someone in a specialised area to communicate clearly with other people in that area. Outside that area, it often makes the speaker seem unaware of the needs of the listener, or makes the listener feel bored, intimidated, unimportant or stupid.

> (6) Break any of these rules sooner than say anything outright barbarous.

Our interpretation of this statement by Orwell is that the rules above are all to do with style: how something is said rather than what is said. And at the end of the day, it is what is said that is important. A speech that followed the first five rules but argued for oppression and corruption, therefore breaking the last rule, would offend Orwell more than one which broke the first five rules but supported equality and freedom.

3.5 The language of persuasion (rhetoric)

Rhetoric is the ancient skill of elegant and persuasive speaking. Although politicians nowadays would not dream of following the original Greek rules, they do often adopt identifiable habits of speech to increase the impact of the ideas.

ACTIVITY 3.2 ═══════════════════════════

2   How many of Orwell's rules are broken by the following sentence, which was produced by the UK water company, Yorkshire Water (and reproduced in *The Daily Telegraph*, 31 January, 1997)? Try rewriting it according to Orwell's rules. How do the two version compare, in your opinion?

> Yorkshire Water has for some time been reviewing proposals that would improve the group's efficiency for the benefit of shareholders by reducing the level of equity to increase gearing whilst intending to maintain the growth in the total cash quantum of the ordinary dividend by 6 to 8pc annually, in real terms, until the year 2000, subject only to there being no material adverse change in the political or regulatory framework within which the group operates.

═══

3.5.1 Figures of speech

One of the challenges politicians face is that they often have to talk about abstract concepts in ways that won't bore people too much. Typically, many people in our culture find concrete entities easier to think about and discuss than abstract concepts (as explored in Chapter 2), and as a consequence, it is common place to find concrete images in political discourse. For example:

> A strong British *economy* (British Conservative Party election pamphlet, 1997).

As discussed in section 3.4 above, the *economy* is regularly referred to in political speeches. It is not a concrete entity; it is an abstract model for thinking about a very large quantity of diverse financial data including rates of inflation, and patterns of employment and spending. However, by applying the **adjective** *strong*, there is an implication that the economy is muscular like a weight-lifter, or perhaps like a healthy organism, a plant which has strong growth, or a well-fed, sturdy animal. It gives us an acceptable concrete image rather than, for example, an image of lists and lists of figures, and pages of graphs. It might be considered strange to think of sets of statistics as a weight-lifter or a plant, but it is very common.

The following phrase also makes use of a common image:

> Germany is *the bully in the playground*
>
> (various British TV news broadcasts,
> referring to the strong and influential position
> of Germany in the European Union)

This phrase includes a metaphor, which is one kind of figure of speech. A figure of speech is any representation which is not literally true. Germany is not literally a bully; Germany could be thought of as an area of land, as a group of people, or as a political concept. The term *bully* is usually used to refer to a single person, which Germany clearly is not. And where is the playground? The metaphor is a linguistic device that provides, in this case, a link between the people of Germany and their political representatives and the idea of a bully in the playground at school. It represents a complicated series of events in international relations with an everyday event that many people will have had direct and negative experience of being bullied at school.

One advantage to a politician of a phrase like this is that it represents something which is complex simply. Another advantage is that by creating a clear image which people can understand easily, and which ties in with their own experience, it is therefore likely to have a strong influence on how the country of Germany is perceived in future by some British people. The phrase has the potential to be useful in the construction of ideology, in other words. Here is one further example of figurative language use:

> The airport is already acknowledged as the *economic motor* of the region
> (Graham Stringer of the Manchester Airport Board on the planned
> construction of a second runway, *The Times*, 16 January, 1997)

We have already considered the difficulty of representing the economy simply. Graham Stringer uses another common phrase: *economic motor*. What exactly does 'economic motor' mean? Stringer's claim may be that Manchester airport is already a major employer, bringing in travellers who need to buy products and services, and providing many local people with jobs. Running the airport itself also provides jobs and revenue in the service, commercial and industrial sectors. It is therefore the 'motor' that 'drives' the economy of the region and is fundamental to it. These meanings are not explicit, but the phrase is perhaps 'catchier' and the meaning more memorable than if Stringer had spelt out exactly what he meant. It also has the advantage of being an image from industry: motors run engines. It is an image of industrial success. The north of England, where Manchester is situated, has been primarily an industrial region, and 'motor' is a powerful image of employment and wealth.

Figures of speech, therefore, have several important functions in political language. They help make abstract ideas easier to think about and they are ideologically powerful since they often link with experiences about which we have strong feelings.

3.5.2 The three-part statement

One of the best-known features of political rhetoric is the use of the 'three-part statement'. This is the linguistic strategy of referring to things in groups of three. For some reason, we seem to find things that are grouped in threes particularly aesthetically pleasing. Goodman (in Cockcroft and Cockcroft, 1992) has looked at the predominance of 'triads, threes and eternal triangles' in cultures from all around the world. She talks about the frequent occurrence of the number three in fairy/folk tales (e.g. *Three Little Pigs*; *Goldilocks and the Three Bears*; *Three Blind Mice*) and of groups of three in films (e.g. *The Good, The Bad and The Ugly*; *Sex, Lies and Videotape*; *Truly, Madly, Deeply*). Political orators all over the world recognise the importance of the three-part statement as a rhetorical device, with perhaps one of the most famous three-part statements being the French *liberté, fraternité, égalité* (*liberty, brotherhood, equality*). Consider the following examples:

- The attempt to create a politically unified Europe is *dangerous, devious and undemocratic* (British Conservative Party election pamphlet, 1997)
- This is the result of four years of Liberal Democrat and Labour *waste, whinge and weakness* (British Conservative Party election pamphlet, 1997)
- We recognise *that a strong country is built from the bottom, not the top; that conformity quickly becomes the enemy of diversity.* And *that the imposition of social blueprints leads to authoritarian centralised government* (British Liberal Democrat manifesto, 1997)

In the third example (we've used a group of three examples!), Paddy Ashdown, the British Liberal Democrat leader, presents his views in three points. Similarly, a 1997 Liberal Democrat election pamphlet used the three-point structure to emphasise what they perceived to be the inadequacies of the government at the time, quoting three promises made by the Conservative Party at the previous General Election and subsequently (allegedly) broken:

Remember what the conservatives said at the last General Election.
'We do not see any need to increase the tax burden' – John Major – 24th March, 1992. The next budget introduced what the **BBC** described as 'colossal' tax increases.

'We have no need and no plans to extend the scope of VAT' – John Major – 27th March, 1992. The next budget introduced VAT on home gas and electricity bills.

'I have no doubt that we will be able to make further reductions in the rate of taxation' – John Major – 1992 General Election Campaign. The Conservatives shortly afterwards introduced tax increases equivalent to 7p in the pound on income tax.

The three-part statement is such a powerful structure that politicians have even used it when they have only one point to make. At the 1996 Labour Party Conference, Tony Blair claimed that the three main commitments of the Labour Party were *education, education, education*, while at the Conservative Party Conference in the same year, that party's main concerns were presented as *unity, unity, unity*.

ACTIVITY 3.3

---

3   Listen to, and record if possible, a politician delivering a speech either in Congress, Parliament or at a political event (such as a Party Conference or Convention, hustings, or TV broadcast). How many times does s/he make use of three-part statements? Are these statements effective? Would they have been more or less effective if they had been delivered in any way other than as a triad?

3.5.3 The rhetorical use of pronouns

The way a political speaker refers to themselves and to their audience can also be very significant. The **pronoun**s applied to the speaker, to their allegiances and to the audience can be used to foreground or hide agency (the person or party who commits a certain action, as discussed above) and responsibility, depending on what the politician is talking about. Consider President Bush's varying use of pronouns below; why do you think he changes from *we* to *I*?

As *we* announced last night, *we* will not attack unarmed soldiers in retreat.
     We have no choice but to consider retreating combat units as a threat and respond accordingly...
     From the beginning of the air operation, nearly six weeks ago, *I* said that *our* efforts are on course and on schedule. This morning, *I* am pleased to say that coalition efforts are ahead of schedule. The liberation of Kuwait is close.

(*The Guardian*, 27 February, 1991)

One explanation for the shift would be that President Bush uses *we* when the focus of his speech is relatively controversial, as it is unclear who *we* refers to, and *I* when he is on safer ground and wanting to claim responsibility for positive achievements.

ACTIVITY 3.4 ▬▬▬

4   Record a political speech from the radio or television, or use data you analysed for the previous activity. What pronouns are used, and to what effect?

3.6 Summary

This chapter started with a discussion of what politics is, and argued that it is an extremely widespread phenomenon, not restricted to people who make their career in national government. It then discussed the importance of ideology in constructing a worldview: that people in a society tend to collaborate in the production of certain value systems and ways of talking about things, which make other ways of thinking or talking seem rather strange or anti-social. This idea was then taken one stage further, as the question was asked: 'is it possible for language to control thought'?, and we considered illustrations from Orwell's *Nineteen Eighty-Four* and 'political correctness'.

The chapter then turned to the use of political rhetoric, exploring ways in which language can be made deliberately obscure and difficult to understand. We looked at figures of speech, and how metaphors can be used to create a concrete image for an abstract concept, to be imprecise about what is really meant, and for ideological potency. We gave some examples of the widely used three-part statement, which is a favourite in political speaking. The chapter concluded with a consideration of pronouns and how it is possible to use pronouns to appear to take credit or disguise responsibility.

The themes in this chapter have tied in closely with those discussed in the previous chapter, considering the extent to which the language we use affects our view of the world. It is important to remember that political language is in use all around us everyday, and that we actually use it ourselves. The next chapter continues these themes, looking at language use in the media, and how language choices can influence our perception of events, their causes and effects.

Suggestions for further reading

Bolinger, Dwight (1980) *Language – The Loaded Weapon*, London: Longman.
   This is a first-year undergraduate level text, which as a whole is very good on many
   of the issues discussed in this book. Chapters 10–12 are particularly relevant to the
   discussion of language and politics.
Fairclough, Norman (1989) *Language and Power*, London: Longman.
   This text looks very closely at the use of language to influence what people accept
   as 'common sense' as a means of manufacturing consent.

Chapter 4

Language and the media

Joanna Thornborrow

4.1 Introduction

The media, which is usually understood to refer to the press, radio and television broadcasting, have become one of the most pervasive phenomenon in our culture. We can also add the World Wide Web to the list of communications media, but we will be dealing here mainly with newspapers and broadcasting media (television and radio). The aim of this chapter is to examine how our knowledge about the world is mediated through the press and broadcasting institutions, and to suggest ways in which the analysis of language can provide insights into how that mediation can affect the **representation** of people, places and events.

The mass media have become one of the principal means through which we gain access to a large part of our information about the world, as well as to much of our entertainment. Because of this, they are a powerful site for the production and circulation of social meanings, i.e. to a great extent, the media decide the significance of things that happen in the world for any given culture, society or social group. The language used by the media to represent particular social and political groups, and to describe newsworthy events, tends to provide the dominant ways available for the rest of us to talk about those groups and events. We will be looking here at some examples of these.

Lastly, as access to TV and radio discourse is widening, more programmes, such as the ever-popular talk shows and phone-ins, are being dedicated to the 'voices' of the ordinary public, rather than limited to journalists, politicians and media experts. Also, with the development of the Internet, a vast amount of information is now available from many different sources. But does this necessarily mean that a broader spectrum of people and opinions are being represented as a result, or do media institutions to a large extent still maintain control of who can talk and what gets said? We will also be addressing this question here.

4.2 The function of the media

We use the media for many different purposes; for information, for entertainment, and for education, through a range of programmes for schools as well as university broadcasts. We listen to the news on radio and television for information about local, national and international events; many people spend hours every week being entertained by a variety of programmes from regular soap operas to weekly quizzes and chat shows. Sometimes, the boundaries become blurred between information and entertainment, and a new term has been coined to refer to programmes which serve both functions: 'infotainment'. Wildlife programmes, docu-dramas and the growing number of talk shows could all be described as having a dual role: to entertain as well as to inform.

The mass media provide the means of access to much information and represent a potentially powerful force in our society. They can select what is news, who gets into the papers and onto television and radio and, most importantly for linguists, the way that those stories get told, and the frameworks in which people get to appear and talk. However, we must be careful when talking about the media as 'they'. Any newspaper story goes through several stages before it appears on the page, and many different people can be involved at each stage. The same is true of broadcast news stories. Rather than seeing the media as being a group of individuals who control and in some way manipulate what we read or watch, we need to think of each medium as a complex institution. This institution is characterised by a set of processes, practices and conventions that the people within it have developed within a particular social and cultural context. These practices have an effect both on what we perceive as news, and on the forms in which we expect to hear or read about it.

The media are always there, and have come to be taken for granted as an integral part of most people's lives. Scannell (1988), in an account of the social role of broadcasting, argues that even the language we use to talk about TV programming reflects this ordinariness, this taken-for-granted place in our lives. The expression 'there's nothing on TV' has come to mean 'there's nothing I want to watch', rather than describing an actual state of affairs where there is really nothing being broadcast if you switch on your set. The fact that, with the increase of 24-hour broadcasting and multiple channels, there is practically always something on TV is now quite unremarkable for most of us.

However, we should not be too quick to see the media as all-powerful, and the public as mere puppets of media control. The relationship is not a straightforward one. The reading, listening and viewing public can also choose not to buy, listen or watch; they can switch off, change allegiances, and in some cases challenge versions of events. For example, as a result of the events surrounding the Princess of Wales' death in August 1997, a new set of laws may be passed in Britain restricting the rights of 'paparazzi' journalists to take intrusive photographs, and this is due in some part at least to the public reaction to her death. On the other hand, the same public were always ready to buy the papers and watch the programmes that featured reports of her both when she was alive, and after her death, and in that sense, the media were providing, and continue to provide, what sells their product.

4.3 Media, language and power

As we noted in section 4.2, one of the most important and interesting aspects of the potential power of the media from a linguistic point of view is the way that people and events get reported. Since the early 1970s, linguists have been interested in the relationship between how a story gets told, and what that might indicate about the point of view that it gets told from (Lee, 1992; Simpson, 1993; Montgomery, 1996). This level of language use is called linguistic representation (see Chapter 2) and we will now look at some linguistic structures that can determine how events are represented, and thus lead to different versions, or views, of the same event.

The extracts below are taken from two reports of a car bomb explosion outside a local police station in County Down, in Northern Ireland on 21 February, 1998. There has been unrest and violence in Northern Ireland for many years, and the political situation is very complex. In brief, the island of Ireland is split into two parts. The predominantly Roman Catholic southern part, the Irish Republic, is a separate nation, which governs itself. The northern part, where a minority of Roman Catholics live amongst a Protestant majority, consists of six counties and is part of the United Kingdom. The six Northern Ireland counties are also referred to as *Ulster*, mainly by those who support the division. The police force in Northern Ireland is called the *RUC*, or *Royal Ulster Constabulary*. Republicans in the Irish Republic want a unified country; this view is represented politically by the party, Sinn Fein, led by Gerry Adams. Sinn Fein has been linked by some people with acts of terrorist violence, and to the terrorist Republican group, the IRA (the Irish Republican Army). There is both strong support and strong opposition in Northern Ireland for the Republican cause. Amongst those who oppose it are the members of the Orange Order, a Protestant organisation which holds military-style marches through the streets of cities in Northern Ireland. To understand the extracts which follow, you may need to refer back to this paragraph if you are not familiar with the Northern Ireland troubles.

The explosion described in the extracts below took place during a round of peace talks early in 1998 between the government of the Irish Republic, Northern Irish political leaders, and the British government. The UDP (the Ulster Democratic Party) had previously been temporarily excluded from the talks, and more recently, the Republican party, Sinn Fein, had been temporarily excluded. We will focus on how the same story is told differently by two British newspapers, *The Daily Telegraph* and *The Guardian*.

Starting with the headlines, we can immediately see differences in the way this story is introduced:

(1)   Bomb blast after ban on Sinn Fein
      (*The Daily Telegraph*, 21 February, 1998)

(2)   Ulster bomb new blow to peace talks
      (*The Guardian*, 21 February, 1998)

Both headlines consist of a series of **noun phrases**: *bomb blast*, *ban*, *Sinn Fein*, *Ulster*, *bomb*, *new blow*, *peace talks*. As is often the case in headline text, these are both grammatically incomplete. We could rewrite (2) as:

[The/an] Ulster bomb [is a] new blow to peace talks

However, this is not so easy to do in (1). A relationship between the two events in this headline has already been established by the presence of the word 'after'. This can be interpreted not just as a temporal link between two events (event one: Sinn Fein was banned, then event two: a bomb exploded), but also as a causal link (event two occurred *because of* event one). This creates a difference in meaning between the two headlines.

The causal link is also present in smaller headlines above the main headline of *The Daily Telegraph* report:

(3)   Adams' anger at talks followed by huge explosion outside RUC
      station

Here, *Adams* refers to Gerry Adams, the Republican leader of Sinn Fein. In this headline, too, we find the same pattern. Two phrases, 'Adams' anger at talks' and 'huge explosion outside RUC station', are linked by the words 'followed by', which have the same meaning as the word 'after' in the main headline, and suggest that there is a link between the explosion and Adams' anger.

Turning next to the first sentence in the two articles, we can find further differences:

(4)   A Republican car bomb devastated a Royal Ulster Constabulary
      station and much of a small town in Northern Ireland shortly before
      midnight last night after Sinn Fein had been ejected from political
      talks for a fortnight.

                                              (*The Daily Telegraph*)

(5)   A massive car bomb exploded outside an RUC police station in a
      predominantly Protestant village in County Down last night, piling
      pressure on the credibility of the IRA cease fire hours after Sinn

Fein was ordered out of the multi-party talks on Northern Ireland's future.

(*The Guardian*)

First, there is a difference in the words, in this case **adjectives**, used to describe the bomb:

a *republican* car bomb
a *massive* car bomb

The Guardian's choice of adjective provides information about the size of the bomb (massive), *The Daily Telegraph*'s choice provides information about whose bomb it was (Republican). Second, there is a difference in the choice of **verbs** used in these sentences:

a republican bomb *devastated* a Royal Ulster Constabulary station
a massive car bomb *exploded* outside an RUC police station

In *The Guardian*'s first sentence, we know what 'exploded' (a massive car bomb), but not what was damaged. Instead, we have information about the position of the bomb (outside an RUC police station in County Down). In *The Daily Telegraph*'s opening sentence, we are given information about what did the devastating (the bomb), and what was devastated (the RUC station). This difference is partly on account of the grammatical nature of the two verbs used, *devastated* and *exploded*. *Devastated* requires additional information (in the form of what was devastated), because of the kind of verb it is (it is called **transitive**), which *exploded* does not (it is called **intransitive**). In other words, you can't just say 'a Republican bomb devastated' without saying what was devastated, whereas you can just say 'a massive car bomb exploded'.

So, in these two opening sentences, different linguistic forms have been chosen in each article, and two different representations of the event have been reported. *The Daily Telegraph* sentence represents two groups of people, the Republicans and the RUC, as being involved in the event; the Republicans own the bomb, the RUC is affected by it. Who does what to whom is also clearly present here, whereas *The Guardian* sentence does not include this information. 'The bomb exploded' is a linguistic structure where neither who was responsible for the explosion, nor what was affected by it, are made grammatically explicit. The choice of one word over another, one type of verb rather than another, or the way elements in a sentence are combined by words like 'after' or 'followed by', will always have an effect on the way any news story is presented, and the way events in it are interpreted.

Another difference in the way this story was reported can be found in the attribution of sources for information given in the text. As newspapers are concerned with the 'factual' reporting of events, one common feature of news stories is that they have to be authenticated by giving a source for the information they contain. These sources can range from official comments to on the spot eyewitness accounts. Some elements in a story are presented as having no named source, as in the following examples:

> *It is thought* that the Police station was unmanned at the time
> *It was announced* that the UDP [the Ulster Democratic Party] […] would be allowed back into the talks on Monday
> *It was thought* that no one was seriously injured.

Sometimes an information source is given as a collective group rather than an individual, e.g. 'security sources had warned'. It is also interesting to compare how the eye witness accounts of the events in these two reports are selected:

> Harry Stevenson, 70, deputy district master of the local Orange Order, said: 'this was the IRA giving their response to democracy. Talking to Republicans has only encouraged them'.
>
> (*The Daily Telegraph*)

> A man who had been walking down the street when the bomb went off said: 'A massive flame went up after a huge blast, then glass and rubble came down from the sky – I thought I was going to die.'
> One said: 'We had just returned when the windows came in around us'.
> Another said: 'The police station has been reduced to a mangled wreckage'.
>
> (*The Guardian*)

The Daily Telegraph report has used the words of a local man who represents the Protestant Orange Order, and he clearly lays the blame for the explosion with the IRA. Although the previous paragraph mentions that 'more than 200 Orangemen and their guests had been holding a dance in the parochial hall next to the police station when the warning came', it is not actually made clear in the text that Harry Stevenson was among them. It is through the specific description of him in the next paragraph as 'deputy district master of the local Orange Order' that readers make the inference that he may have been in the hall. *The Guardian* report, on the other hand, uses the words of an unnamed 'man in the street', and 'customers in the Norman Inn' to give a different type of account of the event, where no blame is attributed for the explosion, only a description of its effect. The overall effect of the linguistic choices of the two newspapers is to give a different focus to the event, with *The Daily Telegraph* having a greater emphasis on the sectarian divisions in Northern Ireland, focusing on the Republican movement and the IRA. The difference in focus can be seen to reflect the different political perspectives of the two newspapers.

The attribution of a source is important to the level of 'factuality' that can be claimed for a story. In the following extract from a story about Princess Diana and British rugby player, Will Carling, the 'facts' of the case are far from clear. Although sources are given, the original source of the information on which the newspaper bases its report is masked by the way this paragraph is written. A complex series of reporting phrases appear to indicate the source, but effectively succeed in making it quite difficult to retrieve. These phrases are italicised in the text below:

> The newspaper *claimed* Mr Carling arranged to take former England foot-baller Gary Lineker to lunch with the princess at Kensington Palace earlier this year. A friend of Mr Carling's *is reported as saying*: "He [Mr Carling] *told* me later Gary had bottled out *saying*, 'that woman's trouble'."
>
> (*The Guardian*, 7 August, 1995)

There are four sources of information mentioned in this passage: Lineker, Carling, Carling's friend, and a newspaper (*News of the World*). Their reports range from the direct 'said' and 'told' to the more mitigated 'is reported as saying' and 'claimed', suggesting that the paper is anxious not to claim outright that this third or fourth hand information is absolute fact.

In this section we have shown how the linguistic choices made in a text can construct different accounts, or linguistic representations, of events in the world. In doing so, we may have mentioned some terms for linguistic structures which are not familiar to you, but if you want to find out more about these structures, and how to use them in an analysis of a media text, you may find it useful to refer to Fairclough (1989: particularly Chapter 5), and Thornborrow and Wareing (1998).

ACTIVITY 4.1

1   Buy two newspapers and compare two versions of the same story. What differences can you detect in the way language is used? Do these differences influence or affect your interpretation of the event?

4.4 Commonsense discourses

The tendency to represent people, situations and events in regular and predictably similar ways results in the linguistic choices that are used in these representations becoming established in our culture as the most usual, prevailing ways of talking or writing about types of people and events. Once something has been represented in a particular way, it becomes more difficult to talk 'around', or 'outside', that representation, to find an alternative way of describing a social group X, or a political event Y. As discussed in Chapter 3, we call these prevailing choices in representation **commonsense** or **dominant discourses** (see also Chapter 2, this volume, and Fairclough, 1989).

An illustration of how one event can become the frame for representing subsequent events is the tendency to refer to any story of American presidential cover-up scandal as some kind of 'gate'. Since Nixon and Watergate, there has been Reagan and 'Irangate', Clinton and 'Whitewatergate', followed by 'Zippergate', and 'Fornigate'. While the history and circumstances of each individual situation may be distinct, the use of the term 'gate' categorises them according to the notion of an American president deliberately setting out to deceive the American public. The category has also been taken up by the British press and has been used in the context of the British royal family. 'Camillagate' was the story of the long-standing relationship between Prince Charles and Camilla Parker-Bowles, which hit the headlines some years after his marriage to Diana, when her problems with him and other members of the royal family had entered the public domain.

4.4.1 The power to change?

If the media are powerful as a site for producing and maintaining dominant discourses, as we have claimed in the previous section, they can also be a possible site for change. One of the most publicly discussed changes in recent years has been the move to use non-sexist language, and to encourage **symmetry** in the representation of men and women. Sometimes the press can be seen to be trying to adopt grammatical forms which are neutral, such as the **third person pronoun** 'they' or 'them' as a non-specified gender **pronoun**.

The following extract is from a story about Texan farmers suing the talk show host Oprah Winfrey for damaging their business when she invited people on to her show to talk about the risks involved in eating American beef:

> And this year *the average American* will chew *their* way through 63lb of Texan beef, compared to only 51lb of chicken and 46.7lb of pork. It's an ill-advised man who stands between *an American* and *his* burgers.
>
> (*The Guardian*, 10 February, 1998)

This extract shows the use of the **unmarked** possessive form *their* (rather than *his* or *her*) in the phrase 'chew their way through' to refer back to the earlier noun phrase 'the average American'. So far, so non-sexist. But in the following sentence, this is not sustained, and we have the **marked** male forms 'it's an ill-advised man' (rather than 'it's an ill-advised person') representing the actor in this sentence as male, and 'an American and his burgers', which also represents the average American as male. (For more on the use of **asymmetrical** language in the representation of gender, see Chapter 5.)

Another way in which the media can have a powerful role in establishing commonsense discourses is in the coinage and use of new terms and concepts. The media are sometimes responsible for labelling certain events or social phenomena, and this label enters the language as a new term, for example, the phrase 'political correctness'. This refers to the practice of paying more careful attention to the use of words and phrases in order to represent social groups in a fairer, more positive manner. However, ironically enough, the current use of the phrase 'political correctness' in many media contexts has taken on a much more negative **connotation**, and being 'politically correct' tends now be an accusation rather than praise, as shown in the phrase: 'the victims of political correctitude' (*Evening Standard*, 27 January, 1998). (See Chapters 1 and 3 for more on 'political correctness'.)

In this section we have introduced the concept of 'dominant discourses' within the context of the media, and have suggested that these discourses are produced by recurring similarities in the way information is represented. We have looked briefly at some examples of linguistic choice in reporting political events, the representation of women, and the concept of political correctness. In the next section we turn to the question of 'voice' in the media, looking at whose voices are represented, and who gets to say what.

4.5 Media voices: accent and register

ACTIVITY 4.2 ▬▬▬▬▬▬▬▬▬▬▬▬▬▬▬▬▬▬▬▬▬▬

2   When you listen to the news on your local radio station, what **accent** does the newsreader have? Is this the same as those on the national, or more prestigious, radio station? Listen to the television news at different times of the day; do you notice any difference in the accents of the newsreaders at these times?

In the early days of news broadcasting in Britain, the accent used almost exclusively by presenters was one called advanced **received pronunciation** (advanced **RP**). This was the accent of the educated and the wealthy, which gave no indication of what part of the country the speaker came from. This accent gave rise to the expression '**BBC** English', so strong was the link between this accent and the British Broadcasting Corporation. This has now given way to what is known as mainstream RP, an accent which sounds less formal than advanced RP, and is the one that most people in Britain generally hear when they listen to newsreaders on national television.

This established use of mainstream RP is linked to the continuing perceived status of RP as an accent of authority. In radio and television discourse, the occurrence of marked regional variation in accent in the national news tends to be organised according to a hierarchy within programmes: the main news readers in the television studio read in standard English, with a mainstream RP accent; while the accents of specialist reporters outside the studio 'at the scene' are much less constrained and may sometimes be regionally marked (for example, one well-known BBC TV journalist and political commentator, John Cole, had a marked Northern Irish accent). Voice-overs in documentaries are also likely to be mainstream RP, while the accents of sports commentators, weather presenters, political commentators and other media 'voices' tend to be more regionally varied.

At one time this difference was especially noticeable on British television when a particular sports journalist would modify slightly his accent depending on which programme he was reporting for. On the national six o'clock evening news he would give the sports news bulletin in a mainstream RP accent, and half an hour later, on the local London South East news, he would shift into a more marked London accent.

Allan Bell (1984) calls this phenomenon '**audience design**' where a speaker changes their style of speech according to the person or people they are addressing. Bell also suggests that since radio and television presenters are addressing a distant, unknown audience of viewers and listeners, then they may design their speech according to certain linguistic 'values' or '**norms**'. In this case, newsreaders may be selecting one **variety** over another according to the conventionally prestigious norms of RP, rather than according to the actual audience they are addressing. This is a particular type of audience design that Bell calls 'referee design'.

4.5.1 Variation in register

Register has been defined as **linguistic variation** according to the context of use (Halliday, 1972). This means that we expect to find language used in different ways according to the situation it occurs in, and according to different types of media. For example, the register of weather forecasting in Britain depends on three features: its topic or **field** (the weather around the country), its **tenor** (the way it is delivered by the presenter), and its communicative **mode** (speech, writing and some visual modes in the form of maps and icons). We expect a weather bulletin to contain technical vocabulary relating to temperature, high and low pressure, cyclones etc., but we also expect the presenter, unlike newscasters, to address the audience directly, by saying things like 'look at this rain moving in from the west here'. On TV weather reports, there is also usually some visual representation of the weather being described, for example a small sun to represent sunshine, arrows for the direction of the wind, and snowflakes for wintry conditions. The register of weather forecasting depends also on the cultural context of the broadcast. The British format has just been described, but the format can vary from country to country.

The same expectations of linguistic register (language variation according to context) apply to other media **genres**, where there are conventions of appropriate language use for specific types of programme. When these conventions are well established, often the form of how something is reported can outweigh the content, or the information itself.

A famous media hoax used a well established media format (the documentary) to broadcast information that was false. A report of a 'spaghetti harvest', broadcast on BBC One's documentary programme *Panorama* on 1 April, 1957 (April 1st being a traditional date for practical jokes), showed strands of pasta growing on trees, while a male RP voice-over provided a serious commentary on traditional spaghetti farming in Italy. Radio, TV and newspapers in the UK still successfully play hoaxes on the public on April 1st. Similarly, though unintentionally, misleading was the radio broadcast in the USA on 30 October, 1938, of Orson Welles' reading of H. G. Wells' short story *The War of the Worlds*. It caused panic amongst listeners who believed that New Jersey was being invaded by Martians.

These occurrences demonstrate the potential power of the broadcast word to be received by the public as authoritative, factual and believable. On the other hand, research into how audiences react to and interpret news programmes (Morley, 1980, 1992; Richardson and Corner, 1986; Moores, 1993) has suggested that the viewing public is not always so ready to believe events as they are presented through the news media, and has other resources for interpreting what it sees and hears on the news.

However, it does remain the case that the media are constantly shaping our expectations about the way different kinds of information are transmitted, and these conventional formats can play an important part in the way we interpret the messages they contain. Language plays a central role in structuring these conventions through the association of particular registers with specific types of programme, such as the language of documentaries, where voice-over commentaries can often produce an effect of authority and objectivity in their account of events on the screen (see Fairclough, 1995).

The effect of an institutional, authoritative, objective voice can be compared to the effect produced by voices which are beginning to be heard on television in new media genres such as BBC Television's *Video Nation* slots. These are very short video film sequences, lasting only a few minutes, made by 'ordinary' (i.e. non-institutional) people, about themselves, or any topic they feel strongly about. The growth of public participation programmes and phone-in radio shows also provides a space for lay people to contribute to the variety of voices represented in the media, as we shall see next, although the final 'gatekeeping' to decide who gets access, and who does not, remains with the broadcasting institutions.

4.6 Public participation in the media

Programmes which involve audience participation, such as *Oprah Winfrey* and *Donahue* in the US, *Kilroy* and *Esther* in Britain, have been growing in popularity and number, and achieve very high viewing ratings. There is some disagreement about whether these programmes provide the opportunity for more democratic debate in the media, or whether they in fact depoliticise important issues by presenting them in this format. Some theorists (e.g. Livingstone and Lunt, 1994) have argued that these programmes open up access to an important public domain for people whose voices and opinions are not usually heard on television, and that talk shows provide a powerful space for the voices of ordinary, lay members of the public to be privileged over the voices of institutional representatives and experts whose opinions and views usually predominate elsewhere in other media genres. Others (e.g. Fairclough, 1995) have argued against this view, saying that audience participation programmes are structured in such a way that the discourse of the experts and the institution is still the framing, dominant discourse, while the discourse of lay participants is always mediated and constrained within the institutional format.

An example of this can be found in a study of the interaction between host and callers to a London talk radio show. Ian Hutchby (1996) explores the strategies available to participants in argument sequences, and shows that typically the caller 'goes first', by stating their position in relation to a particular topic, while the host 'goes second', challenging the caller's opinion without necessarily having to produce one of their own. The following transcript illustrates this phenomenon:

```
1 CALLER:   When you look at e:r the childcare facilities in
2           this country, .hh we're very very low (.) i-on
```

```
3              the league table in Europe of (.) you know if
4              you try to get a child into a nursery it's

5              very difficult in this country. .hh An' in fa:ct it's
6              getting wor::se.
7  HOST:       What's that got to do with it.
8  CALLER:     .phh Well I think whu- what 'at's gotta d-do
9              with it is....
```

(Hutchby, 1996: H:21.11.88:11.1)

This resource of 'going second' in an argument is available to both caller and host, but in this context is principally used by the host, making them interactionally most powerful participant through their position as challenger to a previously stated claim.

Another strategy which also contributes to the interactional power of the TV host over audience participants is illustrated in the following transcript of a sequence in a British talk show, *Kilroy*. Here, the talk of the lay audience member is directed and to some extent controlled by the host's intervention and questioning:

```
1  HOST:    Tell me about this (.) household
2  ALICE:   erm well both my parents are very loving (.)
3           very accepting of lots of things (.) and (.)
4           therefore that rubs off (.) on my sister and
5           I -erm
6  HOST:    -how old are you
7  ALICE:   nineteen
8  HOST:    how old's your sister
9  ALICE:   sixteen
10 HOST:    mmm
11 ALICE:   and erm (1.0) I've lived with both separately (.)
12          I've lived with Dad for the last couple of years
13          -now
14 HOST:    -does Dad have a lover
15 ALICE:   Yes he does (.) -Pedro
16 HOST:                      -You live with Dad and lover
17 ALICE:   yes
18 HOST:    How old were you when you lived with Dad and
19          lover
20 ALICE:   erm (1.0) I was seventeen when I moved to
21          Melbourne
22 HOST:    cause you problems
```

23	ALICE:	no
24	HOST:	did you find it strange
25	ALICE:	no
26	HOST:	find it difficult
27	ALICE:	no it's just like living with any other
28		parent and their lover
29	HOST:	it's just like living with any other parent
30		and their lover

(Thornborrow, 1997: Adoption/Kilroy/1994)

In this extract, Alice is asked by the host to tell the story of how she came to live with her father and his male partner. However, she is not left to tell her own story without the intervention of the host. She starts by focusing on the quality of the relationship between her and her parents (lines 2–5), but the host interrupts her several times, asking her questions which elicit certain kinds of information (about her age, her father's relationship, and how she felt about it), resulting in a story which is jointly produced, rather than a story told by Alice in her own words.

4.7 Summary

In this chapter we have discussed the power of the media to determine what counts as news, and also how it gets represented. We have outlined the conflicting views of the media, on the one hand as organs of democracy, providing essential public information, and on the other, as powerful monopolies which relentlessly pursue their own interests. With the increase of public access to broadcasting space, and particularly with the arrival of the World Wide Web, and its potential for unregulated mass communication, these questions remain central to the debates about the function and power of the mass media. Are they providing an emerging forum for public debate, or are they still closely-monitored institutions with hierarchies of discourse and systems of 'gatekeeping' which continue to control who gets to say what, and how? An analysis of the language and discourse used in mediated contexts provides a valuable way of finding evidence to support or counter these claims.

Suggestions for further reading

Graddol, David and Boyd-Barrett, Oliver (eds) (1994) *Media Texts: Authors and Readers*, Clevedon: Multilingual Matters.
A collection of essays which cover a range of different themes in media discourse, from the style and structure of news stories, the role of visuals, to more theoretical discussions of the concept of 'author', and the interpretive role of the audience.

Simpson, Paul (1993) *Language, Ideology and Point of View*, London: Routledge.
This is an accessible account of the relationship between linguistic forms and point of view in a wide variety of media.

Thornborrow, Joanna and Wareing, Shân (1998) *Patterns in Language: An Introduction to Language and Literary Style*, London: Routledge.
A practical introduction to how to approach texts using linguistic tools of analysis. Chapter 7 deals specifically with examples of media language.

Chapter 5

Language and gender

Shân Wareing

5.1 Introduction

In the preceding chapters, we have focused on the ways in which **representation** in language can have an impact on perception, and on forms of language use which are typical in two contexts: politics and in the media. This chapter also looks at representation and at typical forms of language use, in this case, in relation to gender. We will consider **asymmetrical** representations of women and men, and why these can be considered sexist. We will then look at whether women and men use language in different ways, and the possible reasons for gender based differences in conversational styles. The chapter ends by probing the concept of gender.

It may help to start with an explanation of what is meant by the terms 'sex' and 'gender'. 'Sex' refers to biological category, which is usually fixed before birth. 'Gender' refers to social category, which is associated with certain behaviour. Bicycle design neatly illustrates the difference between the two: bike saddles designed for women are usually wider than saddles designed for men, because women have a wider pelvic girdle (a sex difference). Bikes without a crossbar, so riders can wear skirts, are designed in response to a gender difference, since there is no biological reason why, in some cultures, women wear skirts and men don't.

So what is meant by 'sexism'? Sexist language represents women and men unequally, as if members of one sex were somehow less completely human, less complex, and had fewer rights than members of the other sex. Sexist language also presents stereotypes of women and men, sometimes to the disadvantage of both, but more often to the disadvantage of women.

It is debatable whether language can actually be sexist against men (as opposed to just rude), or only against women. Clearly language can represent men as less complex, less fully human or entitled to fewer rights than women. However, whether this counts as sexist or not can be argued to depend on the distribution of power in society as a whole. Generally speaking, men still hold more 'high status' occupations in this society than women do; men still own more property and earn more than women. There are still more male politicians, more male company directors, more male judges, professors, surgeons, head teachers and film directors. Men also tend to have more physical power; domestic violence appears to be perpetrated more often by men against women than the other way around. It is debatable whether using language to diminish men has the same effect as using language to diminish women, since the power relations underlying the language use are different. We will mainly be looking at sexist language which diminishes women, but one example of language which represents men in demeaning ways appears in section 5.2.6.

5.2 How is English sexist?

Sexist language can be discussed in two ways; first, as the extent to which the English language system is inherently sexist, and second, as the extent to which some ways of using language are sexist. To consider the first approach, the extent to which the English language system is sexist, one of the things we look for is **symmetry** versus **asymmetry** in the vocabulary or **lexis**.

5.2.1 Symmetry and asymmetry

A clear example of symmetry can be found in English terms for horses. *Horse* is a **generic** term which covers animals of both sexes:

(1) generic   *horse*
     female   *mare*
     male   *stallion*
     young   *foal* (either sex)
     young female   *filly*
     young male   *colt*

The terms for human beings follow a similar system, but are not so symmetrical in the way they are used:

(2) generic   *Man*
     female   *woman*
     male   *man*
     young   *child*
     young female   *girl*
     young male   *boy*

Example (2) indicates the ambiguity of the term *Man/man*. Speakers and writers often blur the distinction between the use of the word *Man* generically, to mean women, men, girls and boys, and the use of *man* to mean only men (and not women or children). This is illustrated in example (3) below, where the first mention of *Man* appears to be in its generic sense, but the next sentence makes it clear that in fact *Man* here means men and not women.

(3)   For decades, pubs have been Man's best friend. He could take his wife, his girlfriend, but not his children. But now that's all about to change.
       (News at 10, ITV[1], 3 January, 1995, on changes in the laws regarding children in licensed drinking bars)

Another kind of asymmetry in the way the system shown in (2) is applied, is the use of *girl* to describe adult women, where *man* would almost certainly be used if the reference were to an adult male. Consider this headline and the first sentence of an article from the *Daily Mail* (24 September, 1997):

(4)   **Police girl wins sex bias case by a split verdict**
       A policewoman who allegedly threatened to kill her chief constable and have the legs of a senior officer broken won a controversial sex discrimination case yesterday...
       The 34-year-old officer, who said her high-flying career was ruined by bullying male colleagues, now expects to receive up to £250,000 in compensation...

Girl is used instead of *woman*, probably because of the emphasis on youth as what makes adult females attractive. Since women's status tends to be far more dependent on their attractiveness than men's is (see example (17) below), the use of *girl* to imply that you are not yet 'old' is usually assumed to be a compliment. Would a male police officer ever be called a *police boy* in a headline (especially if he was 34)?

The use of titles is also asymmetrical:

(5)   woman   Miss / Mrs / Ms
       man   Mr

An adult male can be assumed to use the title *Mr* before his family name, unless he has another title such as *Dr* or *Judge*. However, an adult woman (who does not use another title such as *Dr* or *Judge*) may use one of three titles: *Miss, Mrs* or *Ms*. Thus any woman who gives her preferred title on a form is revealing far more information about herself than a man does. *Miss* reveals she is unmarried (or chooses to present herself as such). *Mrs* indicates that she is married. *Ms*, a relatively new title, was introduced to end the inequality in the system but instead you could say that the inequality has increased. Instead of having only one title (which does not reveal marital status, in line with titles for men) there are now three possible titles in circulation, and all three appear alongside *Mr* on most of the forms we have to fill in.

If you choose not to tell the world your marital status by selecting *Ms*, some people will assume you are divorced; others will assume you are a feminist; i.e. the use of *Ms*, if you had the choice of using *Miss* or *Mrs*, can seem to carry information about your political opinions. Furthermore, since the introduction of *Ms*, selecting *Miss* or *Mrs* as your title can seem to indicate that you do not want to appear to be a feminist. Therefore not only do two of the titles women use reveal marital status, all three titles can appear to carry information about the user's political affiliations. This is not a situation men face!

The titles *Miss* and *Mrs* are a reminder of a time when the power relations between women and men were much more markedly unequal than they are today for most women living in Europe or the US. Women were then regarded as the responsibility, or indeed the property, of either their father or their husband. Some forms of marriage service still require women to be 'given away' by their father (or other male relative) to their husband. Women's political and economic rights have changed considerably over the twentieth century, with, amongst other changes, the advent of votes for women, equal opportunities policies, and effective birth control. However, our language still allows us to indicate the marital status of a woman in way that does not exist for men.

5.2.2 Unmarked and marked terms

Another useful concept when analysing sexism is that of **unmarked** and **marked** terms. This is still asymmetry, but of a specific kind. For example, *lion*, an unmarked form, can refer to a male or female lion. However, the term used for a male lion is also *lion*, while a female lion is referred to by a marked term, *lioness* (it is 'marked' because it has the additional suffix *-ess*). It is quite common for 'unmarked' terms to refer to males, while to refer to a female, the terms are 'marked' by adding a suffix. This may make terms for females appear to differ from the 'standard'. For example:

(6) waiter/waitress
     host/hostess
     actor/actress

The marked terms on the right are used less nowadays, and the unmarked terms on the left are often used for women as well as men, which indicates that language and attitudes are changing. However, it is also true that some terms which can apparently refer to females or males, such as *surgeon*, *doctor*, *professor* and *nurse*, are in fact sometimes used as if they really only applied to one gender. People refer to a *lady doctor*, a *woman professor* or *woman surgeon*, implying that the norm is male, and to a *male nurse*, implying that the norm is female. It should be noted that nurses are of lower status than the other occupations mentioned. Therefore one way which these examples can be interpreted as sexist is that they imply that 'normal' (or, in the case of the medical profession, 'high status') people are men.

5.2.3 Semantic derogation

The process of words which refer to women acquiring demeaning or sexual **connotations** has been widely observed, and has been termed **semantic derogation**. (*Semantic* is a linguistic term referring to meaning; *derogation* means 'to cause to seem inferior'). Examples (7) to (10) illustrate this process.

(7) gentleman or lord/lady

Lady is used in contexts where is it highly improbable that *gentleman* or *lord* would be used. In the UK, *lady* is commonly used to form the expressions: *dinner lady* (a woman who serves meals to schoolchildren), *lollipop lady* (a woman who helps school children to cross roads) and *charlady* (a domestic cleaner). If men were filling these roles, would you expect them to be referred to as *dinner gentlemen*, or *dinner lords*? As *lollipop lords* or *lollipop gentlemen*? As *charlords*? Probably not! *Lady* is used in contexts where *man* or a gender-free term is used if the job is done by a male (*lollipop man* and *cleaner* are in common use, for example).

(8) master/mistress

'He is my master' usually means 'he is my boss' or 'he has more power than me'. 'She is my mistress' is most likely to be interpreted as meaning 'she is my illicit lover'. This demonstrates two phenomena; first that words for women tend to lose status (being someone's illicit lover usually is a much less powerful position than being their boss), and second, that words for women often end up referring to women in a sexual capacity. This has clearly happened to *mistress* and not to *master*. Even the term 'woman' is also sometimes used to refer to women as sexual activity, as in the phrase *wine, women and song*.

(9) sir/madam

Sir and *madam* can both be used to refer to high status people, but *madam*, unlike *sir*, is also used to refer to a brothel keeper.

(10) bachelor /spinster or old maid

All three terms refer to an unmarried person, but *spinster* and *old maid* appear to be rarely used nowadays, perhaps because their associations are so negative. *Bachelor*, however, usually has positive connotations. *The bachelor life* and *a bachelor pad* (an apartment for a single man) are generally regarded as glamorous; a bachelor is someone who has succeeded in not getting tied down. *Spinster* and *old maid* on the other hand suggest to many people someone old, grey, ugly, and unable to 'get a man'. *Bachelor girl* can be used to refer to an unmarried woman, to avoid the stigma of the other terms; however, this expression follows the pattern of unmarked and marked terms discussed above (*bachelor* is the 'norm', *bachelor girl* the marked form).

The examples cited above are all asymmetrical, and diminish women rather than men, by representing women as the property of men, as being of lower status, and as being primarily sexual beings. If we agree with the arguments laid out in Chapter 2, these usages not only represent women unequally, they may also contribute to women receiving unfair treatment.

―――――――――――――――――――――――――――――――――― **ACTIVITY 5.1**

1   Many of the examples in this chapter come from British newspapers. If you are interested in this area, you could conduct a small research project by buying a selection of newspapers over a few days, and collecting as many examples as you can find of asymmetrical references to women and men. If your newspapers are not British, are there still examples of sexism? Or do you think your national newspapers are less sexist, or perhaps sexist in other ways?

5.2.4 Sexism in discourse

In section 5.2, it was stated that sometimes sexism is not located in specific words but in the **discourse**, that is, by meanings created in a whole utterance or sentence, or a longer text. Below are some examples of apparently non-gender specific terms being used in a context which in fact shows they are being used to refer exclusively to men. The information which indicates that the use is specific is contained elsewhere in the discourse. Sometimes this additional information is described as **disambiguating** the generic term (that is, it indicates more exactly to what the term refers). *Generic* (non-gender specific) terms are shown in *italic*; GENDER SPECIFIC terms are in SMALL CAPITALS.

(11) *People* feel entitled to the car, the GIRL, etc. If *they*'re let down, *they* blame *themselves*.

(Oliver James, quoted by Emma Cook in
The Independent, 31 August, 1997)

(12) *Your* car says a lot about *you*, *you* big HUNKY STUD.
Drive a Ferrari? *You're sporty and rich*. A Rolls Royce? *Successful and dignified*. The Daihatsu Hijet MPV? Infallible in the sack*. Think about it. Why else would a MAN need a car that carries a family of six?

(Car advert *Daily Mail* 7 August, 1997)

(13) . . . *several of Hollywood's most powerful players* have arrangements with what in pre-palimony terms were 'common-law WIVES' – Kurt and Goldie, Tim and Susan, and Hugh and Elizabeth – one has to wonder: why do *stars* bother to get married at all?

(Alison Powell, *The Guide* (*The Guardian* newspaper's weekly guide to arts and entertainment), 13 September, 1997)

(14) *They* haven't talked to *their* WIVES, *their children* or *their dogs* about the programme.

(BBC spokeswoman denying programme makers leaked details of a controversial interview with Princess Diana, reported in
Time Out, 22–29 November, 1995)

(15) According to disapproving church writers, the *Vikings* were addicted to drink, gluttony and WOMEN.

(The Jorvik Viking History Centre, York (seen in 1997))

ACTIVITY 5.2 ▬▬▬▬▬▬▬▬▬▬▬▬▬▬▬▬▬▬

2   In example (16) below, can you identify the gender specific references and the generic, or gender neutral, references in these descriptions of dress codes in London restaurants?

* can the phrase *infallible in the sack* refer to both women and men, or only to men?

(16) **WHO DRESSES FOR DINNER?**
The Causerie Restaurant, Claridges's Hotel
The rule of jacket and tie at all times has become more relaxed. The public rooms require smartness without formality; the restaurant remains firmly jacket and tie. Those who come without a tie are invited to choose one from a selection held at the door – 'all very fine ties'. The restaurant used to ask any gentleman who removed his jacket during the meal to put it on again, but this practice appears to be dying out. The recalcitrant 'star' who came in less than formal clothes would be admitted, but respectfully asked to improve next time.

The Ritz
Tries very hard to ensure no denims or trainers. Smart casual is the norm for breakfast, while at lunch, tea and dinner, jacket and tie are mandatory. A spokeswoman draws attention to 20 silk Turnbull and Asser ties, and a selection of jackets, for guests who do not provide their own. Ladies' only requirement is to be smart: 'It's hard with the ladies, but we tend not to make an issue of it'.

The River Café, Hammersmith
Owned by the wife of architect Sir Richard Rogers, and one of the most fashionable restaurants in London, it has no code at all, but a spokesman did indicate that bare chests would not be allowed, 'although people haven't actually started stripping off', he adds.
(James Bristow, *The Independent*, 20 September, 1996)

You will probably have noticed that 'guests' are assumed in all three paragraphs to be male, since jackets and ties are rarely regarded as appropriate formal wear for women, and the Ritz paragraph distinguishes explicitly between *guests* and *ladies*. You may also have noticed that the owner of the River Café is not identified by name at all, only by her relationship to her husband!

5.2.5 Insults and obscenities

One aspect of sexism in language which we have not discussed yet is probably the most obvious kind: direct insults which are aimed at women rather than men. For example, in a short article titled 'Selina still has star quality', this comparison of three British television presenters, Selina Scott, Angela Rippon and Anna Ford, is made:

(17) She [Scott] made Angela Rippon and Anna Ford look like a couple
of sock-knitting crones

(John Junor 1980, cited by Peter McKay in
the *Daily Mail* 22 September, 1997)

The comparison is made solely in terms of the three women's appearance. Junor
and McKay both apparently regard Scott as more worthy of success than Rippon
and Ford because they consider her more attractive. To emphasise how comparatively unattractive he finds Rippon and Ford, Junor invokes a stereotype of old
women: that they knit socks, and that they are ugly. It is hard to imagine a similar
assessment of male presenters, based on looks and stereotypes of old men.

ACTIVITY 5.3

3   Insults and obscene words are often to do with sexual behaviour and parts
of the body. To investigate whether there is a sexist bias in insults and
obscene terms, make a list of as many as you can think of (you can do this
on your own, or in class). Now group the terms you have listed into separate lists according to what they describe. Compare the length of your different lists, and the kind of terms they contain (for example, are they
funny? blasphemous? very obscene or only mildly? to do with sexual
behaviour or with body parts?): Decide whether your lists provide you
with evidence of sexism in English.

It is common, as a result of this activity, to find that there are far more
terms to describe promiscuous women than men, that insults for women are
often harsher and less funny, and that the words that many people find most
obscene describe women's sexual organs, not men's. (See also Chapters 6 and 7
for examples of insult terms centred on ethnicity and age.)

5.2.6 Sexism against men?

In introducing this section, I raised the question of whether language could be
sexist against men. The following example seems to illustrate the other side of
the coin:

(18) Last week I asked for alternative suggestions for the phrase *toy boy*.
Hundreds have poured in from men and women. Here's my pick of

the best: HRT (Husband Replacement Therapy), Youthfool, Wrinkle picker, Joy Boy, GIBBET (Good In Bed But Extremely Temporary), Mantress, Sugar laddie, POW (Prefers Older Women), Mutton Fodder and Booster Rooster. Glad Lad, Juvenile Lead, Studlet, Born-Later-Babe, Bimboy, Bounty Hunter, Nappy Chappy, Ego Booster, Mini Mate, Play Mite, Lap Chap and Tom Kitten. Muscle Tussle, Handsome Sansom, Younger Monger, Romp Tot, Cub Class, Game Boy and Sapling. Homelette, Boncubine, Little Soldier, Beddyboy, Passion Puppy, Honkybonk, Kideology Kid and Himbo.

(*Daily Mail*, 28 May, 1997)

Do you think the sexist effect in example (18) is the same as in the previous examples discussed? Do you think there is a difference between sexism directed at women and at men, or does sexism always have the same effect?

5.3 Do women and men talk differently?

Perhaps some of the examples discussed above seem to you more likely to be used by women or by men. There is plenty of anecdotal evidence around that there are differences in the way men and women talk. A common stereotype is that women talk more than men; perhaps you have heard people say things like: 'women never stop talking'. Women's talk is often described in terms seldom used about men's talk: *gossip*, *chatter*, *nag*, *rabbit*, *yak*, and *natter* are all terms used to refer predominantly to women's conversations. They all imply that women's talk is plentiful but rather pointless. (See also Chapters 6 and 7 on the value placed on the language or talk of other minority groups.)

There has been a considerable amount of research in this area, and the findings have been that there are sometimes quite dramatic differences in the ways men and women talk. Sometimes these are the opposite of what you might expect. For example, the evidence strongly suggests that men on the whole talk far more than women, in contradiction of the stereotype. This is an important finding, because it shows **ideology** at work (as discussed in Chapter 3). It is so much a part of our 'common sense' that women talk more than men, that we tend to assume it's true despite plentiful evidence around us to the contrary. The fact that we do tend to believe that women talk too much, when research shows men on average talk more than women, also indicates how women, and women's activities, have tended to be undervalued.

The differences between women's and men's use of language are remarkably many and varied. For example, there is evidence at the level of **phonology** that women and men may vary in their pronunciation. There isn't enough space in this chapter to investigate this area, but if you are interested you should read Trudgill (1972), Milroy (1987), Thomas (1989) and Coates (1993: 61–86). There is also evidence of **syntactic** differences, i.e., the kinds of grammatical constructions we use (see Coates, 1993: 76–7). Although these areas are worthy of much greater discussion, in this chapter we will concentrate on the area of discoursal differences, that is, variation in the kinds of things we talk about, and how we conduct conversations.

5.3.1 How much talk?

As stated above, stereotypes of women's and men's talking styles usually portray women talking far more than men (see Coates, 1993: 16–37, for an overview of common stereotypes and prejudices). As also stated above, men (and boys) in fact appear from the research to talk more in mixed sex groups than women (and girls) do. Studies on this which you might want to check for more information include Fishman, 1980; Spender, 1980; Swann, 1989. Spender (1990: 41–2) gives an overview of the research. The proportions most frequently quoted are that in a mixed sex conversation, the average amount of time for which a man will talk will be approximately twice as long as the average amount for which a woman will talk. There is evidence that women who talk for more than one third of the available time will be regarded by others as talking too much.

This unevenness in how much women and men are expected to talk is also found in school classrooms, where boys talk more in front of the whole class than girls do, and absorb more of the teacher's time. As a consequence of this research, changes to teaching styles in the UK were made to distribute the amount of classroom talk, and the teacher's time, more fairly.

5.3.2 Turn construction and interruption

One of the very famous findings from research into language and gender differences is the extent to which men interrupt women. It appears that men interrupt women more than they interrupt other men, far more than women interrupt men, and more than women interrupt other women (see Coates, 1993: 107–13; and for a critical review, see James and Clarke, 1993). The finding that men interrupt women so frequently is often argued to indicate that men act as if they have more right than women to speak in mixed sex conversations, and that women act as if they had less right to speak than men.

The research in this area also discovered that women, particularly in single sex conversations, are more likely to overlap one another's talk than men are.

This overlapping talk differs from interruptions because two or more speakers can continue talking at the same time on the same topic without any apparent sense of their right to speak being violated. This data is often used to argue that women value co-operation and collaboration very highly in their conversations, while men perhaps feel uncomfortable with the degree of intimacy that overlapping talk involves.

5.3.3 Back channel support

Research suggests women are often more active than men in supportive roles in conversation. It appears that women give more **back channel support** than men do. Back channel support is the verbal and non-verbal feedback listeners give to speakers. Listeners can give feedback by saying things like *mmm*, *uhuh*, *yeah*, and by nodding, smiling, frowning, and by other body language including gestures and body posture. People who have written on this include Zimmerman and West (1975); Fishman (1983); Coates (1989); Jenkins and Cheshire (1990).

Not only do the studies suggest that women give more back channel support than men, some studies suggest that women's sense of when it is appropriate to give back channel support is more 'finely tuned' than men's, so that the speaker really feels they are being listened to. Not giving back channel support is usually reported as making the speaker feel unsure of themselves, and can lead to the speaker hesitating, repeating themselves and sometimes to their just ceasing to speak. If you are interested in testing this out, experiment with giving different amounts of back channel support and monitor the effect it has on the conversation.

5.3.4 Mitigated and aggravated forms

Women have been shown in some studies to use more **hedges** and **epistemic modal forms** than men. Hedges are linguistic forms which 'dilute' an assertion; for example: *sort of*, *like*, *I think*, and *kind of*. Epistemic modal forms indicate explicitly the speaker's attitude towards their utterance. For example, *should*, *would*, *could*, *may* and *might* (which are all **modal auxiliary verbs**) can be used to indicate you don't want to sound completely certain about something. Other words with a similar function are *perhaps*, *really* and *maybe*. Compare these two statements:

(a)   I'm going upstairs to study now
(b)   I guess perhaps I really could think about going upstairs to study now

The studies suggest that women exploit hedges and epistemic modal forms more than men, although why this should be is disputed. Some scholars claim it is because women are less confident than men and feel nervous about asserting anything too strongly (see Lakoff, 1975, one of the first people to publish on this area). Other studies claim that women prefer to avoid conflict and so use forms which, by being less direct, allow disagreement to take place without explicit confrontation.

Here is an example of a 15-year-old girl using hedges to mitigate the force of her statement, in which she is questioning the interpretation made by another girl of a character in a play they are studying in school:

> Laura: But (.) but (.) *do you not think* that's *just* a big a. (.) it *could* be *just* a big act (1) he *might* not

(The dots in brackets indicate a pause shorter than 0.5 of a second; the figure 1 in brackets indicates a pause of one second.)

Laura is suggesting that her classmate's interpretation is wrong and that the character is just putting on 'a big act'. To make her objection, however, she uses very mitigating language, emphasised here with italics.

5.3.5 Topic development

Another way women's and men's conversations appear to vary is in the topics they choose to discuss. Women, it is said, select more personal topics: their family, their emotions and their friendships. Men, on the other hand, are said to prefer more impersonal topics, often based on factual or technical knowledge, such as football, cars, or home improvements. These require fewer intimate revelations, and also emphasise the exchange of information as the reason for the conversation. Women's conversations, it is claimed, focus more on the development and maintenance of the relationship between speakers, fostered by the exchange of intimate details and supportive listening (as discussed above).

ACTIVITY 5.4

4   Ask permission to tape a group of people talking. Transcribe approximately three minutes' worth of conversation and see which of the features discussed above you notice. Does your recording follow the gender-specific uses outlined above? This is a time-consuming activity, but it is worthwhile because you can learn so much from the process.

5.4 Possible explanations

So why might these differences exist? The situation is different from those which give rise to people speaking different languages or different **dialects**, which are usually associated with geographical or social distance. Women and men, on the other hand, grow up in the same families, go to school together, work together and socialise together.

5.4.1 Dominance

One explanation offered for these variations is 'dominance' theory, which takes the difference in power between women and men as the main cause of discoursal variation. As stated above, it is statistically the case that men tend to have more power than women, physically, financially and in workplace hierarchies. The ways we talk may be a reflection of the material differences between the sexes, and may also reinforce those differences, making them seem 'normal', part of the 'natural order of things'.

Research which supports this explanation includes Fishman (1980), and DeFrancisco (1991). The strength of this explanation is particularly clear in some situations, such as business meetings, where women often report that they have difficulty in gaining the floor (i.e. the right to speak), that they are more often interrupted, and that their points are not taken as seriously as men's are.

5.4.2 Difference

Two of the problems with dominance theory are that first, it may appear to cast all women as 'powerless victims', and second, it casts men as undermining, excluding and demeaning women. 'Difference theory' is a response to these difficulties. It suggests that women and men develop different styles of talking because, in fact, they are segregated at important stages of their lives. Deborah Tannen's work (1990, 1991) is often taken as an illustration of difference theory.

According to 'difference' theory, playing in single sex groups as children, and having same sex friendships in adult life, leads men and women to have separate 'sub-cultures' each of which have their own 'sub-cultural norms', that is, rules for behaviour and in particular, talking. Within their own sub-cultural groups, women's and men's conversational norms work perfectly well for what they want to accomplish. Women, the theory explains, desire from their relationships collaboration, intimacy, equality, understanding, support and approval. Men, on the other hand, allegedly place a greater premium on status and independence, and are less concerned about overt disagreement and inequality in their relationships. The rub comes when women and men try to communicate with one another: their different styles can lead to misunderstandings.

Some people link these characteristics to biological factors: that men's different hormonal balance means they are more aggressive than women. Others link it to socialisation: that girls are rewarded very early for behaving politely and putting the needs of others before their own, but are told off more than little boys for rough behaviour. Little boys, on the other hand, are praised for being 'active' and 'spirited'. These gendered socialisation patterns are not neutral, as you will probably have noticed: they still prepare women for being less socially powerful than men.

5.4.3 Analysis of gender

The weakness of both the models described above is that there is a tendency to regard 'women' as being all more or less the same: talking in the same ways and having the same expectations from relationships. In fact differences of age, nationality, religion, class, sexual orientation, regional and cultural background mean that two women may have different ideas of what it means to be 'a woman', and different expectations of their friendships and sexual relationships. Equally, men are not an homogenous group with shared values, but have diverse ways of thinking about their identity.

Another way of looking at the differences between the ways in which women and men use language is to see the differences in the way we use language as part of what creates our perception of gender. Newborn babies cannot easily be identified as 'girls' or 'boys' if they are dressed identically. However, in the UK, babies are frequently dressed in ways to make their gender clear, for example by the colours of their clothes. The use of colour to indicate gender is particularly marked when it comes to dressing boys. Many British people would feel quite disturbed by the thought of dressing a baby boy in pink. We use clothes, and other physical attributes we control such as our jewellery, hairstyles and use of makeup, to indicate our gender. Similarly, perhaps women and men adopt certain styles of talking as part of the process of demonstrating to the world what their gender is.

Finally, it is worth considering how many of the differences we observe are linked less to what people actually do when they talk and more to our perception of gender, and how we interpret the differences we notice. For example, in studies of interruption, it is notoriously difficult to agree on exactly what an interruption is and when one has occurred, making it a slightly ambiguous area. And because of this ambiguity, it is easy for our expectations to affect what we notice, and how we interpret what we notice, while ignoring other evidence which does not fit so neatly into our preconceptions.

5.5 Summary

In this chapter we looked first at sexism in English, created through asymmetry, marked and unmarked terms, and semantic derogation. We also looked at how it's possible to be sexist in discourse using terms which in another context might not be sexist at all. You were asked to consider whether it is possible to be sexist about men in the same way as it is about women. Bearing in mind the arguments made in Chapter 2, that representation reflects, and has an effect on, the way we perceive the world, you might consider whether the evidence of sexism in language is also evidence of sexism in society.

In the second part of the chapter, we looked at differences in the way women and men talk, and how evidence of these differences sometimes contradicts our 'common-sense' ideas. Two possible explanatory theories were put forward: dominance and difference theory. We ended with a word of warning: that it is very hard to be objective in our analysis of gender, since our perceptions in this area can easily be distorted by our expectations.

Note

1   Commercial television in the U.K.

Suggestions for further reading

Cameron, Deborah (1998) *The Feminist Critique of Language*, 2nd edn, London: Routledge.
    A wide and fascinating range of essays on the topic of women and language.
Coates, Jennifer (1993) *Women, Men and Language*, 2nd edn, London: Longman.
    The definitive overview of differences in women's and men's speech (phonological, syntactic and discoursal), written in a clear, accessible style.
Mills, Sara (1995) *Feminist Stylistics*, London: Routledge.
    Sexist language and how to analyse it: examples from literature, songs and advertisements.

Chapter 6

Language and ethnicity

Ishtla Singh

6.1 Introduction

This chapter explores language use in the context of ethnicity. We will look mainly at how language is used to **represent** ethnicity and at some of the consequences of this. We will also examine how different groups use language as an important marker of their ethnic identity. Before tackling these issues, however, we need to first address the question of what ethnicity means to people.

6.2 Defining ethnicity

If you were to take a quick poll on what the terms 'ethnic' and 'ethnicity' meant, the chances are you would get a mixed bag of definitions. Some might say 'to be ethnic is to be black', or 'ethnicity is to do with your roots, or your culture', or 'ethnicity means race'. These all contain a kernel of truth, since 'ethnic' is ultimately derived from the Greek word *ethnos* or 'nation'; and a nation is defined as a community which has a common history, cultural tradition and language. Since we each have cultural, historical and linguistic affiliations, we each also have an ethnic identity, in terms of which we can be (and often are) labelled. However, an individual can have more than one ethnic label, ranging from those they choose to those that are decided for them.

Two related concepts which are often used in discussions about ethnic groupings are 'ethnic majority' and 'ethnic minority'. The former term normally refers to the ethnic groups that hold social and political power in nations and the latter to groups which have very little or none. An ethnic majority is made up of the cultural group that has been dominant in shaping a nation's infrastructure, for example, its governmental and educational systems. The cultural affiliations of the ethnic majority (its religious beliefs and its language use, for example) also become primary because that group has the power to enforce them through the institutions they establish. People then come to see the things that have been shaped by the beliefs of the ethnic majority as the norm, and everything else as atypical. Thus, the terms 'ethnic' and 'ethnicity' are often used to refer to anything not part of the mainstream culture. For example, a telecast in Britain of *The Clothes Show* covered the British Hairdressing Awards, and the winner of the 'Afro-hair category' was said, by the presenter, to be 'exploring new directions for dressing ethnic hair' (**BBC** 1, 30 November, 1997). The presenter on a cookery programme broadcast on the same day on Channel 5[1] said of a dish of chicken with coconut curried couscous that 'the couscous [was] infused with all those ethnic flavours' (*Utter Nutter*, Channel 5, 30 November, 1997). The British supermarket chain ASDA has, in some of its branches, an 'Indian' counter, where customers can buy a package consisting of two curries, two pilau rice dishes and six 'mini ethnic' snacks. In all of these examples, we can see that the use of 'ethnic' really means 'different', since it is used in relation to various things: a hair type found in Africa, flavours that can be found in Middle Eastern and Eastern cooking, and East Indian food. What they all have in common is that they belong to ethnic minorities in Britain, and therefore symbolise differences from the 'normal' culture of the ethnic majority.

In many cases an ethnic majority is also made up of the bulk of a nation's population, and an ethnic minority of a numerically smaller group. However, it is important to note that just because a group is large in terms of actual numbers, it does not necessarily follow that they will have social and political power. In the sixteenth to nineteenth centuries, for example, many European powers colonised West Indian islands, setting up sugar plantations cultivated by imported African slaves. Each island had a few large plantations, each home to a European planter, who had perhaps been accompanied by his immediate family, and about 50–60 slaves. So in most islands, African slaves actually outnumbered their European masters. For example, it has been estimated that in 1684 in Barbados (an island colonised by Britain), there were 19,508 British but 62,136 African slaves (Watts, 1987: 311). However, this numerically larger group of slaves had no actual power, and few (if any) social and human rights. They were in fact an ethnic minority socially and politically.

One of the things you might have noticed from this example is that the cultural and historical dissimilarities between ethnic groups can be expressed in terms of differences of race and/or nationality. The Europeans and Africans were distinct from each other not only in terms of where they came from, their religious beliefs, their cultural practices and the languages they spoke, but also in terms of their racial characteristics. So we could label the ethnic majority as 'white'/'European'/'white European', and the ethnic minority as 'black'/ 'African'/'black African' respectively. Because labels of 'white' and 'black' are explicitly racial ones, using them can sometimes direct people into thinking of ethnic differences as being equivalent to racial differences, hence definitions such as 'to be ethnic is to be black'. And the use of 'ethnic' in relation to the features or customs of black or non-white groups which we saw exemplified earlier in 'ethnic hair' 'ethnic flavours' and 'ethnic snacks' both reflects and reinforces the connection between 'ethnic' and 'black'.

Because your ethnic identity includes so many different characteristics about yourself, you can often simultaneously be part of different ethnic groupings. For example, in modern Britain, we could say that on one level there are three major long-established ethnic groups: the English, the Welsh and the Scots. Although all three are termed 'British', they also have separate ethnic identities and differ from one another in terms of their histories and cultural practices.

The fact that people can have multiple layers of ethnic identity was neatly illustrated on a 1997 advertisement on BBC Radio 1 for a helpline for victims of racial harassment. It took the form first of two men, one English, the other Scottish, arguing in a pub. The two traded insults based on the other's individual ethnic identity. A third man, with an East Indian **accent**, then intervened and the Englishman and Scotsman then claimed solidarity as 'real' British, turning on the member of the British East Indian minority group. A Frenchman then waded into the foray, which caused the Englishman, Scotsman and East Indian to claim solidarity as 'British' and to carry on a well-established tradition of hostility with France. An American then stepped in, causing the Frenchman and the 'British' to merge into 'Europeans'. The sketch ended with the appearance of a Martian, which then united the rest as 'Earth humans'.

Because the concept of ethnic identity incorporates many characteristics, its definition is not clear-cut or uniform. Individuals can have multiple layers of ethnic identity, each of which can be encoded in an ethnic label. These labels encapsulate traits that are perceived to be important, and it is to the power of such naming that we turn in section 6.3.

ACTIVITY 6.1

1   Think about and list all the characteristics that you think go into making up ethnic identity. Ask members of friend and family groups to do the same. Do your definitions differ greatly? Which traits are most often emphasised and which are not?

6.3 The language of prejudice

As we said above, ethnic majorities are groups that hold social and political power and, therefore, whose practices and beliefs become established as a norm. Everything that does not conform to this norm is perceived as different and peripheral. This also holds true in the context of ethnic labelling. Ethnic majorities can, and do, label minority groups in ways which emphasise the latter's status as outsiders. Furthermore, because these labels originate from the dominant group, they easily become entrenched in usage. We will now look at two of the most common practices in emphasising the otherness of ethnic groups: (1) the use of **marked** terminology to create an opposition between 'us' and 'them'; and (2) the use of negative labelling.

6.3.1 Markedness and 'us' and 'them'

The 1997 Radio 1 advertisement outlined on p. 86 illustrated not only the various levels of ethnic identity that individuals can have, but also the separation of groups into what can be referred to as 'us' and 'them'. When the Englishman insults the Scotsman on his nationality, he is expressing opinions on behalf of his group: 'we' English who hate 'you' Scots. The same goes for the Scotsman's insults to the English. As the different characters come in, the 'us' and 'them' groups grow: 'we' real British unite against the 'them' of the East Indian immigrant community; 'we' British against the 'them' of France; the 'we' of Europe against the 'them' of America; and finally, the 'we' of Earth against the 'them' of another planet. The same divisions happen in reality, with modern ethnic majority and minority groups all over the world. Ethnic majorities tend to assume that minorities in their respective countries have to accommodate to the norm. In terms of 'us' and 'them', the majority stance can be expressed as '"they" [the minority] live in "our" land and as part of "our" culture. "They" therefore should learn "our" language and behave as much as possible like "we" do.' In such situations, the majority's ethnic identity becomes invisible (because it is 'normal') and that of others, marked.

An illustration of the invisible majority and marked minority can be seen in the following examples from the British and American press:

(1) President Bill Clinton has denied having oral sex with work experience girl Monica Lewinsky, who visited him 37 times, and of lying about it under oath. He claims Monica's a friend of his black secretary, Betty Currie.

(Daily Mail, 12 March, 1998)

(2) Finally, 23 months after the murder, a 21 year old black inmate in Michigan told a cellmate: 'I killed Sal Mineo'.

(National Enquirer, 3 March, 1998)

Of the five people mentioned in these extracts, the ethnicity of only two is mentioned: that of the 'black secretary' and that of the 'black inmate'. The white ethnicity of the others is **unmarked**, since they are the norm, and the outside nature of the minority black group is made distinctive by the use of a label that emphasises their difference from the mainstream, in a context where it is irrelevant.

When ethnic labels encode and convey negative attitudes held by the speaker, the effect of their use in marked contexts can be far-reaching. We will now explore in more detail the nature of negative labelling.

6.3.2 Negative labelling

As we have seen, the ethnicity of a majority group often becomes invisible, unlike that of minorities. It is, therefore, much easier to create and emphasise a negative perception of a minority's ethnicity through the labels that are accorded to them. In order to understand this fully, we need to place it in the wider framework of the relationship between language and perception discussed in Chapter 2.

Chapter 2 discussed the Saussurean theory that the words of a language are a set of linguistic signs that consist of a concept and a label. These two elements are completely interwoven, so much so that the label becomes the concept, and vice versa. In other words, you can't visualise the concept without the label and, in addition, you don't have to stop and think about the meaning of most of the words that you use every day. You instinctively 'know' them because the two elements, concept and label are working together. We inherit the linguistic signs of the **speech community** we are born into, and there seems to be evidence that the meanings of those signs influence the way in which we can then perceive the world around us. These ideas go a long way towards explaining the power of negative labelling. (See also Chapters 5 and 7 for gender- and age-related labels.)

ACTIVITY 6.2 ━━━━━━━━━━━━━━━━━━━━━━━━━━━━━━

2   One way of discovering how a particular minority group is viewed by the majority is to look at the number of insult terms that exist for that group. Make a list of all the ethnically or racially marked insult terms that you can think of. Now group them according to the ethnic groups they refer to. The group which has the most, and/or the most extreme, insult terms directed at them is usually the group which is held in the lowest esteem.

━━━━━━━━━━━━━━━━━━━━━━━━━━━━━━

Negative labelling can occur in two main ways. The use of racist terms is one of the most obvious means but so is simply labelling people mainly in terms of their ethnic identity. Both types of usage are effective because of their status as 'labels of primary potency' (Allport, 1990: 248). Allport points out that we use a range of different terms to describe people, but there are some 'salient and powerful' labels that stand out among the rest. These tend to be ones that describe groups that are perceived to be distinct from the mainstream, such as those denoting ethnicity or describing some sort of incapacity. Because they stand out, these 'labels of primary potency... prevent alternative classification' (Allport, 1990: 248). In other words, they direct our perception of the described person. Allport gives a clear illustration of how influential such labels are in an example from Irving Lee:

> I knew a man who had lost the use of both eyes. He was called a 'blind man'. He could also be called an expert typist, a conscientious worker, a good student, a careful listener, a man who wanted a job. But he couldn't get a job in the department store order room where employees sat and typed orders which came over the telephone. The personnel man was impatient to get the interview over. 'But you're a blind man' he kept saying, and one could almost feel his silent assumption that somehow the incapacity in one aspect made the man incapable in every other. So blinded by the label was the interviewer that he could not be persuaded to look beyond it.
>
> (1990: 248)

Similarly, when a group's ethnicity is continuously marked, as we saw in the examples above, we focus on it. If the sense is repeatedly not affirmative, negative ethnic stereotypes are perpetuated. Andersen (1988) for instance illustrates how *black* is often connected to negative words like *hate*, *fight*, *riot*, and van Dijk (1993) shows how negative topics such as crime become 'over-ethnicised'. Where topics are positive, ethnic identity is less focused; the topic becomes 'de-ethnicised', as this letter to press indicates:

> Can you explain why black Englishmen and women who win Olympic medals or excel at games are described as 'English' while those who riot and throw petrol bombs are almost inevitably 'West Indian'?
>
> (reproduced in van Dijk, 1991: 212)

When terms denoting colour, race and ethnicity are mainly used in negative ways the inability to see such groups in any other way becomes reinforced.

An example that neatly draws together the two components of markedness and negative labelling can be seen in the following excerpt from the *Daily Star* (3 March, 1998) which reported that a large number of tickets for the 1998 World Cup football games had already been bought by French fans. The headline read 'Frogs need a good kicking':

French history is littered with acts of plunder, greed and cowardice. The way they've grabbed the lion's share of World Cup tickets is typical of their slimy continental ways. So good on EU [European Union] bosses for threatening savage fines if they don't hand some back. The EU mustn't back down. As we proved at Agincourt and Waterloo, a good kicking on their gallic derrieres is the only language the greedy frogs understand.

There is a very clear distinction in this piece between 'us' (the British) and 'them' (the French): 'they' are greedy and slimy (like the rest of continental Europe but unlike 'us'); 'their' history is full of deeds of plunder and cowardice (but 'ours' is not); 'they' therefore need a good kicking and 'we' are the ones to do it, since 'we've' done it before and because 'we' have always had a sense of fair play, courage and high moral standards. The qualities attributed to the French reflect and reinforce a negative stereotype long held by the British (in particular, the English) about this nation of people. This typecasting is so dominant that labels such as 'French', 'gallic' and 'frog' do not always have to be used with reference to stereotypes. In utterances such as these, we can clearly see the concept and the label working together: the simple use of *frog* or *French* is enough to convey all the negative perceptions behind the term. This is the reason why a headline such as 'Frogs need a good kicking' is possible: the derogatory label immediately summons the reader's negative perceptions of the French and so draws them into approving the idea that they 'need a good kicking'. Readers who share negative perceptions of the French are more likely, on seeing the headline, not to think 'why do we have to punish the French?' but instead 'what have they done now?'

So far in this discussion, we have seen that labelling groups in terms of their ethnicity can disempower them through the creation of potent negative stereotypes. Groups that are negatively labelled by the majority sometimes attempt to reclaim those terms, turning them instead into positive markers of group identity. For example, when I was a teenager at school in Trinidad, West Indies (a multiethnic society), a prefect of Afro-Caribbean ethnicity frequently addressed our class (comprising females mainly of Afro-Caribbean and Indo-Caribbean ethnicity) as 'niggers', a term which is widely proscribed. In such a context, the term was not considered or treated as offensive to the majority, who could claim ethnic solidarity with her and each other as non-white. However, her companion prefect (of white British ethnicity) could not, and did not, use such a term, since to do so would recreate an uneasy colonial relationship between a socio-politically powerful white majority and correspondingly powerless black minority.

Debate over the use of the taboo term 'nigger' recently surfaced with the release of Quentin Tarantino's film *Jackie Brown* (1997). Tarantino claimed that his penchant for realistic dialogue resulted in his black ghetto characters frequently referring to each other by the term:

Ordell's [one of the main black characters]...a black guy who throws the word around a lot, it's part of the way he talks...that's just who he is and where he comes from....If you're writing a black dialect, there are certain words you need to make it musical, and 'nigger' is one of them.

(James, 1998: 8).

He therefore seemed to think that he was capturing, and in a sense, celebrating the 'natural' cadences of a certain type of African-American speech. Black director and producer Spike Lee however, criticised Tarantino's script, stating that since the black characters are fictional, what is ultimately the source of the taboo term is Tarantino's white voice, one which, by virtue of its place in the majority group, cannot use such terminology in any positive way.

Such issues are not easily resolved but they do show that it is difficult to totally reclaim certain labels as positive markers of ethnic identity. Because they continue to be used as terms of ethnic abuse, and ultimately because ethnic prejudice continues to occur, they retain currency as negatively potent labels.

Another means by which ethnic minorities can claim solidarity and assert their ethnic identity is through language use. This is also fraught with difficulties, as we will see in section 6.4.

━━━ **ACTIVITY 6.3**

3   Look through a newspaper or magazine for articles where people are labelled in terms of their ethnicity (as in the examples in sections 6.3.1 and 6.3.2). Determine the context of usage (that is, decide whether the mention of ethnic identity is relevant to the article). What is the result of including such information on your perception? Let a friend read the article and without revealing your awareness of the use of marked terms, ask them to summarise it for you. Has the ethnic labelling used in the article influenced their perceptions?

6.4 Language use as a marker of ethnic identity

Despite the fact that the otherness of ethnic minority groups is often emphasised by majorities, members of the former can (and do) choose to maintain their distinctiveness from the mainstream. Members of ethnic minorities will continue to participate in cultural, religious and linguistic practices which differentiate them from the norm. In terms of language use, this can mean preserving a mother tongue which is different to that utilised and made official by the ethnic major-ity. Such choices are not always perceived favourably by members of majorities, who have the power to curtail and obstruct them. In order to illustrate these points, we will now look briefly at the status of Ebonics in America and of lan-guages other than English primarily in Britain.

6.4.1 Ebonics

In 1990, it was reported that there were approximately 30 million African-Americans in the US (or 12 per cent of the total population). A substantial proportion of these (80–90 per cent) are estimated to speak a **variety** which is known as Ebonics (a blend of *ebony* 'black' and *phonics* 'sounds'), or African American Vernacular English (AAVE). Ebonics has been studied over the years by various linguists and has been established as a systematic and normally functioning spoken human language, but few members of European-American communities and not all members of African-American communities positively recognise it as such. Part of the problem with the acceptance of Ebonics is because, as a variety of English which has marked differences from standard US English, it is widely regarded as the 'bad' English of 'lazy' or 'ignorant' speakers. (See Chapter 10 for a discussion of standard and non-standard varieties of English.)

Ebonics provided a focal point for public debate in 1996, when the Oak-land Board of Education in America passed a resolution to officially recognise its use in the classroom. The Board had realised that the grades of many African-American children in reading and writing skills, both of which are carried out in standard US English, were 'substantially below ... norms' (*USA Today*, Decem-ber, 1996) and that this was very likely due to the fact that their cultural and lin-guistic differences from the ethnic majority were marginalised or ignored. They were therefore 'bewildered, then angered, and finally alienated from the schools where their language and self-esteem are belittled by a seemingly insensitive system'. It must be noted however, that even though the resolution seems to be biased towards validating the speech of the African-American community, its ultimate aim was to facilitate the acquisition of the majority language. The Board therefore recommended that schools teach students that a language form like Ebonics does have rules of grammar and **phonology** and that these, along with different vocabulary items, make it distinctive from standard US English. In this way, students would feel more positive not only about African-American culture and language, but also about acquiring literacy skills in standard US English.

Despite the fact that integration to the norm was the Board's eventual goal, the resolution did not meet with widespread support, and was eventually dropped. This may seem somewhat odd if we go along with the idea that there is an expectation of ethnic minorities to accommodate to the majority's norms (see section 6.3.1). However, as Lippi-Green (1997: 188) points out, the issue is not straightforward. Ebonics is, and has been, constantly vilified as 'the language of black trash', 'the lazy verbiage of the ghetto' and as a 'disability' which consists of 'speaking English and violating the correct rules of grammar'. Such statements though, are not so much judgements about the language as about its speakers. The 'real trouble' with Ebonics is that to recognise it (even as a temporary stepping stone to acquisition of the majority tongue) is to also acknowledge that 'there is a distinct, healthy, functioning African-American culture which is not white, and which does not want to be white' (ibid.: 178). This is an uncomfortable idea in a country which promotes the notion of 'one nation, indivisible':

> In the 1960s we put an official end to racial segregation in schooling, housing, public places and the workplace. What does it mean to say that there is an African American culture distinct enough from other American cultures to have its own variety of English, a variety that persists in the face of overt stigmatization?
>
> (ibid.: 178)

This maintenance of 'otherness' is seen by some members of the ethnic majority and of the African-American minority (for whom acquisition of standard US English is 'a fact of life' for fulfilling social and educational aspirations) as a 'wilful act of rebellion: destructive, hurtful' (ibid.: 184). To have passed the Oakland Board's resolution would have been to legitimise and give authority to behaviour, and to a group, that is perceived as threatening to social stability and majority political ideals. This feeling was so strong that Donald McHenry, former US Ambassador to the United Nations and an African-American, stated that he did 'not approve of Black English...in our [American] society...we ought to eliminate those differences which are either the basis or result of divisiveness in our society' (ibid.: 190).

For many African-Americans there is a tension between these two linguistic varieties. On the one hand, standard US English is the 'language of wider communication' and is needed for social and economic survival or advancement. On the other hand there remains what Lippi-Green (ibid.: 191) calls 'evidence of mistrust of blacks who assimilate too well' to mainstream varieties who may be viewed with 'suspicion and scepticism'. She quotes a black adolescent who:

> indicates how serious an offence it is to cross the line linguistically [from AAVE to more mainstream US English]: 'over at my school, if they – first

> time they catch you talking white, they'll never let it go. Even if you just quit talking like that, they'll never let it go!'
>
> (Lippi-Green, 1997: 191)

A similar situation is evident in the UK, where British Black English varieties are also regarded as 'bad' English and are not recognised in the life of the majority community. Speakers of Black Englishes (also referred to as 'Patois') have the same tensions as those in African-American communities and similar views of mistrust:

> My sister, she's a right little snobby . . . if she came here now she'd speak plain English, but she can speak Patois better than me. She speaks it to me, to some of her coloured friends who she knows speak Patois, but to her snobby coloured friends she speaks English. She talks Queen English, brebber. She's the snotty one of the family.
>
> (Edwards, 1986: 121)

So using the language of the wider community can be seen as denial or even betrayal of cultural and ethnic identity.

Like Patois in the UK, Ebonics and the community to which it belongs remain officially unacknowledged by the ethnic majority in the US. However, it persists as the language which binds together a large percentage of the African-American population, which must mean that its speakers 'get something from their communities and from each other that is missing in the world which is held up to them as superior and better' (Lippi-Green, 1997: 201).

6.4.2 Languages other than English

Although both the UK and the US are regarded as English-speaking nations, both countries have a variety of other languages within their shores. After World War II, Britain became home to a substantial proportion of immigrants from its overseas colonies. The largest number came from the Indian subcontinent (India, Pakistan, Bangladesh and Sri Lanka), complete with native languages such as Hindi, Punjabi, Bengali, Tamil and Gujerati to add to the other languages, both indigenous and immigrant, which already existed in Britain. Immigrants from the same districts tended to settle in communities in different areas in Britain's cities, where they could form a support network. The maintenance of cultural and religious practices, as well as of their native languages, was consequently facilitated among those groups. These markers of their ethnic identity would therefore have served as symbols of their solidarity as a group distinct from the majority.

Many of the British-born children of these communities however, have tended to become multilingual, versed in the language used in the home and in British English in both its standard and local forms (Andersen, 1988: 222), but this is not the case for all and some children can still have 'virtually no English' when they first enter school (ibid.: 225). Even so, though Britain is home to more than 1 million people who originate from the Indian subcontinent (Stubbs, 1985: 36), their languages are not officially recognised by the State, and schools have been slow to respond to either the monolingualism (in their mother tongue) or multilingualism of their minority pupils. Until the mid-1970s, educational policy concentrated on integrating such children quickly into the mainstream culture and into use of the majority language. Children were therefore taken out of the everyday school environment and 'immersed' in English by being placed instead in special centres where the use of standard British English alone was permitted. Evidence to suggest that the maintenance of the mother tongue has educational benefits and that suppression of it is debilitating has led to a growing awareness of the needs of such groups. Nevertheless, it is important to note that the effect on educational provision has been limited, and that languages other than English still have no political status in Britain.

In the US, languages such as Spanish suffer similar stigmatisation. In 1998 a virtual ban on bilingual teaching for Hispanic-American children whose English may be limited was imposed in California. Children entering school who speak predominantly Spanish are instead to receive immersion English before returning to mainstream schooling. The education secretary condemned the move saying that it would place children in 'an educational straitjacket' (quoted in *The Guardian*, 1 May, 1998). Others have suggested that the measure could reduce the number of such children reaching college, already at a low level, and have described it as 'mean spirited and mean minded' (ibid.).

As we saw in 6.4.1 failure to recognise the validity of another language has to do with attitudes towards the speakers of these languages. In Britain there is an ambiguity towards bilingual speakers and languages are seen in a status hierarchy. The child who is bilingual in English plus a prestigious language such as French or German because s/he happens to have one English and one French or German parent (an 'élite' bilingual), is much admired and her/his bilingualism is seen as an asset while the bilingualism of children whose languages are Gujerati or Tamil is undervalued or even ignored. This may be partly to do with the perceived status of the language in question, partly to do with the status of the speaker, and partly to do with the isolation of the élite bilingual whose linguistic diversity is not seen as a threat to the majority population (see also Chapter 11).

Yet despite stigmatisation, languages other than English persist in Britain, because their speakers retain them as markers of ethnic solidarity. Andersen (1988: 224) states that many young British bilinguals increasingly prefer to use their family's native language when possible. Parmar (1982) exemplifies the power of marking ethnic solidarity through language use in an account of an incident where a group of Gujerati-speaking women ostracised their supervisor, a member of the ethnic majority. According to the **informant**, the supervisor rebuked one of the women for speaking in Gujerati, and generally belittled the group's command of English. They therefore deliberately began to use Gujerati in her presence, often speaking about nothing in particular but effectively turning her into an outsider to a norm. As Andersen (1988: 224) states, 'talking another language, black to black, is a start to taking power back'. The reclaiming of this power can cause great discomfort to those who have been accustomed to wielding it.

6.5 Summary

We can conclude that language use in the construction of ethnic identity involves issues which are far from straightforward or easily resolved. The terms 'ethnic' and 'ethnic identity' comprise characteristics that we consider important when defining who we and others are, both as individuals and as part of larger groups. Despite the fact that everyone has an ethnic identity, it tends to be emphasised mainly for minority groups, who are treated largely as outsiders to the majority norm. The 'alien' identity of ethnic minorities is accentuated by the ways in which they are represented by the majority. The effect of this is that the distinctive nature of minority groups is constantly reflected through labels of primary potency. This representation in turn reinforces the perception of these groups as different and, sometimes, as threateningly distinct from the norm. To diminish the threat, accommodation to the norm on every practical level, including language use, is therefore encouraged or imposed by the majority. At the same time however, minority groups actively maintain their distinctiveness from a norm which ostracises them, and express positive in-group solidarity. One of the ways in which they do this is through language use: in attempting to reclaim abusive terminology and in preserving their native tongues in the face of opposition, they are rejecting the labels and norms imposed by the majority and 'taking power back' (Andersen, 1988: 224).

Note

1   A commercial television channel in the UK.

Suggestions for further reading

Lippi-Green, Rosina (1997) *English with an Accent: Language, Ideology and Discrimination in the US*, London: Routledge.
Suitable for undergraduates, this text explores the creation and maintenance of social tensions between ethnic majority and minority groups in the US. Chapter 9 deals specifically with issues surrounding the use of AAVE (African American Vernacular English), also known as Ebonics.
Van Dijk, T.A. (1987) *Communicating Racism: Ethnic Prejudice in Talk and Thought*, London: Sage.
This text is also suitable for undergraduate use, though students at introductory level may find some bits difficult. Nevertheless, Chapter 3 provides an interesting discussion of how social prejudice against minority groups is manifested in institutional set-ups and particularly in media discourse.

Chapter 7

Language and age

Jean Stilwell Peccei

7.1 Introduction: what has age got to do with language?

How would you describe yourself? Usually, quite a few possibilities come to mind. For example, I am a woman, an American who has lived in England for 30 years, a 51-year-old 'baby boomer', and a university lecturer (just to name a few of my 'identities'). And, just as I have a variety of identities, I also have a variety of ways of speaking. Although in all cases I am speaking English, the language I use when I talk informally to friends of my own generation can be quite different from the one I use when I talk with my grandmother in California or when I give a lecture in London. The way I talk to my husband is not the same way I talk to my grown sons. And the way I talk to my sons now is quite different from the way I talked to them when they were toddlers.

As Hudson (1980) has pointed out, we make a very subtle use of the language variability that is available to us. It allows us as speakers to locate ourselves in a multi-dimensional society and as hearers to locate others in that society as well. Age, like gender, profession, social class, and geographic or ethnic origin, has often been studied as one of the factors that locates us in society and causes **language variation**. One of the ways that I described myself was by my age and generation: *a 51-year-old 'baby boomer'*, and one of the factors that I felt would influence the way I talk in a given situation was the age of my conversational partner. To see how the ages of the speakers can give conversations a characteristic 'flavour', look at the three conversations below. Which one involves two teenage girls, which one involves an adult and a toddler, and which one involves an elderly person and a younger adult?

(1) A: what – what are these pictures doing here?
     B: careful of them, darling. Gangan (*grandmother*) painted them.
     A: me like a little one best.
     B: do you?
     A: which one do you like first? a big one or a little one?
     B: I like that white one.

(Fletcher, 1988: 545)

(2) A: it's your cheque, love. [2 second pause] yeah.
     B: [4 second pause] how much for?

A: God! [2 second pause] shall I just read what it says to you? [3 second pause] dear sir or madam you are entitled to supplementary benefit of a hundred-and-fifty pounds for the articles listed overleaf.

B: oh

A: for a cooker. [*stove* in American English] so you've got a hundred-and-fifty pounds for a new cooker. er from Social. Social Security because you're on supplementary benefit all right? [. . .] so you've got a hundred-and-fifty pounds. and that is to get a cooker with my love, all right? [1.5 second pause] aren't you lucky? eh? didn't we do well?

(Adapted from Atkinson and Coupland, 1988)

(3) A: Anna's so weird

B: pardon? [laughter]

A: Anna. sometimes kind of hyper hyper

B: and sometimes kind of lowper lowper

A: no and [laughter] sometimes kind of 'We should care for the animals of this world', you know

(Coates, 1996)

Apart from the topics of the conversations, you probably used certain features of the language to give you clues about the ages of the speakers. In extract (1), A is three years old and B is her mother. We notice that the toddler has a serviceable but somewhat 'imperfect command' of her native language and that her mother appears to be using a slightly simpler and clearer form of the language than you would expect to be used with another adult. We also notice the mother's use of a 'pet name' *darling* when speaking to the child and a 'baby-talk' word for *grandmother*. In extract (2), A is a home help and B is her elderly client. You perhaps noticed that the conversation contains long pauses between the turns, making it seem that B is having a hard time 'taking in' what is being said to her and then making a response. Did you notice that A seems to have assumed this since she sometimes does not wait for B's answer to a question, repeats what she says several times and 'translates' the contents of the letter for B. Interestingly, like the mother speaking to her child in extract (1), the home help uses 'pet names' with her client: *love*, and *my love*. In extract (3), A and B are both 15 years old. In contrast to extract (2), we notice that their conversation seems quite fluent. Each speaker comes in quite rapidly after the previous speaker's turn has ended. In contrast to Extract 1, the structure of their sentences appears quite 'adult'. There are no sentences like *me like a little one best* .What might also give the game away is some of the vocabulary used by the girls: *weird* and *hyper hyper*.

Our everyday experience yields many examples of vocabulary used by teenagers and young adults which often appear to need 'translations' for older age groups. My 20-year-old British students added a new meaning for *pants* (as in *underpants*) to my vocabulary. They said it was roughly equivalent to *terrible* as in *That was a pants exam*. Age-related differences in vocabulary are often the ones most easily noticed by people, but there are other slightly less obvious linguistic differences between age groups as well. For example, the sociolinguist Labov (1972a), found that older New Yorkers were less likely to pronounce the 'r' in words like *fourth* and *floor* than were younger speakers, while Chambers and Trudgill (1980) found that in Norwich, England the pronunciation of the 'e' in words like *bell* and *tell* varied according to the age of the speaker.

ACTIVITY 7.1

1   Make a collection of current slang words used by children and teenagers. Ask people of different ages if they can give you a definition for those words. Do people of different age groups have differing perceptions of what those words mean and how they are used?

So far, we have touched on some of the ways in which the ages of speakers (and their conversational partners) will cause variations in the particular form of the language being used. However, there is another aspect to the language and age issue. Language is a fundamental human activity through which we communicate our particular **representation** of the world. It is primarily through language that cultural values and beliefs are transmitted from one member of a society to another and from one generation to the next. Thus, we can often see within the structure of a language reflections of the way that a particular culture views the world, and the kinds of distinctions that are held to be important. Age distinctions are frequently reflected in the world's languages. For example, in Italian, as in many languages, the use of certain **pronouns** is partly governed by the ages of the speaker and the hearer. Comanche, an **Amerindian** language spoken in the southern Plains region of the US, had a special version with its own pronunciation patterns and vocabulary which was used with children under five years old (see Casagrande, 1948). Closer to home, look at the opening sentences in these two newspaper articles:

(4)   Senior citizen Tom Ackles risked his own life to save a drowning dog
        – a beloved neighborhood pet that had fallen through the ice on a

frozen lake. The 66-year-old retired college janitor got a frantic call from a neighbour that a large dog was drowning in a nearby lake.

(National Enquirer, 24 February, 1998)

(5)   Lifeguards had to intervene to separate two brawling pensioners during an early morning swimming session.... Their dispute spilled out on to the pool side with both men clambering out of the water and squaring up to each other.

(The Daily Telegraph, 14 November, 1997)

Did you notice that at the very beginning of each article special terms which refer to their age group are used to describe the men: *senior citizen* in the American extract and *pensioner* in the British extract? We will return to this issue in section 7.2 where we will look more closely at how different age groups are represented in English..

In this chapter we will be concentrating on language issues at the two extreme ends of the lifespan, children under five, and the 'elderly', who we will provisionally define as people over 65. Two factors make these groups particularly useful for exploring the relationship between language, society and power. First, children and the elderly have a high degree of cultural salience in most societies. That is, they are clearly differentiated from the rest of society not only by their special social, economic and legal status but also by the language which is used to describe and categorise them. Second, there are aspects of the communicative abilities of these two groups which can sometimes be quite different from that of the 'middle segment' of the lifespan. By looking at these factors, we can explore the relationship between the way we talk to children and the elderly and the more general attitudes of our society towards the status of its youngest and oldest members.

7.2 How can a language reflect the status of children and older people?

In this section we will be looking at the importance of age as a cultural category and the way that our language might reflect a special status for the young and the old.

7.2.1 Age as an important cultural category

How often have you filled in a form where you were asked for your date of birth? It would be hard to imagine a culture which did not use age as a social category and as a means for determining duties, rights and privileges. Your age can determine whether you attend school, marry, drink alcohol, vote, draw a pension, or get into the movies at half price. To see just how important age labels can be, unscramble the words in (a)–(d) below, and put them into the order which seems most 'natural' to you.

(a) *intelligent woman the old*   (c) *dishonest man young the*

(b) *singer the teenage attractive*   (d) *middle-aged the nurse kind*

Most people produce the following:

(a) *the intelligent old woman*   (c) *the dishonest young man*

(b) *the attractive teenage singer*   (d) *the kind middle-aged nurse*

In every case, the age description is placed closer to the 'the person' than the other description. There is a very strong tendency in English to place the **adjective** expressing the most 'defining' characteristic closest to the **noun**. What might seem to be a 'natural' word order for these phrases is really a reflection of which of the two characteristics we consider to be more important for classifying people. Even though intelligence, honesty, physical attractiveness and kindness are all important to us, they somehow seem to be secondary to a person's age. As Turner (1973) has pointed out, a word order like *the old intelligent woman* can seem a bit odd not because it violates any rule of grammar but because it does not reflect our habitual way of thinking.

ACTIVITY 7.2

2   Collect a series of articles about people of different ages. Take a look to see how many explicitly age-related terms appear. As we saw in extracts (4) and (5), the participants' advanced age seemed particularly newsworthy. Would a minor fight between two people at a local swimming pool normally make it into the pages of a national newspaper? Do you notice any other age groups receiving this kind of treatment in your collection? If so, in what sorts of situations?

7.2.2 Labelling age groups

Write down all the labels you can think of which can be used for people under five; between 20 and 60; and over 65, for example *baby, woman, person*. (For now, omit any derogatory expressions.)

Below are some of the most common terms.

Under 5	20–60	Over 65
person	person	person
child	adult	adult
youngster	grown-up	grown-up
girl	mature person	mature person
boy	woman	woman
minor	man	man
newborn	lady	lady
kid/kiddy	gentleman	gentleman
tot		aged (as in the aged)
neonate		oldster
infant		elderly person
baby		elder
toddler		senior citizen
		retired person
		pensioner
		OAP (old age pensioner)

Given today's life expectancy, the under-fives and over-65s account for only about a quarter of the lifespan, yet they seem to have a disproportionately large number of specialised age group labels. Did you notice that even though all the expressions used to label the 20–60 group could have been used just as accurately for the people over 65, it might not have occurred to you to use them? The first words that come to mind are often those which specifically single out the over-65s as having a special status, such as *elderly person*, *senior citizen*, *pensioner*. If you did use some of the same terms that you listed for the 20–60 group, you may have added *old* or *elderly*. Explicit age marking also occurs with expressions for the very young, although for this group, size is also used as an age marker: *little/young child*, *tiny/young tot*.

7.2.3 Talking about age groups: underlying evaluations of early childhood and old age

Have you ever noticed that some adjectives seem to 'belong' to a particular age group? Words like *wise, dignified, cantankerous, frail* for the elderly and *bouncing, cute, bratty, misbehaved* for young children are a few examples. On the other hand, have you also noticed that there seem to be several adjectives, both positive and negative, like *little, dear, sweet, fussy, cranky, stubborn, foolish* that are used very frequently to describe both these groups? Expressions such as *second childhood* for old age make this cultural equation between children and the elderly quite explicit.

(6) It is important to recall that the term 'child' was initially used to describe anyone of low status, without regard for their age. Being a child continues to express more about power relationships than chronology, although the two are intimately intertwined. Children's powerlessness reflects their limited access to economic resources, their exclusion from political participation and the corresponding cultural image of childhood as a state of weakness, dependency and incompetence.

(Franklin, 1995: 9)

(7) Elderly woman, Morocco: I have no liberty. It is simply that my children have taken me in their charge.

(Tout, 1993: 25)

(8) Woman who cares for her elderly mother, USA: I 'listen' to her requests but do what I think best.

(Coupland and Nussbaum, 1993: 233)

Childhood and old age are often viewed as particularly problematic and vulnerable life stages, requiring special attention from the rest of society. There are the terms *paediatrician* and *geriatrician* for doctors who specialise in treating children and the elderly, but no special term for doctors who concentrate on 20 to 60 year olds. We have *Save the Children* and *Help the Aged*, but no charities called *Save the Adults* or *Help the Grown-Ups*. *Aid to Dependent Children* and *Medicare* in the US and *Child Benefit* and *Old Age Pension* in the UK are just a few examples of economic resources that governments target specifically to these age groups. We also find special legal institutions designed to protect them. Children are in the care of their parents or guardians and are extremely limited by law in the choices they can make. You may even have left *person* off the list of terms for the under-fives. The legal term *minor* makes direct reference to this aspect of childhood. Elderly people who become too frail to manage their own affairs may appoint someone to act for them, or where mental frailty is involved, guardians may be appointed for them. While the over-65s, as a group, have more legal independence than children, there is one restriction which can have quite far-reaching consequences for their status in society. In most occupations, they are normally required to retire at the age of 65.

(9) Elderly man, Morocco: Nobody bothers with me. When I had means they were all here, but now that I have nothing, nobody knows me.

(Tout, 1993: 24)

(10) Nurse at a day hospital for the elderly, UK: All they've got to give is their memories. And that's why you find old people are always going on about the past... because that's all they've got to give to say thank you.

(Coupland and Nussbaum, 1993: 68)

Very young children are financially dependent on their parents, and even those who inherit or earn money in their childhood are not free to spend it as they wish until they *come of age*. The physical limitations that sometimes accompany the ageing process as well as retirement norms mean that most people over 65 are no longer 'earning a living'. Some of the labels for the over-65s make specific reference to this aspect of their identity: *retired person*, *pensioner*, and *OAP*. Lack of financial independence can be particularly problematic for the elderly. While it is assumed that children will one day become 'productive' members of society, people over 65 are often seen (and see themselves) as no longer capable of contributing to the general prosperity of their families or of the wider society, a potential 'burden' rather than an 'investment'.

One way of seeing whether particular groups might have a low, or at least problematic, status is to look specifically at the number of negative, demeaning or insulting terms in the language which are exclusive to that group (see also Chapters 5 and 6 for negative terms related to gender and ethnicity.) The loss of status resulting from physical and economic dependence can be seen in a **thesaurus**. You will find that there are virtually no insulting or demeaning terms that are exclusive to the middle of the lifespan, but there are several for children, often accompanied by *young* or *little*. Examples are *brat*, *punk*, *whelp*, *whippersnapper*. When we look at demeaning or insulting terms for older people, the choice is, unfortunately, vast. The terms *fogey*, *hag*, *biddy*, *fossil*, *geezer*, *codger*, *crone*, *duffer*, *bag*, *wrinklies* (a term that appeared in the UK in the 1990s), are just a few examples. Most of these words can be made even more derogatory when preceded by *old*. Perhaps because of this, many people over 65 reject the label *old* entirely as a way of describing their age group, finding that it focuses too much on the negative aspects of ageing. In an American study described in Coupland, Coupland, and Giles (1991), the researchers found that the expressions *senior citizen* and *retired person* had positive **connotations** of 'active', 'strong', 'progressive' and 'happy', while, *aged, elderly*, and *old person* were much more negatively evaluated. The researchers had three age-groups carry out the rating task (17–44; 45–64; 65+) and found that all three groups tended to agree on the evaluations.

This raises some interesting questions about the complex relationship between language and thought, a subject which was the focus of Chapter 2. Our language might reflect underlying attitudes to children and the elderly, but does it also shape them? If so, would getting rid of ageist language also get rid of ageist attitudes? Would the use of more 'positive' words change our negative perceptions of old age? Or might it be the case that new socio-economic circumstances will lead to changed attitudes towards older people and then to a change in the way we talk about them? At the time of this writing, the older members of the generation born just after World War II are less than 15 years away from retirement age. The population bulge resulting from the 'baby boom' makes this generation a powerful voting bloc. Post-war prosperity, smaller families, and increased career opportunities for women mean that when they retire, this generation will have considerably more economic power than their predecessors. Medical advances allowing many more people to have a healthy and active old age might possibly change our perceptions of what it is to be 'old'. However, not all 'baby boomers' are relying solely on changing socio-economic circumstances to solve the problem. In *Declining to Decline: Cultural Combat and the Politics of Midlife* (1997), Margaret Gullette places a very strong emphasis on ageing as a socially constructed process and urges that 'we who are in our forties and beyond, older and wiser than we once were, must write our own age-positive autobiographies' (in Breines, 1997: 29).

ACTIVITY 7.3 ━━━━━━━━━━━━━━━━━━━━━━━━━━━

3   Ask 10 people to write down the first four words that come to mind for three different ages: three, 23, and 83. Compare the age groups in terms of the proportion of words that refer to:
- positive and negative qualities
- physical qualities; mental/emotional qualities; legal or socio-economic status.
- age itself, e.g., *youthful*, *elderly*, etc.

7.3 Talking to young children and the elderly

In this section we turn from looking at the way the very young and the very old are talked about and look at the way these groups are talked to.

7.3.1 Language characteristics of the under-5s and over-65s

Very young children's language takes its characteristic 'style' from the fact they are apprentice speakers. During the first five years of life, children are still in the process of acquiring the grammar of their native language and a 'working' vocabulary. Young children's speech also has a characteristic 'sound'. First, the pitch of their voice is quite high relative to that of adults. Second, their early pronunciations of words can be quite different from the adult versions.

Unlike young children, the over-65s are experienced language users. However many people believe that old age inevitably results in a decline of communicative ability. Although there is evidence to suggest that older people may require slightly longer processing time to produce and understand complex sentences, numerous studies have shown that the normal ageing process in itself does not result in a significant loss of verbal skill unless serious illnesses, such as a stroke or Alzheimer's Disease, intervene. In some types of **discourse**, such as complex story-telling, elderly speakers generally outperform younger speakers. However, hearing often becomes less acute as people get older, and this can lead to a reduced understanding of rapid or whispered speech, or speech in a noisy environment. The 'elderly' voice, like a young child's, is instantly recognisable. The normal ageing of the vocal cords and muscles controlling breathing and facial movement results in slower speech and a voice which has a higher pitch and weaker volume and resonance than that of younger adults.

It is important to remember, however, that the way a person sounds is quite separate from what that person is actually saying. The problem for elderly speakers is that people do not always make that distinction. Just as different **accents** can lead hearers to make all sorts of stereotyped and often inaccurate judgements about everything from the honesty to the education level of the speaker (see Chapter 11), the sound of an elderly person's voice can immediately link the hearer into a whole set of beliefs about old age which may or may not be true of that particular person.

ACTIVITY 7.4

4   You and I *speak*. Children *babble* and *chatter*. Old people *drone* and *witter*. Or do they? Chapters 5, 6, 10 and 11 show how the talk of people in other 'low status' groups is often devalued or described in negative terms. See if this might hold true for young children and the elderly by examining descriptions of their talk in literature, the media and in your own conversations.

7.3.2 Child Directed Language

Child Directed Language (CDL), sometimes called 'Baby Talk' or 'Motherese', is a special style used in speech to young children and has been extensively studied over the past 30 years. It has several characteristics, some of which were illustrated in extract 1.

- calling the child by name, often using a 'pet' name or term of endearment
- shorter, grammatically simpler sentences
- more repetition
- more use of questions or question tags (*That's nice, isn't it?*)
- use of 'baby-talk' words
- expanding on and/or finishing a child's utterance

CDL also has a characteristic 'sound':

- higher pitch
- slower speed
- more pauses, particularly between phrases.
- clearer, more 'distinct' pronunciation
- exaggerated intonation (some words in the sentence heavily emphasised, and a very prominent rising tone used for questions)

Observational studies of parents' conversations with their children have also highlighted several common features in the way the interaction proceeds. Young children are usually perceived to be incompetent turn-takers with older speakers having expectations that their contributions will be irrelevant or delayed. The younger the child, the more likely their attempts to initiate a new topic will be ignored by older speakers and the more likely they are to be interrupted or overlapped (two speakers talking simultaneously). There is a relatively high proportion of 'directive' and 'instructive' talk from adults, either by blunt commands: *be careful*, *don't do that*, or by 'talking over' (talking about people in their presence and referring to them as *we* or *she/he*.) Here is an example:

(11) c = Child, T.; m = Mother. C wants to turn on the lawn sprinklers. A researcher is present.

> c: Mommy.
> m: T. has a little problem with patience. We're working on patience. What is patience, T.?
> c: Nothing.
> m: Come on.

c: I want to turn them . . . M: (at the same time) What is . . .

c: on now.

M: patience? Can you remember?

(Ervin-Tripp, 1979: 402)

7.3.3 Similarities between Child Directed Language and 'Elder Directed' Language

In section 7.1 we noted that there seemed to be several parallels between the speech style used by the home help to her elderly client and that of the mother talking to her child. Coupland *et al.* (1991) review several studies which confirm the similarity between CDL and the speech style which is often used with the elderly, particularly by their caregivers. These similarities involve both the content of the talk: simpler sentences, more questions and repetitions, use of pet names, etc. and the sound of the talk: slower, louder, higher pitch, exaggerated intonation, etc. As the next extract illustrates, there can also be similarities in the ways speakers interact with young children and the elderly, interrupting and overlapping them, treating the person's contribution as irrelevant to the conversation, and using directive language, especially 'talking over'.

(12) [–] indicates unintelligible syllable(s); HH = home help; CL = elderly client; D = Relative of CL.

HH: How are you today?

CL: Oh I [–] I've

CL: got a [–] D: (at the same time) She's a bit down today because we're leaving

HH: I guessed that's what it would be today

Later discussing cakes which have been left for CL who is still present

D: They're in there and I'm hoping. They're in the fridge you see. I'm hoping she will go in there and take them and eat them.

HH: That's right yeah don't waste . . .

(adapted from Atkinson and Coupland, 1988)

7.3.4 Why might these similarities occur?

One of the original explanations for the use of CDL was that parents used it as a language-teaching tool. And indeed, there are some aspects of CDL which could potentially be of help to novice speakers. The problem is that variations in the amount of CDL which children receive do not seem to significantly affect their progress in acquiring their native language. And, as Ochs (1991) points out, not all cultures use this type of talk with young children. So, if CDL is not primarily a teaching tool, why is it used in some cultures?

One proposal is that one of its primary uses is to ensure understanding in someone who is not believed to be a fully competent language user. This might account for the considerable similarities between CDL and the language used with the elderly. Its use could therefore be closely connected to cultural expectations and stereotypes about people in these groups. **Matched guise experiments** have shown that speakers with an 'elderly' voice tend to be rated as vulnerable, forgetful and incompetent more often than speakers with younger voices (see Chapter 11 for an explanation of matched guise techniques). The low expectations of the elderly resulting from cultural stereotyping of old age as an inevitable decline in physical and mental capacity is illustrated in the following extract between a home help (HH) and her elderly client (CL):

(13) CL: Well I don't know your name anyway

HH: Ann.

CL: Ann...

CL: mmm   HH: (at the same time) Right.

CL: I don't need to know your surname do I?

HH: (2 second pause) Well you can know it. It's Campbell, but I don't think you'll remember it, will you. (laughs)

CL: (2 second pause, sounds annoyed) What do you mean I won't remember it? I'm not dim.

(adapted from Atkinson and Coupland, 1988)

Another proposed explanation for the use of CDL is that it asserts the power of the caregiver in relation to the child, establishing the caregiver's right to command compliance. When young children are taught the socially appropriate way to 'ask', the message is often that adults can make demands of children but children must make polite requests of adults.

(14) MOTHER: I beg your pardon?

CHILD: What?

MOTHER: Are you ordering me to do it?

CHILD: Mmm, I don't know, Momma.

MOTHER: Can't you say 'Mommy, would you please make me some?'

(Becker, 1988: 178)

The emphasis on unequal power relations between adult and child fits in with our observations about conversational interaction between children and the elderly on the one hand and their caregivers on the other, where the more powerful speaker tends to use interruption, overlapping, and 'talking over'. While the use of questions and question tags by caregivers can help elicit conversation, it also allows them to 'direct' the responses of their conversational partners. Tag questions can be especially controlling because they explicitly seek agreement with the speaker. Atkinson and Coupland (1988) have suggested that using CDL with the elderly can reflect not only a cultural equation between these two groups which is potentially demeaning to elderly people but also a deliberate strategy to constrain and marginalise them, particularly in institutional settings.

However, there is another dimension to the use of CDL which is seemingly in contradiction to this proposal. That is, some aspects of CDL might reflect an attitude of affection and nurturance toward the recipient and a willingness to accommodate to their needs. Cromer (1991) has pointed out that affectionate talk to lovers and pets is also characterised by higher pitch, exaggerated intonation, pet names and baby-talk words. And, while no one is likely to appreciate being interrupted or talked over, a negative reaction by the elderly to pet names and repetition accompanied by slower, louder and simpler speech cannot be taken for granted. Coupland *et al.*'s (1991) review of studies involving elderly people's evaluations of this style of talk have shown that some found it patronising or demeaning and negatively evaluated caregivers who used it. Others, particularly those who were very frail or suffering from deafness or short-term memory loss found it nurturing and 'encouraging' and a help in understanding and participating in the conversation.

7.4 Conclusion

At the beginning of this chapter, I asked you to identify the approximate ages of the speakers in three conversations. We will end with the same sort of task.

(15) A: what have you been eating?

B: eating

A: you haven't been eating that spinach have you

B: (laughs) spin

A: you know what Pop...happens to Popeye when he eats his spinach

(adapted from Atkinson and Coupland, 1988)

(16) Dominic, I'm putting some people in the bus. Now drive off. Down to

the end. . . . Drive off down to the village, darling. . . . Now are you
going to do that?

(Harris and Coltheart, 1986: 79)

(17) I remember love – the beauty, the ecstasy!
Then – how it hurt!
Forgetting helped time dissolve the hurt and pain
of defeated expectation.

(Thorsheim and Roberts, 1990: 123)

Extract 15 is a conversation between a home help, A, and her elderly client, B.
The speaker in extract 16 is four years old. She is explaining how to play a game
to her two-year-old brother. Extract 17 was written by an 80-year-old retirement
home resident in the US. If you were surprised by the ages of some of the speakers in these extracts, it simply shows that there is a very complex relationship
between physical, mental and social factors in determining a person's use of
language and how others perceive and react to that language.

7.5 Summary

In this chapter we have seen that age is an important cultural category, an identity marker, and a factor in producing language variation within a **speech community**. The way we talk about young children and the elderly reflects their
special status in our society, a status which is partly determined by the amount
of social and economic power which these groups possess. There are parallels
between talk addressed to young children and talk to the elderly. These parallels
cannot be explained entirely by physical and mental immaturity in the case of
young children or by physical and mental decline in the case of the elderly. The
status of young children and the elderly in our society, and culturally determined
beliefs and stereotypes about their communicative abilities, can play a significant role in producing these parallels.

As a final thought, the following excerpt is from a somewhat tongue-in-
cheek review of a television documentary about au pairs. Analyse the language
looking particularly at any references to children's socio-economic status, the
'characteristic' attributes of young children which have been highlighted, and
the degree to which the piece reflects cultural attitudes toward childhood (or
turns them on their head).

Say what you like about Paul Newman, I regard him as the acceptable face
of capitalism. His physiognomy may be prominently displayed on the side

of every jar of his high-priced spaghetti sauces, but that's okay by me because he gives 100 per cent of his profits to a children's charity. Lloyd Grossman, who also sticks his face on his pasta sauce bottles, ensures that his profits go to an equally deserving cause (Lloyd's bank), and I'm planning to follow suit by marketing Vic's own brand of olive oil, made from freshly pressed olives. No, on second thoughts, I think I'll market Vic's baby oil instead, made from freshly-pressed babies. Mmmm, great on salads.

I doubt if anyone who watched last night's *Cutting Edge* would need much persuading to operate the baby crusher. We all know that children are little, noisy, stupid people who don't pay rent but, worse still, here were dozens of precocious and over-indulged American brats, all fed on rocket fuel and all screeching "mommy" through voice boxes seemingly powered by the windchest of a Harrison & Harrison cathedral organ...

(Victor Lewis-Smith, 'Days of Whine, Not Roses', *Evening Standard* 4 March, 1998)

Suggestions for further reading

Maxim, J. and Bryan, K. (1994) *Language of the Elderly*, London: Whurr.
> Although this is an advanced undergraduate level book, it is clearly written and explains the relevant linguistic terminology before applying it to the analysis of elderly people's language. It provides a wealth of information on both the normal ageing process and age-related illnesses and their effects on communication with the elderly. It also discusses wider social issues related to the ageing process, including attitudes to old age and the effects of social isolation on the elderly.

Gleason, J. (ed.) (1997) *The Development of Language (4th edn)*, Boston: Allyn & Bacon.
> This undergraduate text book provides a series of accessible and well illustrated articles on all aspects of children's language development. The article on 'Language in Social Contexts' is particularly useful for pursuing some of the issues raised in this chapter.

Coupland, N. and Nussbaum, J. (eds) (1993) *Discourse and Lifespan Identity*, London: Sage.
> This advanced undergraduate book contains a series of very interesting articles on the relationship between language, self-identity and social interaction throughout the lifespan. The discussions are supported by a wide range of data from speakers of all ages.

Chapter 8

Language and class

Jason Jones

8.1 Introduction

A given language will never be used in exactly the same way by every one of its speakers, as we have already explored in Chapters 5, 6 and 7. Speakers vary considerably in their use of language, and this variation can be caused by a number of things. One of these things is class and this chapter explores the connection between a person's social class and the **linguistic variety** that they use: in other words, the way in which their social background affects the way they speak.

The chapter begins by considering **accent** and **dialect** and the relationship between regional and social variation and social position. We then highlight some of the issues involved in defining social class, before considering some of the methods that have been used by sociolinguists to determine the social class of different groups of people in their studies of **linguistic variation**.

8.2 Linguistic variation and social class

8.2.1 Accent and dialect: regional and social variation

All speakers have both an accent and a dialect. The term 'accent' refers to pronunciation. For instance, to speak with a regional accent is to pronounce your words in a manner associated with a certain geographical area. 'Dialect' refers to grammar and vocabulary (or **lexis**). For example, according to which region of the UK you come from, you might use the word *bairn* as opposed to *child*; according to which country you come from, you might use the word *diaper* as opposed to *nappy*. Similarly, according to which region of the UK or the US you come from, you might use a form like *I might could do it* as opposed to *I might be able to do it*. (For more examples of dialect differences, see Trudgill (1990).) In spoken language a dialect is often associated with a particular accent, so a speaker who uses a regional dialect will also be more than likely to have the corresponding regional accent.

Not all dialects and accents are regional though. Both the UK and the US have standard varieties of English and these varieties are also dialects, albeit prestigious ones. As prestigious dialects they are social rather than regional; that is they are preferred by particular (usually higher) social groups, and in particular (usually more formal) social situations. Standard English is often equated with 'correct English' and in Britain is also known by terms which reflect its status, such as 'Queen's English' or '**BBC** English'. (See Chapter 10 for a discussion of standard English.) Although there is a standard dialect, there is not a standard pronunciation of English in the UK. There are, however prestige **norms**, the most prestigious accent being known as **RP** (**Received Pronunciation**) which, like standard English, has a social rather than regional distribution. Probably the most widely recognised prestige form of pronunciation in Britain is that associated with formal broadcasting, such as the BBC national news. In the US it is speakers from the midwest that provide a widely recognised norm.

However, it is not in practice possible to separate regional and social linguistic varieties so clearly: regional dialects are usually social dialects too. Speakers of the variety of a given geographical area tend also to be associated with a certain position on the social scale. In the example above, the speaker who uses the form *I might could do it* is unlikely to be a member of the higher social classes. So two people may come from the same geographical area or region, but how they talk will also depend on their social position. For example, although she comes from London, Queen Elizabeth does not speak in the same way as a London cab driver.

Because we associate features of speech with particular social groups, we also expect members of these groups to behave in linguistically appropriate ways. Consider this extract from a reader's letter to *The Sunday Telegraph* (21 December, 1997):

> Many teachers have not known how to speak properly for years and I'm sure this partly explains the lack of esteem in which they are now held. I recently heard a bank manager telling someone that they should 'fink' seriously about something or other – this would have been unheard of some years ago. On television the other day there was a vicar[1] holding forth in a raging Cockney accent – for God's sake!

'Fink' is an example of a form of pronunciation typical of London and the south east of England (though also spreading to other urban centres). The 'th' in words like *three*, *think*, *Kath*, or *Arthur* is pronounced as 'f', giving *free*, *fink*, *Kaff*, *Arfer*. It is a highly stigmatised form of pronunciation in the UK. 'Cockney' is the name given to the accent and dialect of the East End area of London, which also has, among other things, the *fink* pronunciation and which is also highly stigmatised. People who are classed as 'professionals', such as teachers, bank managers and vicars, are usually considered to occupy comparatively high positions on the social scale and are not expected to use such stigmatised forms. The extract above demonstrates how it is assumed that such people will (or

should) automatically speak the **prestige variety**, the variety which society associates with education and high social standing. In the UK, this means speaking
standard English with an RP accent, whatever region or area you might come
from.

The social stigma attributed to a regional accent is also illustrated in an
article which appeared in the *Washington Post* (16 December, 1997) on speakers
with a New York accent, labelled 'Noo Yawkese'. The report explains that such
speakers have an extra 'uncharted and rather unappetizing **vowel**' in words like
bad (pronounced '*bayuhd*'), which, it is claimed, is:

> to the ears of a great many Americans, . . . part and parcel of a regional
> accent that sounds like hell. Outsiders associate the New York accent with
> someone who is fast-talking, sleazy, hucksterish and low-brow.

According to a speech pathologist interviewed for the article, 'Noo Yawkese has a
whole quality of sound that is abrasive to the ears', and the accent is described by
a Bronx-born aspiring actress as being 'quite limiting', having 'soured countless
auditions' she has attended.

Of course, there is nothing inherent in any given variety that makes it 'bad'
or 'good'; it is very often the case that the stereotypical view of a geographical
area and the people within it causes the associated linguistic variety to be seen
in the same light. Urban areas and accents are often stigmatised and this is why
people might feel that there is something wrong with a vicar (a positively viewed
occupation) speaking with a Cockney (a negatively viewed) accent, or why all
speakers with a New York accent tend to be viewed in negative terms. (See
Chapter 11 for a discussion of attitudes to language use.)

8.2.2 Accent and dialect: a clue to social information

The expectation that we can gain social information from accent is widespread.
You only have to look at some of the canonical literature to see how the social
position of a given character is often indicated by the type of accent or dialect
they use. For example, one of the central themes of many of Charles Dickens'
novels is that of society and the social class divisions that separate the rich from
the poor. Many of Dickens' characters are portrayed as archetypal members of
either the rich and privileged classes or the poor, working classes. Their membership of one or other of these groups is usually reflected in the way they speak.

The literary use of linguistic variation to highlight social class divisions
is made explicit in D.H. Lawrence's *Lady Chatterley's Lover* (1928). Here, the
working class background of the gamekeeper Mellors is mirrored by his broad

East Midlands[2] speech, while Lady Chatterley's use of a standard linguistic variety indicates her elevated social position. This is implicit in the speech of each of these characters throughout the novel, but in the following extract Lawrence draws greater attention to the social distance between the two lovers by emphasising the specific differences between their respective uses of language:

> "Tha mun come one naight ter th' cottage, afore tha goos; sholl ter?" he asked, lifting his eyebrows as he looked at her, his hands dangling between his knees.
> "Sholl ter?" she echoed, teasing.
> He smiled.
> "Ay, sholl ter?" he repeated.
> "Ay!" she said, imitating the dialect sound.
> "Yi!" he said.
> "Yi!" she repeated.
> "An' slaip wi' me," he said. "It needs that. When sholt come?"
> "When sholl I?" she said.
> "Nay," he said, "tha canna do't. When sholt come then?" ...
> ... He laughed. Her attempts at the dialect were so ludicrous, somehow.
> "'Coom then, tha mun goo!" he said.
> "Mun I?" she said.
> "Maun Ah!" he corrected.
> "Why should I say *maun* when you say *mun*?" she protested. "You're not playing fair".
>
> (Lawrence, 1961: 184–85)

In this extract, Lawrence's characters are explicitly aware of the social distance between them, and also of the fact that their different ways of speaking reflect this distance.

The reason that these characterisations are used to communicate information about social position and class division is that we, the readers, are expected to share a common attitude towards linguistic varieties, a popular perception of which varieties are 'high' and which are 'low'. Lawrence is distinguishing between **unmarked** and **marked** varieties (varieties which are considered to be the norm and those which are seen as deviating from that norm) and he shows this in the spelling system he adopts.

Lady Chatterley's speech (except when she is imitating Mellors) is represented with standard **orthography** (spelling conventions), while Mellors' speech is consistently written in spelling which attempts to approximate his accent: *slaip* for *sleep*, *coom* for *come*, *goo* for *go* and so on. It is Mellors' accent that is marked here; Lawrence writes Mellors' *shall* as *sholl* to reflect that character's pronunciation, and yet Lady Chatterley's *should* is not an exact **phonetic** representation of the way she speaks. Check your pronunciation of this word. Lady Chatterley is likely to have pronounced *should* as *shud*, not pronouncing the 'o' or the 'l'. Lawrence sees no need to attempt to approximate his spelling to Lady Chatterley's prestige variety, even though standard orthography does not, in reality, represent such pronunciation. So, in deciding not to follow standard spelling conventions in representing Mellors' way of speaking, Lawrence is marking Mellors' accent as being different from the norm. In so doing, Lawrence is drawing attention to Mellors' social position, and is exploiting the relationship between linguistic variety and social class.

ACTIVITY 8.1 ▬▬▬▬▬▬▬▬▬▬▬▬▬▬▬▬▬▬▬▬▬▬

1   Find two examples of an author using unconventional spelling as a means of indicating the social class of her/his characters. You might like to compare an earlier and a more modern work of literature. Is it always the characters from the lower social classes whose speech is marked in this way?

8.3 Does social class really affect language?

We have seen that we have expectations that people in certain social positions will speak in certain ways, but is it the case that social class affects language in reality, not just in our expectations or in literature? In other words, is it really true that the higher a person is on the social scale, the more their speech will reflect prestige norms?

Well, it seems that the answer to this is 'yes'. Those of you who live in Britain may have observed that people who belong to the highest social classes tend not to have a particularly 'broad' regional accent and dialect, or, at least, they don't have a variety that can be easily identified as belonging to a particular region. Standard linguistic forms are used throughout Britain, with little variation. As we move further down the social scale, we find greater regional variation. This situation is illustrated by the two 'cone' diagrams below. Figure 8.1 represents social and regional variation in dialects (grammar and lexis only), while Figure 8.2 represents social and regional variation in accents (pronunciation). Both diagrams emphasise the point that it is impossible to separate regional and social variation: they are two sides of the same coin.

In Figure 8.1, the most prestigious variety is standard English, and in Figure 8.2 Received Pronunciation has the most prestige. Figure 8.1 shows that

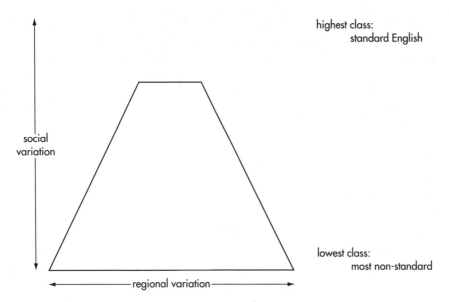

highest class:
standard English

social
variation

lowest class:
most non-standard

regional variation

Figure 8.1 Social and regional variation in dialects
Source: After Trudgill (1983a: 29–30)

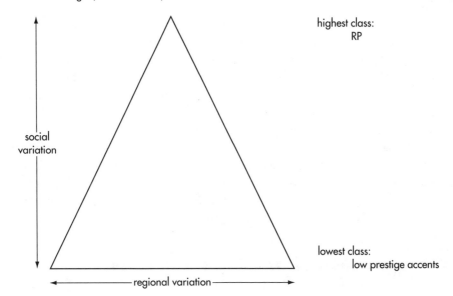

highest class:
RP

social
variation

lowest class:
low prestige accents

regional variation

Figure 8.2 Social and regional variation in accents
Source: After Trudgill (1983a: 29–30)

speakers at the top of the social scale (i.e. at the top of the 'cone') speak standard English with very little regional variation; any variation that is apparent will usually occur between two (or more) equally standard forms. For example, *he's a man who likes his beer* or *he's a man that likes his beer* are both acceptable forms in standard English, and it is quite likely that it will be speakers' regional backgrounds that dictate which form they use. But the further down the social scale we go, the greater the regional variation, so that we encounter additional forms such as *he's a man at likes his beer*, *he's a man as likes his beer*, *he's a man what likes his beer*, *he's a man he likes his beer* and *he's a man likes his beer* (after Trudgill, 1983a: 29–30). Each of these is a non-standard form and each belongs to a different regional variety. The same pattern of variation can be seen in **lexical items**. *WC*, *lavatory* and *toilet* are all acceptable in standard English, and all refer to the same thing. But *bog*, *lav*, *privy*, *dunny* and *John* are all non-standard words for the same object, and are not only features of lower social varieties, but also can be categorised in terms of regional usage.

Figure 8.2 represents variation in pronunciation. The main difference between the two diagrams is that there is no regional variation in the accent used by the speakers of the highest social class. This is why we see a point at the top of the 'cone', rather than a plateau. This means that speakers at the top of the social scale tend to pronounce their words with the same accent (i.e. RP) regardless of their regional background. But, as with dialect variation, the further we move down the social class scale, the greater spread of regional pronunciation we find.

It is important to point out that these diagrams are representative of the situation in Britain only: in other countries where English is spoken, it is more likely that people who belong to the higher social classes will speak with at least a regional accent. It is also important to bear in mind that even with reference to Britain, these two diagrams are generalised representations of regional and social variation, and that different combinations of social class and linguistic variety are possible. For example, it is entirely possible for a person from any other position on the social scale to speak standard English or use RP and they may well do so on appropriate occasions (see also Chapters 10 and 11). It is also possible to speak standard English without having an RP accent. Nevertheless, these two diagrams give a useful illustration of the way the relationship between prestige, social class and linguistic variety works in Britain.

8.4 The problem of defining social class

Up to now we have used the term 'social class' as if we all have a common idea of what it actually is. But trying to define precisely what social class is, and exactly what criteria you would base an assessment of someone's social class on is actually quite hard. Social class is a difficult concept to pin down.

When we talk about being 'higher' or 'lower' on the social scale, or about 'higher' and 'lower' social classes, we are making the assumption that society can be **stratified** according to class. Stratification means dividing something into

hierarchical layers so that one layer is above or higher up than another one. People on each layer have similarities with each other and are considered equals, but they are different from, and not equal to, the people on the other layers. In the case of social class, we commonly talk of 'upper', 'middle' and 'lower' or 'working' class stratification. But the question of defining what it is that differentiates members of one social class from those of another still remains. As Wolfram and Schilling-Estes (1998: 152) put it:

> We would hardly mistake a chief executive officer of a major corporation who resides in a spacious house in a special part of town for an uneducated, unskilled labourer from the 'wrong side of the tracks'. The reality of social stratification seems obvious, but identifying the unique set of traits that correlate with social status differences in a reliable way is not always that simple.

━━━━━ ACTIVITY 8.2

2   Before we look at other people's definitions of social class, check your own intuitions by making a list of the major factors which you feel combine to determine a person's social class, indicating their order of importance. How many factors did you come up with? Compare your list with a friend's. Did you differ in terms of which factors you felt were the most important? Did one of you come up with anything that the other one didn't?

It's quite likely that your lists have much in common: you might have mentioned things like parentage, education, occupation and economic means. But you might also find that there are differences in both the content of your lists and the order of importance you put things in, or the emphasis you placed on them.

Surveys too can emphasise or focus on specific social factors. For example, a survey conducted in 1997 in London, England (*THES*, 18 April, 1997) revealed that people living in certain areas of London have a statistically much greater chance of entering higher education[3] (HE) at the age of 18 than people living in certain other areas of London. It's generally agreed that participation in HE in Britain is still very much class-based, and that there are greater numbers of students from middle-class backgrounds than there are working-class students. This being the case, in suggesting that there is a direct link between the area you come from (defined by postal (zip) code) and your chances of going to college or university, this report is making the comment that a person's social class can be defined by the area they live in.

Another basis for defining social class is money; this may well have been the first thing you put on your list. The popular equation between social class and money is illustrated by a British initiative for encouraging people to save money in tax-exempt investment accounts. This was put forward as a scheme which would benefit 'the many and not just the few' (*The Independent*, 3 December, 1997). It was emphasised that previous tax-free savings schemes, which required a high level of investment, had benefited only middle-class and high-income investors. So here wealth and middle class go together. But does this connection always hold?

The main problem with equating social class with money in this way is that it is not only (or always) the middle classes that have money. A report published in 1997 proposed a new classification scheme for social class divisions in Britain. Like traditional classification schemes, this new scheme defined social class on the sole basis of occupation. Unlike previous schemes, it also officially recognised the existence of an 'underclass': the unemployed. The new class divisions proposed were as follows:

Class 1: Professionals and senior managers: doctors, lawyers, teachers, fund managers, executive directors, professors, editors, managers (with more than 25 staff under them), top civil servants.

Class 2: Associate professionals and junior managers: nurses, social workers, estate agents, lab technicians, supervisors, managers with fewer than 25 staff under them, journalists, entertainers, actors.

Class 3: Intermediate occupations: sales managers, secretaries, nursery nurses, computer operators, stage hands.

Class 4: Self employed non-professionals: driving instructors, builders.

Class 5: Other supervisors, craft jobs: charge hands,[4] plumbers, telephone fitters.

Class 6: Routine jobs: truck drivers, assembly line workers.

Class 7: Elementary jobs: labourers, waiters, cleaners.

Class 8: Unemployed.

(David Walker, *The Independent*, 15 December, 1997)

One of the things you might have noticed about the groups of jobs in each of these eight categories is that the further down the scale you go, the less well paid the jobs often are. So, on first sight, what this classification seems to say is that the more money a person earns, the higher up the social scale they are. But some of the jobs included in the lower divisions can actually provide a fairly high income. A plumber, defined solely by her/his occupation, would fall into one of the lower social classes, but plumbers can have a comparatively high income. Equally, some of the occupations listed in some of the higher class divisions, such as nursing or social work, are ones which are not always the most well paid. So if we take economic means as the main factor in defining social class, a conflict of factors emerges. This report acknowledges this conflict and bases its evaluation of social class on the level of responsibility a particular job entails, on whether people 'give orders or take them', rather than the income attached to it.

A model based on occupation can also be applied to social class in the US.

Class 1: Major professionals: executives of large concerns

Class 2: Lesser professionals: executives of medium-sized concerns

Class 3: Semi-professionals: administrators of small businesses

Class 4: Technicians: owners of very small businesses

Class 5: Skilled workers

Class 6: Semi-skilled workers

Class 7: Unskilled workers

(Wolfram and Schilling-Estes, 1998: 152)

Again, people are ranked according to the job they do and there are similarities between the levels proposed here and those proposed for occupations in the UK.

Although there are difficulties relying on any one feature in isolation to determine social class, you will probably have realised that those we have considered are not unconnected. For instance, housing (or the area in which you live) relates to income, as does occupation. Occupation also relates to education, which is another factor often considered in defining social class. And all these factors relate in different ways to gender and ethnicity. So, researchers who are interested in language and social class tend to use defined formulas for quantifying social class based on the analysis of a combination of characteristics and factors.

> Ultimately, social class distinctions seem to be based upon status and power, where, roughly speaking, status refers to the amount of respect and deference accorded to a person and power refers to the social and material resources a person can command, as well as the ability to make decisions and influence events.
>
> (Wolfram and Schilling-Estes, 1998: 152)

In the next section you will see how sociolinguists interested in explaining the connection between social class and linguistic variation have approached the task of determining the social class of their **informants**.

8.5 Research into the relationship between language and social class

Different sociolinguistic studies have used combinations of factors in calculating social class. For instance, Labov's (1966) major study of linguistic variation in New York City calculated social class according to the criteria of education, occupation and income, resulting in categories of lower class, working class, lower middle class and upper middle class. Shuy *et al.*'s (1968) study in Detroit used education, occupation and residence to distinguish upper and lower middle class, and upper and lower working class. In the UK, Trudgill used income, education, housing, locality and father's occupation to classify his informants. In the following sections we will look in more detail at Trudgill's study and at Labov's 'department store' study in New York City.

However, it is important to note that these now 'classic' studies of linguistic variation are based on 'consensus' views of social class. That is, that members of a society agree on norms of behaviour and (usually) aspire to prestige norms. Other linguists have concentrated on other explanations for linguistic variation such as the influence of social networks (see Milroy (1987), for example) and have considered 'conflict' views of social division (see for example, Milroy and Milroy (1998)) where the maintenance of stigmatised forms is viewed as a positive marker of group membership and non-acceptance of the norms of more prestigious social groups (see also Chapters 6, 9 and 10).

8.5.1 William Labov: the social stratification of 'r' in New York City department stores

In 1962, the American sociolinguist, William Labov, conducted a survey of the relationship between social class and linguistic variation in New York City (Labov, 1966; 1972b). He wanted to find out whether the presence or absence of a pronounced 'r' in words like *mother*, *bird*, and *sugar* was determined by a speaker's social class. In New York City (NYC), the prestige variety has pronounced 'r' (known as **postvocalic 'r'**), and lack of this feature is stigmatised. Note that the NYC situation is the reverse of that in Britain, where the prestige variety is 'r'-less (that is, *mother* is pronounced *muthuh* and so on) and only a small number of non-prestige varieties have postvocalic 'r'.

Labov believed that the higher the social class of the speaker, the more instances of postvocalic 'r' he would record from them. In order to test this hypothesis, he carried out a study of speakers in three NYC department stores. These three stores were carefully chosen so as to present an accurate cross-section of society. Labov assumed that, by selecting stores from 'the top, middle and bottom of the price and fashion scale' (Labov, 1972b: 45), he could expect first that the customers would be socially stratified, and second that the sales people in each of the department stores would reflect this in their speech styles. He supported this second assumption by citing C. Wright Mills who 'points out that salesgirls [sic][5] in large department stores tend to borrow prestige from their customers, or at least make an effort in that direction'. So they would 'borrow' the prestige speech style; postvocalic 'r'.

The three stores chosen by Labov were Saks Fifth Avenue (highest social ranking), Macy's (middle social ranking) and S. Klein (lowest social ranking). Labov's main criteria for judging the social status of these three stores were the kinds of products they sold, the price of their products, and, very importantly, the newspapers in which they advertised:

> Perhaps no other element of class behaviour is so sharply differentiated in New York City as that of the newspaper which people read; many surveys have shown that the *Daily News* is the paper read first and foremost by working class people, while the *New York Times* draws its readership from the middle class.
>
> (Labov, 1972b: 47)

In terms of prices, Saks' were the highest, followed by those in Macy's, and then by S. Klein's. As far as advertising was concerned, Labov found that Saks only ever advertised in the *New York Times* (a 'quality' newspaper); Macy's advertised mainly in the *Daily News* (a 'popular' newspaper) but sometimes in the *New York Times*; and S. Klein advertised almost exclusively in the *Daily News*.

The location of the department store was also an important factor on which the evaluation of social position was based. So, although one of Labov's indicators was economic wealth, he also used a combination of other factors as a means of determining social class.

Labov's method of observation was to approach sales assistants in each store and ask the location of a particular department, to which he already knew the answer would be *fourth floor* (in which, as the spelling indicates, there are two places where it is possible to pronounce postvocalic 'r'). Labov also believed that speakers tend to shift towards the prestige variety when paying more attention to their speech, and in order to test this, he pretended that he had not heard the informant's response the first time, and asked them to repeat it. In this way, Labov hoped to elicit a more 'careful' style of speech, in addition to the 'casual' style of the first response. Figure 8.3 shows a simplified version of the results of the investigation.

Figure 8.3 shows the pronunciation of postvocalic 'r' as a percentage of the number of times it could have been pronounced. The horizontal axis shows the

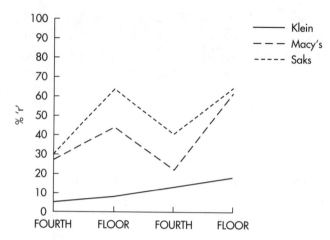

Figure 8.3 Simplified version of Labov's results
Source: Labov (1972b: 52)

two occasions on which 'fourth floor' was produced. Speakers from Klein's pronounced the 'r' infrequently, with a very small increase on each occasion they had the opportunity to pronounce the 'r'. Speakers from Saks and Macy's pronounced the 'r' in a similar pattern of frequency to each other although informants in Sak's pronounced the 'r' more often. Speakers in all three stores showed a tendency to increase their pronounciation of 'r' when they repeated 'fourth floor': that is, when, according to Labov, they were being more 'careful' with their speech. It is clear that, according to Labov's results, the presence or absence of postvocalic 'r' was indeed related to social class, such that the pronunciation of 'r' in words like *mother* and *bird* was more common for speakers wishing to project a higher social position. Interestingly, when Joy Fowler replicated Labov's study in 1986,[6] she found almost exactly the same pattern of social stratification. Thus, we can say that the presence of postvocalic 'r' in the accents of NYC speakers is socially stratified.

8.5.2 Peter Trudgill: the social differentiation of English in Norwich

Another famous large-scale sociolinguistic investigation was conducted by the British sociolinguist Peter Trudgill in Norwich, England in the late 1960s and early 1970s (Trudgill, 1974). Trudgill's primary interest was to find out whether social factors played a part in the way the people of Norwich spoke, his basic assumption being that the higher a person's social class, the closer to the prestige variety their speech would be.

To test this hypothesis, Trudgill took a sample of 60 speakers randomly selected from the electoral register, in equal numbers from four separate areas of

Norwich. These areas were carefully chosen to reflect a wide variety of housing and an accurate cross-section of the population. Trudgill used a detailed method of calculating each individual's social class, which he called the Social Index Scale. This was a six-point scale, according to which each individual informant was given a score ranging from 0 to 5 for each of the following: occupation (type of employment); income; education; housing; locality; and father's occupation. On the basis of the total scores he categorised social class as follows:

19 and over	middle middle class	(MMC)
15–18	lower middle class	(LMC)
11–14	upper working class	(UWC)
7–10	middle working class	(MWC)
3–6	lower working class	(LWC)

None of Trudgill's informants was classified as anything higher than middle middle class; this is simply because it was unusual to find anyone of a higher social class living in the areas of Norwich in which Trudgill was working. There is, of course, no reason why a score on the Social Index Scale could not be assigned to such groups of people if they were present in an investigator's sample area.

Creating situations of varying formality, Trudgill then elicited linguistic data from each of the informants. The procedure consisted of eliciting four 'styles' of speech: 'word list style' (WLS), the most formal style, in which the informant read words from a list in front of them; 'reading passage style' (RPS), slightly less formal than WLS, requiring the informant to read a passage of prose containing a number of the words included in the word list; 'formal style' (FS), less formal again, which comprised the main part of the interview; 'casual style' (CS), the least formal style, for which informants were asked to recount a funny story. Trudgill's four styles assumed a 'scale of formality', working on the assumption that the more formal the style was, the more attention the speaker would pay to their speech. As in Labov's study, the resultant 'careful' speech would be closer to the prestige variety.

One of the linguistic features Trudgill was interested in was the way in which speakers pronounced 'ing' at the end of words like *running*, *singing* and *raining*. He believed that the higher the social class of the speaker, the more likely they were to say things like *running* rather than *runnin'*, while the further down the social scale the informant was, the greater the likelihood of them saying things like *singin'* instead of *singing*.

Figure 8.4 shows each social group's score for this feature; this score shows the number of times they said *-in'* rather than *-ing* as a percentage of the number of times a word with this suffix occurred. Thus, a score of 0 indicates

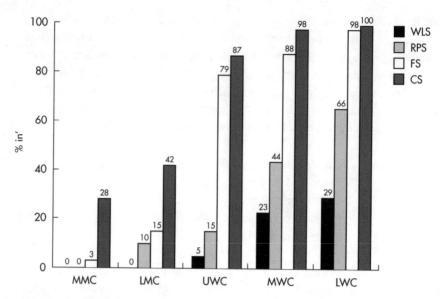

Figure 8.4 Results of Trudgill's sociolinguistic survey, Norwich
Source: Trudgill (1974: 92)

exclusive use of *-ing* (as in the prestige variety), while a score of 100 signifies exclusive use of *-in'*.

Figure 8.4 shows that, for the pronunciation of 'ing', the higher the social class of the speakers, the closer their speech is to the prestige variety. The assumption that speech also moves closer to the prestige variety in direct proportion to an increase in formality (and thus attention to speech) is also borne out. In fact, the middle middle class use exclusively *-ing* in the two most formal styles (WLS and RPS), while the lower working class use only *-in'* in casual style, when they are assumed to be the least 'careful' with their speech. This pattern was also apparent for other linguistic features that Trudgill investigated.

Like Labov's in NYC, Trudgill's research in Norwich illustrates that the higher a person's position on the social scale, the closer their linguistic variety is to prestige norms. Another interesting point suggested by both investigations is that, when they wish to, people can change the way they speak in accordance with the demands of the situation. You can see this if you look at the way in which the speech of Trudgill's informants became closer to the prestige variety in line with the steady increase in the 'formality' of the situation, as did the speech style of Labov's informants when repeating the statement *fourth floor*.

8.6 Summary

This chapter has looked at the relationship between regional and social variation and the connection that holds between a linguistic variety and social class. This connection might be perceived (based on prevailing attitudes regarding linguistic norms) or based on a more reliable assessment of a speaker's social class, calculated by a variety of different means. We have looked at the difficulties in objectively determining the social class of speakers and at the way in which linguists have approached this problem in their investigations into linguistic variation. The results of such investigations suggest that the higher a person's social class, the closer their linguistic variety will be to prestige norms. In addition, speakers will change their speech, adopting more or less prestigious styles, in accordance with the perceived demands of a given situation.

Notes

1   In the Church of England (the Anglican Church), the vicar is the priest in charge of a parish. Vicars have a relatively high social status in the UK.
2   East Midlands is the area in central England around the city of Nottingham.
3   In the UK, 'higher education' refers to college or university level study.
4   A charge hand is a supervisor who ranks slightly lower than a foreman.
5   The use of the Latin term *sic* indicates a correct transcription of the original, even though this may not be a term the present writer would use or condone. In this case, a non-gender marked term would be preferred, such as 'sales personnel' or 'sales staff'.
6   Fowler's restudy of the social stratification of (r) in NYC department stores replicated Labov's survey in every detail but one: she had to substitute May's for Klein's, as Klein's was no longer in business. A detailed summary of Fowler's findings may be found in Labov (1994).

Suggestions for further reading

Labov, William (1972b) 'The social stratification of (r) in New York City department stores', in *Sociolinguistic Patterns*, Philadelphia: University of Pennsylvania Press.
     This gives a full account of the methodology and findings of the investigation outlined in section 8.4.1.
Trudgill, Peter (1983a) *Sociolinguistics: An Introduction to Language and Society*, Harmondsworth: Penguin.
     This first year undergraduate level text contains a chapter on language and social class, which covers many of the issues raised in the present chapter and which also gives a more detailed account of Trudgill's investigation of language and social class in Norwich, England.
Wardhaugh, Ronald (1992) *An Introduction to Sociolinguistics*, 2nd edn, Oxford: Blackwell.
     The chapter on regional and social variation gives good coverage of the sociolinguistic findings in this area.

Chapter 9

Language and identity

Joanna Thornborrow

9.1 Introduction

One of the most fundamental ways we have of establishing our identity, and of shaping other people's views of who we are, is through our use of language. This chapter continues the theme established in Chapters 5, 6, 7 and 8 about how people use language to construct a social identity (or identities) for themselves, and also about how social groups and communities use language as a means of identifying their members, and of establishing their boundaries.

Because language is so important in the construction of individual and social identities, it can also be a powerful means of exercising social control. Identifying yourself as belonging to a particular group or community often means adopting the linguistic conventions of that group, and this is not just in relation to the words you use, but also in relation to the way that you say them. The way those conventions are defined and maintained is usually controlled by the group rather than the individual. In this chapter we will also look briefly at how language relates to national and political identities.

9.2 What do we mean by linguistic identity?

How you talk, along with other kinds of social codes such as how you dress or how you behave, is an important way of displaying who you are; in other words, of indicating your social identity. This question of identity, who we are, how we perceive ourselves, and how others perceive us, is not simply defined by factors such as where we were born and brought up, who our parents are/were, and which socio-economic group we happen to belong to. Identity, whether it is on an individual, social or institutional level, is something which we are constantly building and negotiating all our lives through our interaction with others. Identity is also multi-faceted: people switch into different roles at different times in different situations, and each of those contexts may require a shift into different, sometimes conflicting, identities for the people involved. One of the ways in which we accomplish and display this shift is through the language we use.

How can language indicate this kind of information? Various factors come into play here. First of all, on the individual level, where you grew up, where you went to school, how wealthy (or not) your family were, will to some extent be displayed through the **variety** of the language that you speak. Often the most immediately obvious difference in the way that people speak is in their **accent** (the **phonological** level of language), but there are also grammatical **variations** between speakers (see also Chapters 8 and 10) and, in Britain at least, someone's accent and **dialect** will always carry a great deal of information about them. They can indicate not only their regional origin, but also their social class and, to some extent, the kind of education they had.

It is often the case that children change the way they talk if they move from one region of Britain to another, sometimes even from one school to another. As a personal example, I was born and brought up in Cumbria, in the north-west of England, in a middle class family. I attended a small private school until the age of 11, when I went to the local secondary school, and then my accent changed. From fairly mainstream **RP**, I began to sound much more regionally marked as a Cumbrian. When I was 14 years old, my parents moved to the Midlands, and my accent changed again, and I began to sound less Cumbrian and more mainstream RP again. After leaving school I went to a northern university, and shifted back into using some of the sounds I had left behind in Cumbria.

The way that I spoke was also commented on by people in the places where I lived. In the Midlands, new friends referred to me as a 'primitive northerner'; when back visiting old friends in the north, they said I talked like a southerner. Later, while at university, I visited my sister in the south of England where her friends commented on how different I sounded from her. In order to fit into a new community, one of the most powerful resources I had at my disposal to show that I was just like the new group of young people I was spending my time with was the way I spoke. Significantly, this was not the same way either my parents or my sister spoke. So within the same family, even within the same generation, there can be a very wide diversity in the way different family members sound.

The importance of accent as a label of identity is evident in so far as this is the aspect of their language that speakers most frequently change, either to disguise their membership of, or distance themselves from, a particular social or regional group, or to move closer to another group they want to belong to. However, linguistic identity is not just a matter of using one dialect or **code** (the term sociolinguists use to refer to language varieties as systems of communication) rather than another, or one accent rather than another. It is also a matter of how we use language with others; in other words, how we communicate and interact with others through talk.

9.3 Language and the construction of personal identities

In this section we will be looking first at how personal identities are socially constructed through the use of names, naming practices and rituals. We will also look at systems of **address**, i.e. the way you refer to someone when you are talking to them directly, and how speakers use language to classify and identify each other through these systems.

9.3.1 Names and naming practices

One of the most obvious linguistic means of establishing people's identity is through the giving and using of names. We are distinguished from other members of a group by our name, which sets us apart as an individual, as different from others, even though we might share other attributes, like belonging to the same family, or the same school class. In Britain and the US, Western cultures distinguish between given (first) name and family (last) name, the given name being chosen, the family name being traditionally the father's family name. In some cultures, for example in Russia, people are identified further by names which designate them as 'son of x' or 'daughter of y'. These names are called patronymics. In Icelandic, it is the patronymic name that is used as the family name, so this changes from generation to generation.

ACTIVITY 9.1 ━━━━━━━━━━━━━━━━━━━━━━━━━━

1   What kind of identity does your name give you? How do you feel if someone uses it wrongly? Think of all the different ways people can name you (e.g. nickname or pet name, title plus full name) and how these construct different identities for you in different contexts.

━━━━━━━━━━━━━━━━━━━━━━━━━━━━━━━━━━━━━━

Names can sometimes carry important meanings for individual identity, as expressed by Zambian writer Felly Nkweto Simmonds:

Friends ask me why I don't just drop my non-African names. It would be a good idea, but not a practical one. In reality, my reason has nothing to do with practicality, it has to do with my own identity. For better, for worse, my names locate me in time and space. It gives me a sense of my own history that I not only share specifically with a generation of people in Africa but also with all Africans in the Diaspora.

I belong to a time. The twentieth century. A time of fragmentation, a time of rebirth. I need to understand and know myself from that position. It is the only position I have, wherever I am. In both my private and my public life. I'm also lucky. Naming myself differently to suit the occasion allows me the space to experience all my subjective realities and identities (we all have many) in a way that does not imply fragmentation, but coherence.

(Nkweto Simmonds, 1998: 36)

The naming practices and rituals of social groups are often similarly important ceremonies, and vary from culture to culture. The following passage describes the Hindu practice of choosing a child's name:

Later that same day the priest was called, and he was known to be a good man and a holy one; and one, moreover, who could read the patra, the astrological almanac, and cast a horoscope and tell in a minute the luck of a child; what it should guard against as it grew up and the name it should have in consonance with its horoscope.

(Naipaul, 1976: 26)

In the Hindu religion as practised in Trinidad up until about 30 years ago, a child was given two names. One, called the 'rasi' name, was determined by reading the 'patra', which gives the astrological positions of the stars at the time of the birth of the child. The function of this name was to give the child strength, but it was not used to address them, as anyone who knew your 'rasi' name could possess or manipulate you if they wished. A second name was also given to address the child by, also based on the 'patra', and its function was to protect the child and give them as much good fortune as possible according to their predicted horoscope. Both names were conferred at a naming ceremony at the first full moon after birth.

The giving of a name can also be part of the acceptance of an individual into a particular culture or religion, establishing individual identity but also simultaneously a religious identity (for example the bar/bat mitzvah in the Jewish religion, or the giving of a saint's name at confirmation in the Roman Catholic faith).

The attribution of names is only part of the story, however. Once you have your name, how people use it becomes very important. The way names are used in interaction is central to the process of constructing individual identities within a group. In one of his lectures, the American sociologist, Harvey Sacks (1995), describes the relevance of how names are used in introduction sequences for establishing not only who people are, but what they can call each other. Introductions can be **symmetrical**, in so far as speakers can choose to introduce people as being of the same type and status, or belonging to the same group, for example by using both first names as in:

Jim this is Alice

or as **asymmetrical**, i.e. being of a different type, as in:

Jim this is Dr Jones

This choice of names by the person doing the introducing can have an effect on how the rest of the conversation proceeds, and Sacks suggests that when you put people 'into a state of talk' by introducing them, you are not just giving them a name to use but that 'the choice of a name is already informative to them of more that they can use in conducting their conversation' (1995: Lecture 6).

What you get called is not necessarily a matter of personal choice though. Names can cause problems, particularly if they don't fit in with the conventions of a community. Children's playground practice of 'calling someone names' is also a powerful resource for a dominant group to enforce their dominance and marginalize others. Simmonds again comments that:

> [i]n public, at conferences, for example, I insist that my full name appears on my name tag. In a society that cannot accommodate names that come from 'other' cultures, this can be a frustrating exercise. It is no wonder that many Black children will Anglicise their names to avoid playground taunts ... and much worse.
>
> (Nkweto Simmonds, 1998)

9.3.2 Systems of address

It is not only the name you have, but the way that people use it in different contexts which helps to establish your identity within that context. The way that other speakers refer to you can depend on the degree of formality, of intimacy and of relative status of all the participants involved in the interaction. Think of the people you know and how you have to address them; for example, by first name (*Mary*), by title and last name (*Ms A, Mr B, Dr C*), by some kind of deferential form (*sir, ma'am*). These systems of address are culturally determined. For example, it is customary in France to address members of the legal profession as *maître*, whereas in Britain there is no equivalent professional label to use when directly addressing a lawyer, but there is if you are addressing a judge: *your honour* or *m'lord* or *m'lady*. To disregard the rules can lead to some form of disapproval or sanction, or at worst, be interpreted as an insult.

The way that address terms are used can have important implications and effects on the participants in a conversational exchange. In her study of American address terms, Susan Ervin-Tripp describes a famous triple insult based on the choice of address terms by a white American policeman in addressing a black American doctor:

"What's your name boy?"
"Dr Poussaint. I'm a physician."
"What's your first name, boy?"
"Alvin."

(Ervin-Tripp, 1980: 22)

She shows how by using the address term 'boy', the policeman is deliberately insulting the doctor by not acknowledging his age, rank or status. Poussaint responds by giving his title and last name, and in doing so he indicates that he is not complying with the white policeman's use of an address term that places him in a socially inferior position. The policeman's next question shows that he does not consider the response 'Dr Poussaint' from a black adult male as a suitable answer to his question. In asking for his first name and again addressing him inappropriately as 'boy', the policeman is repeating his earlier insult and assigning the doctor to the rank of 'child' or 'inferior'. In his choice of address terms, he is signalling his refusal to recognise the doctor's adult status and professional rank. The effect of this sequence was experienced and recorded by Dr Poussaint as 'profound humiliation' (Ervin-Tripp, 1980: 18).

The way that the **second person pronoun** (you) is used in many languages can also be a linguistic indicator of social identity, used to construct social relations of solidarity, intimacy or distance (see Crystal, 1987). The so-called T/V distinction (based on the French **pronoun** system where *tu* is the familiar form of address, and *vous* the formal, polite form) in second person pronouns has now been lost in English, where social relations are no longer encoded in the pronoun system. But in many other European languages speakers have a choice between addressing someone with the informal, intimate second person pronoun (*tu/du* in Spanish and German), or the formal, distancing second person pronoun (*Usted/Sie*).

In a language with complex **honorific** markers, like Japanese, a speaker must learn the social hierarchy of respect and condescension, and their place within that hierarchy, in order to produce grammatically correct pronoun forms

(Mühlhäusler and Harré, 1990). For example, the **first person pronoun** *watashi* (I) is used by men to mark formal status, but by women to mark neutral status (Crystal, 1987). In Russian, the choice of address pronoun is governed by a range of complex individual and social considerations; group membership is indicated by the use of the familiar *ty* form between speakers, for example between people who come from the same village, while individual emotional states of closeness, anger, respect and love can also be signalled by switching to *ty* rather than *vy*, the more formal, distancing form.

So the words you choose to address people by are important ways of showing how you situate yourself in relation to others, of creating social distance or intimacy, of marking deference, condescension or insult through the conventions of the address system of a language.

9.4 Language and the construction of group identities

We next examine how people can construct their social identity by categorising themselves (or being categorised by others) as belonging to a social group through particular types of **representation**. We will also look at how speakers' choice of linguistic code, or variety, plays an important role in establishing their group identity. We'll illustrate these ideas with some of the findings of research on the relationship between language and group identity, looking at such aspects as shared **linguistic norms** within a group, the role of **speech communities** (this term refers to social groupings which can range in size from a whole region, to a city street, to a teenage gang), and the definition of social categories and group boundaries.

9.4.1 Identity and representation

In places where there is social conflict there will often be linguistic conflict too, about whose words are used, and about which terms are used by which group of people to identify themselves and their opponents. People often have to work to establish their own identity categories, to name their particular social group, and stake their claim in owning their representations of themselves. In a discussion of these kinds of categories, Sacks (1995) analyses the case of teenage groups in the US during the 1960s who used the term 'hotrodders' to describe themselves, and makes the following observation:

> If a kid is driving, he's seen as a teenager driving, and he's seen via the category 'teenager,' compared to the variety of things he could be categorised

as. His problem, then, initially, is that he is in fact going to be typed; where for one, the category 'teenager' is a category owned by adults.

(Sacks, 1995: Lecture 7)

The point Sacks is making here is that social categories, or labels of identity, are frequently imposed on some groups by others, who may be in a more powerful position than they are, or may be using the label to make some kind of social judgement about them. We do not always control the categories people use to define our identity, or the cultural assumptions that accompany them. In Sacks' example above, the important thing for this group was to be in a position to own their own category, 'hotrodder', rather than have one imposed upon them by another group. Sacks suggests that one of the ways that kids work towards establishing independence from adults, and also exert some form of control over who gets to be a member of a particular group, is to develop their own set of categories rather than be defined by terms used by others, whose values they do not share.

9.4.2 Ingroups and outgroups

Your social identity is not something you can always determine on your own; it is also bound up with how others perceive you. In fact, it would be difficult to conceive of identity as a purely individual matter. Your perception of yourself as an individual can only be in relation to others, and your status within a social group. This status can be constructed through language use in various ways.

As with other kinds of social codes which people use to display membership of a social group, like dress codes, certain kinds of linguistic behaviour also signal your identity in relation to a group, as well as your position within it. Being able to show that you can use linguistic terms appropriately according to the norms associated with a particular group helps to establish your membership of it, both to other members of the group, the **ingroup**, and those outside it, the **outgroup**. Furthermore, adhering to the linguistic norms of one group may position you very clearly as showing that you do not belong to others.

In his study of the language used by members of street gangs in New York, William Labov (1972c) found that the core members of groups shared the most linguistic similarities. Although all the members of these gangs were perceived as speaking the non-standard 'Black English Vernacular' (BEV), it was those boys who were at the centre of the group, and who were perceived by the other boys as its core members, whose speech showed the strongest and most consistent use of the **vernacular**. Labov also found that the more integrated a boy was into the 'vernacular' culture of the gang, the more his use of language would be consistent with the vernacular, non-standard grammar used by those members at the core of the group. Those on the periphery of the gang culture, referred to by the gang's own category label of 'lames', would show a greater degree of distance from the vernacular. So membership of a group, and the position you hold within that group, either as a core member or as a peripheral member, is accomplished in considerable measure through the language that you use.

Often, language use fits in with other indicators of social identity and group membership, such as style of clothes, type of haircut, and taste in music. In a study of high school students in the Detroit suburbs in the 1980s, Penelope Eckert found that there were two social categories: students who participated in all school activities and who would go on to college were referred to and referred to themselves as 'jocks'; students whose lives were based outside school in the local area and who were destined for the blue-collar workforce were referred to, and referred to themselves, as 'burnouts'. These two categories were the defining identities of all the adolescents, boys and girls, within the school. Other students who did not see themselves as belonging to these two extremes of the school community nevertheless defined themselves in relation to them as 'in betweens' (Eckert, 1997: 69). The linguistic patterns also mirrored this categorisation, with the burnout girls having the strongest local urban accent overall, and the jock girls having the strongest suburban accent.

Other investigations have also revealed that even slight variation can be significant enough to signal affiliation with one group, and correspondingly, disaffiliation with another. Beth Thomas (1988) found that in a mining community in South Wales, women who lived on the same street used different sounds from each other according to whether they attended either the Congregational, Methodist or Baptist church locally. The variation was therefore linked to the particular religious community which the women belonged to and identified with. Labov (1972d), in his study of the island community in Martha's Vineyard, Massachusetts, also noted the variation between the speech patterns of those islanders who identified with the traditional fishing community, even among those who had left the island to go to college but had later returned to take up employment there, and the summer community of holidaymakers from the mainland. The sound changes he identified clearly functioned to establish the local inhabitants who identified with the island's traditional fishing industry as different from the visitors and those involved with them.

The process can also work the other way, when speakers adopt the speech patterns of a group they do not belong to, but which, for whatever reason, they see as prestigious, or they aspire to belong to. This can be a short-term strategy, where a speaker temporarily moves towards the speech of a group for a particular communicative effect, or a long-term one, where a speaker gradually shifts their patterns of speech to match those of the target group. The short-term occasional strategic use of the speech of another group has been termed **crossing** by Ben Rampton (1995) in his study of the use of **Creole** in Britain by 'outgroup' speakers (in this case adolescents whose ethnic backgrounds were white Anglo, Bangladeshi, Indian or Pakistani). He found that their perception of Creole as *tough* and *cool* meant that its use was 'strongly tied to a sense of youth and class identity':

> **Informants** generally credited black adolescents with the leading role in the multiracial vernacular, introducing elements that others subsequently adopted. In this way, for example, 'innit' was analysed as being originally black, and young people most often ascribed Creole roots to new words in the local English vernacular.
>
> (Rampton, 1995: 128)

Some varieties of language are more prestigious than others, and what counts as the prestige form can vary according to the context and type of linguistic activity. One example of this was in the early 1960s, when British pop singers often produced sounds (such as the **vowel** sounds in words like *dance*, *girl*, *life* or *love*) with stereotypical American pronunciation. One explanation that has been suggested for this is that because of long-standing American domination within the field of popular music, British singers were attempting 'to model their singing style on that of those who do it best and who one admires most' (Trudgill, 1983b: 144). As the status of British pop music rose during the 1960s and early 70s, this feature became less frequent, and with the advent of punk rock music and 'new wave' bands in the mid 1970s, whose 'primary audience was British urban working-class youth' (Trudgill, 1983b: 154), things changed again. The use of American features declined, while non-standard, low prestige features associated with southern English pronunciation (such as a **glottal stop** in a word like *better*) and non-standard grammatical forms (such as **multiple negation**) became more frequent, as these bands moved towards adopting a British working class identity. These non-standard, **covert prestige** forms have not replaced the American sounds in British pop music, but rather co-exist with them.

━━━ ACTIVITY 9.2

2   Think of any 'in' words or phrases which are used currently by your own peer group. What kind of words are they? Where do they come from? What happens if someone outside your peer group uses them? Why do you think this is the case?

9.5 Linguistic variation and the construction of identity

9.5.1 Stylistic variation and language choice

Defining common systems of representation and adherence to ingroup linguistic norms are not the only means by which people display their affiliation to (or disaffiliation from) a social group. We also position ourselves in relation to others by the way that we talk in different kinds of interaction. People do not always talk in exactly the same way all the time: they don't always pronounce words the same way, and they don't always use the same grammatical forms (for example *you was* rather than *you were)*. This kind of variation in speech is usually referred to as **style-shifting** (see also Chapter 8).

One of the theories explaining this variation in style is that speakers take into account who they are talking to, and alter their speech style accordingly. This concept of **audience design** (Bell, 1984) provides a theoretical account of the reasons why speakers change the way they talk depending on the situation and context they are talking in. This account is based on the premiss that people are mainly seeking to show solidarity and approval in their dealings with others, and one way that speakers can do this is through linguistic **convergence,** i.e. by changing their patterns of speech to fit more closely with those of the person they happen to be talking to (Giles and Powesland, 1975; Giles and Sinclair, 1979).

Linguistic convergence can, however, backfire, as it can be perceived by the hearer as patronising, ingratiating or even mocking behaviour. This is particularly the case when standard speakers converge towards non-standard, low prestige forms. The imitation of another person's speech can be interpreted as linguistic behaviour that is designed to insult, by emphasising the difference between speakers, rather than behaviour that is designed to display solidarity. In a study of young adolescents' use of Creole in London, Roger Hewitt found that young black Creole speakers were usually quite hostile to their white peers' use of Creole, which was perceived not just as parody but as a display of power:

> [W]hite Creole use was regarded (a) as derisive parody, and hence as an assertion of white superiority, and (b) as a further white appropriation of one of the sources of power – 'it seems as if they are stealing our language'.
>
> (Hewitt, 1986: 162)

There seems, then, to be a relationship between social questions of power and status, and the way in which speakers accommodate to each other in their use of language. Who converges with who is an important issue in any speech situation where the participants have different social status.

In some situations, speakers may choose not to converge, but instead to either maintain their own variety (linguistic maintenance), or move to a more extreme variety of their dialect (linguistic **divergence**), in order to emphasise the difference between themselves and the person or people they are talking to. An example of this comes from Jenny Cheshire's (1982) study of the use of non-standard English in adolescent peer groups in Reading, England. Cheshire recorded her informants' speech both within the peer group and within the more formal setting of the classroom. In line with common practice, most of her informants produced more standard forms in school, converging with the standard norms of the institutional environment. One of her informants, however, increased his use of non-standard forms, diverging from the expected linguistic variety and thus emphasising his distance from and non-acceptance of the school's norms. Viv Edwards (1997) reports similar linguistic signals given by children who diverge from expected norms by using their variety of Black English in the classroom as an expression, not only of solidarity with the black peer group, but of distance from and exclusion of the outgroup (teachers and/or white children).

Speakers may wish to be identified with different groups at different times, and their linguistic patterns may produce a shift, whether it be between different varieties of a language, or from one language to another. The question of group affiliation and identity can determine the choices a speaker makes about how to speak and, for bi or multilinguals, which language to use.

When a choice is made between two different languages, the question of identity becomes even more marked, particularly when the choice is bound up with the national and political status of a language. Monica Heller (1982) describes how, in Quebec, speakers have to deal with the issue of which language to use before the business of the talk gets underway. In choosing French rather than English, or vice versa, speakers are always making a statement about how they align themselves in terms of national and political identities. Heller describes an instance of a call to a bilingual hospital where the conversation between the hospital clerk and the patient has been conducted in English, until the clerk reads out the patient's name (Robert Saint Pierre) in French. The caller corrects the clerk angrily, by repeating his name using the English pronunciation, thereby claiming his identity as an English speaker despite the 'Frenchness' of his name (Heller, 1982: 118).

9.5.2 Power and linguistic imperialism

A sense of cultural identity is often centred on a particular language and speakers' perceptions of the connection between the languages they use and that identity is well documented (see for example Gumperz, 1982a; Alladina and

Edwards, 1991; Gal, 1998). Language rights and recognition are often important issues in socio-political conflicts all around the world. Maintenance of a minority language within a majority culture (such as Spanish in the US, Gujerati in the UK) is often associated with the maintenance of a minority's values and with the continuation of its unique cultural identity (see Chapter 6). Loss of a language can also be associated with a loss of cultural identity.

Languages can be lost for a variety of reasons. For example, speakers may choose to shift from one language to another as social conditions change, or one language may be imposed and another suppressed by a dominant power. In the fictional account below of the historical relationship between Denmark and Greenland, the principal character draws on the intricate relationship between language and identity and describes her feeling that in losing her ability to speak her mother tongue, she is also losing her Greenlandic identity:

> When we moved from the village school to Qaanaaq, we had teachers who didn't know one word of Greenlandic, nor did they have any plans to learn it. They told us that, for those who excelled, there would be an admission ticket to Denmark and a degree and a way out of the Arctic misery. This golden ascent would take place in Danish. This was when the foundation was being laid for the politics of the sixties. Which led to Greenland officially becoming "Denmark's northernmost county", and the Inuit were officially supposed to be called "Northern Danes" and "be educated to the same rights as all other Danes", as the prime minister put it.
>
> That's how the foundation is laid. Then you arrive in Denmark and six months pass and it feels as if you will never forget your mother tongue. It's the language you think in, they way you remember your past. Then you meet a Greenlander on the street. You exchange a few words. And suddenly you have to search for a completely ordinary word. Another six months pass. A girlfriend takes you along to the Greenlanders' House on Lov Lane. That's where you discover that your own Greenlandic can be picked apart with a fingernail.
>
> (Hoeg, 1996: 105)

The passage also illustrates the implications that language use has for wider issues of social, ethnic and national identities. The reference here to the passage to Danish education as 'the golden ascent' which 'would take place in Danish' shows how the ability to speak a language can either enable or restrict access to social and institutional structures, privileging one community of speakers over another.

9.6 Summary

In this chapter we have looked at the construction of personal identities through the use of names and systems of address, and at the construction of group identity through types of representation and adherence to linguistic norms. We have seen how linguistic variation plays a part in the expression of solidarity with, or distance from, group norms, and how language is connected with cultural identity. In this way we have investigated linguistic identity from the point of view of the individual and the group, as well as the institutional and cultural practices of a community of speakers. As always, however useful these categories have been for the purposes of discussion, in practice they overlap and the boundaries between them are probably less clearly defined than is perhaps implied here. The relationship between language and identity will always involve a complex mix of individual, social and political factors which work to construct people as belonging to a social group, or to exclude them from it.

Suggestions for further reading

The question of identity is a thread that runs through many studies in sociolinguistics. This is reflected to a large extent in many of the chapters in this book which have been concerned with identities of gender, age, ethnicity and social class, so much of the reading already suggested will be relevant here. However, one of the first collections bringing together a variety of work in this area is:

Gumperz, John (1982b) (ed.) *Language and Social Identity*, Cambridge: Cambridge University Press.

If you want to read a concise and interesting critical account of research in language and social identity, try:

Ochs, Elinor (1993) 'Constructing social identity: a language socialisation perspective', *Research on Language and Social Interaction*, 26(3): 287–306.

Chapter 10

The standard English debate

Linda Thomas

10.1 Introduction

Of the many different **dialects** of English both within the UK and beyond it, the dialect known as standard English has special status. Standard English is the dialect of institutions such as government and the law; it is the dialect of literacy and education; it is the dialect taught as 'English' to foreign learners; and it is the dialect of the higher social classes. It is therefore the prestige form of English. However, the word 'debate' in the title to this chapter indicates that the idea of a standard English is not a straightforward one, and we will investigate ideas about standard English, as well as ways in which to define it. We will also look at some of the problems involved in trying to get a clear linguistic definition of standard English based on its grammar, and at some social and ideological definitions of standard English. Part of the **ideology** of standard English is that it is the 'correct' form of the language and that other **varieties** are 'incorrect'. Some well established English usages which don't happen to belong to the standard, such as **multiple negation** and the use of *ain't* as in *I ain't got none*, are therefore stigmatised. The debate about standard English centres around such differences in grammar and the notion that one variety (standard English) is linguistically superior to the others. We will also look at the central role that standard English holds in the debate on English teaching within the school.

10.2 What is standard English?

10.2.1 Beginning a definition

It is important first of all to draw a distinction between the terms 'dialect' and '**accent**' as discussions about standard and non-standard English technically refer to dialect, not to accent (see also Chapter 8). Linguistically, accent relates to pronunciation; dialect relates to words and grammar. In theory, and for the purposes of discussion, it's possible to separate accent and dialect, although in practice the two go together, at least in spoken English. It's not possible to talk without both an accent (pronunciation) and a dialect (words or **lexis**, and grammar) and traditional studies of regional dialects usually incorporate accent within their descriptions of a dialect area. Examples of different accents could include words like *hair* and *here* which for some speakers sound the same as each other, and for others sound different from each other; or different pronunciations of the same word, such as *fishin'* and *fishing*, or *aks* and *ask*. Different dialects on the other hand can use totally different words for the same thing, such

---

ACTIVITY 10.1

---

1 Different varieties of English use different words. Think about your own variety of English by deciding which word you would use to describe the following:

(a) the place where pedestrians walk alongside the road
(b) the object that you turn (or open) to let water flow from a pipe
(c) a compartment for transporting people or goods vertically within a building
(d) a railway system below ground
(e) a woollen garment worn on a chilly summer evening
(f) discarded waste or unwanted or useless items
(g) a short, sleeveless garment worn over a shirt, often under a suit
(h) fuel for a car
(i) the hinged part of the car that gives access to the engine

Your answers to this exercise may include the following:

(a)	pavement	sidewalk
(b)	tap	faucet
(c)	lift	elevator
(d)	underground	subway
(e)	jumper	sweater
(f)	rubbish	garbage
(g)	waistcoat	vest
(h)	petrol	gas
(i)	bonnet	hood

The list on the left reflects British English usage and that on the right, American English usage. Do your own replies seem to be more in line with British or American vocabulary? You may find your answers have words from both lists (*sweater* for example is used in both varieties). If you have words that don't appear here, do you think they are words in local or general use? Check your list with your friends.

---

as *autumn* and *fall*, or *wee* and *little*; or different grammatical constructions, such as *I ain't got none* as opposed to *I haven't got any* or *I don't have any*. Although dialect and accent are technically separate entities, they are often treated as the same thing because of their close connection. However, in our discussion, the terms 'standard English' and 'non-standard English' will refer to different dialects, not accents, of English.

Having said that standard English is a dialect, this is unfortunately where the easy part of any linguistic definition stops; there is no comprehensive linguistic description of standard English. Although there are plenty of grammar books which describe standard usage, standard English is, like other dialects, difficult to isolate and put linguistic boundaries around, and we'll come back to some reasons for this in due course. To make matters more complicated, there are also different varieties of standard English worldwide. The two main standard varieties, standard American English and standard English English, whilst sharing many similarities, also have their differences. Unless otherwise stated, the variety of standard English under discussion in the rest of this chapter is standard English English, although the notions of prestige to be developed here may apply equally to other varieties in other countries.

As it isn't easy to define what standard English is, it might be beneficial to start with an example of what it isn't. We mentioned in the introduction that multiple negation (the use of more than one negative in an expression) is not standard English. If you use this form in an utterance like *I didn't say nothing*, you stand to be 'corrected' by someone who thinks they are in a position to judge your language use. So why is this the case when multiple negation is a form which so many people use? To begin to answer this, we need to turn to history and the time when grammarians were working on the **codification** (we'll come back to this term in section 10.2.2 below) of standard English. Milroy and Milroy (1985) point out that multiple negation was a normal feature of English up until the seventeenth century. However, by the end of the eighteenth century, grammarians had decided that this form was not acceptable. They had decided to suppress forms like *I didn't say nothing* and promote forms like *I didn't say anything* on the grounds that multiple negation was illogical. Arguments against the use of multiple negation are still made on the grounds of logic. It is said that it is not logical to use two negatives, as two negatives, at least in mathematics, make a positive. Under this argument, *I didn't say nothing* really means *I said something*. However, given that this is one of the most widespread non-standard forms of English in Britain today, it seems that the 'logical' interpretation is not one that speakers readily employ. Despite the mathematical evidence, speakers understand *I didn't say nothing* and *I didn't say anything* to mean the same thing (and we have yet to meet anyone who interprets *you ain't seen nothing yet* in the so-called logical way). Milroy and Milroy also point out that multiple negation remains a normal feature in the standard forms of many other languages, so it seems that the kind of logic which applies to mathematical relations doesn't apply quite so readily to linguistic ones.

Although the appeal to logic doesn't quite work, multiple negation remains a stigmatised form and this is also partly because it is, like many non-standard forms, a socially distributed form. This means that speakers from one social class are less likely to use it than speakers from another social class. The higher up the social scale you go, the less likely you are to use non-standard forms like multiple negation, and the more likely you are to be a standard English speaker. Standard English is, not coincidentally, the dialect of the middle and upper classes and its forms are prestigious forms. It is the dialect that attracts positive **adjectives** like 'good', 'correct', 'pure' or 'proper' and similarly bestows upon its speakers terms like 'articulate', 'educated' and 'intelligent'. Features of other dialects or varieties of English, social, regional, and sometimes national, tend to be judged negatively when compared to it, as in the case of multiple negation. These aspects of the definition of standard English are social ones and we will keep returning to this social dimension in the rest of this chapter.

10.2.2 Standard English, history and society

The development of a standard form of a language is tied up with the development of a national and cultural identity, and a national standardised language becomes a symbol of that identity. When English began to rise to prominence in England, replacing French and Latin as the prestige languages, it became necessary to chose a variety from the many different varieties of English which were used at the time, to develop as a standard. There is not space here to detail the history of standard English, but writers who have show how the selection and development of the standard variety was often based on social and political, rather than linguistic, choices (see Milroy and Milroy, 1985; Crowley, 1989; Leith, 1992). For instance, the variety which was chosen for promotion was one based on that of the south-east Midlands[1] area. This was a variety already achieving prominence, not on linguistic grounds, but on grounds of the concentration of learning, politics and commerce in the region; that is, on grounds of power and influence. If the political, social and commercial centre of England had been elsewhere, the current standard form of the language would look different, since it would have been based on a different English variety.

Once a variety is selected, the standardisation process continues with codification. Codification means that scholars and academics analyse and write down the vocabulary and grammatical patterns and structures of the selected variety in dictionaries and grammar books. For English, much of this codification work took place in the eighteenth century. The patterns and structures that are written down then become grammatical 'rules'.

Standardisation and codification involves what Milroy and Milroy call 'the suppression of optional variability' (1985: 8). This means that where there are two or more forms in use, two or more ways of saying the same thing, only one is selected as standard. We saw an example of this in multiple negation. Another example they give is the choice of *from*, in the expression *different from*, as opposed to *different to* or *different than*. Milroy and Milroy suggest that although there are reasonable arguments to support the choice of any of the three candidates, *from*, *to*, and *than*, the decision to choose *different from* as the standard form was entirely arbitrary in linguistic terms. It rested instead on 'the observed usage of the "best people" at that time' (1985: 17); in other words, it was a socially determined decision. Incidentally, *different than* is the standard form in the English of the US, which just shows how arbitrary a decision can be, and it is still a feature of British English.

Once codification (the writing down of the 'rules') takes place, the dictionaries and grammar books become 'authorities' which people can consult to find out what standard usage, which readily becomes associated with 'correct' or 'good' usage, is. So one form, the now standard form, becomes dominant. The alternative forms that are not adopted as the standard do not disappear, but, as in the examples we have looked at, remain in use. However, as standard forms become 'correct', the forms designated non-standard become 'incorrect' and are stigmatised. Instead of being able to opt for one form or another, only one has recognition as 'proper English' and so takes precedence, while the other is suppressed. Grammar books, instead of being descriptions of what speakers do with their language, are made to become prescriptions on what they should do, and non-standard forms, despite a long history, and continued use, are seen as sub-standard forms. It then becomes difficult to remember that the selection of one dialect and its forms over others for promotion as the standard is only as a result of historical accident, not linguistic superiority.

However, the idea that there can be only one variety of English is an idealised notion. As we saw in Chapters 6 and 9, cultural and social identity is complex, and the language variety you use is, as Cheshire and Milroy (1993: 18) explain, a linguistic 'badge' of your identity, indicating who you are, where you come from and who you share social and cultural links with. There are many such linguistic 'badges' or varieties of English. Standard English itself is the badge of identity of particular social groups in the same way that non-standard varieties are. So even though standard English is considered to be the correct form of English, it is not an easy prospect simply to adopt it as your own if you come from a different social group. Changing your language variety and conforming to the

norms of another social group means changing the badge of your identity (as discussed in Chapter 9).

There is, however, a tension between standard and non-standard usage. Milroy and Milroy (1985) point out that, even if the universal adoption of the standard has failed, promotion of the ideology of a standard has been very successful. There is a belief among most people in Britain that there is a correct way of using English even if they don't use it that way themselves. And it is still the language habits of the 'best people' which are used, both in the UK and the US, to provide the examples of 'proper' English and 'correctness' which constitute the standard. But, as Rosina Lippi-Green (1997) points out, whilst reasons may be put forward for using prestige groups to dictate usage, there is nothing objective about doing so. The choice of models for standard English is not a neutral one, and standard English is not, therefore, a neutral variety. Because it belongs to a social group, it is defined by that group and is still determined less by what it is, than by who speaks it.

━━━━━━━━━━━━━━━━━━━━━━━━━━━━━ ACTIVITY 10.2

2   Think about your own speech. Have you ever been corrected by someone on your language use? What kinds of things have they objected to? They may have objected to features of your pronunciation (such as saying *bu'er* not *butter*, or *gonna* not *going to*) or they may have objected to features of your grammar (such as saying *I don't know nobody* instead of *I don't know anybody*, or *we was* instead of *we were*). Check with the generation older and/or younger than you. Were they or are they corrected by other people, and was it or is it for the same kinds of features that you have been corrected for, or for different ones?

10.3 The linguistic definition of standard English

10.3.1 Linguistic variation

One of the reasons it is difficult to give an exact linguistic definition of standard English is because language varies in its use. This means that you will choose different kinds of words and put them together in different kinds of ways according to the situation or context. Most people are aware that they use different styles of spoken language during a typical day depending on the situations they find themselves in. Social contexts are infinitely varied but can include: where you are (at home, in the office, in the pub or bar); who you are talking to, for instance in terms of status (your boss), age (your grandmother), or intimacy (your best friend); what you are talking about (the state of the nation's economy, your opinion of a work of art, last night's date). Written language also varies according to its purpose and audience, so a note to your friend looks nothing like a novel, a newspaper editorial, or an academic textbook. To a large extent the style of language you use will depend on the formality of the context and the amount of planning that is involved. For example, a casual conversation between you and a close friend is an informal event which won't be planned in advance. What you say, and how you say it, will occur spontaneously as the conversation develops. On the other hand, in a more formal situation, such as giving a speech or lecture, you will plan what you say, and the way you say it, more carefully. Written language tends to occur in more formal contexts than spoken language, so it usually requires more planning. In most cases, written English will be in standard English.[2]

There are many grammar books, dictionaries and guides to English usage which describe and give advice on the standard English that appears in writing. When you are writing you can refer to them to check your own usage, although such reference books don't always agree with each other, and as Mackinnon (1996: 356) illustrates, sometimes their judgements are based on nothing more substantial than the prevailing attitude to a particular construction, rather than on grammar.[3] Disagreements aside, these books are widely used for guidance on what constitutes standard English. Unfortunately, there is often also a tendency to apply these judgements, which are about written English, to spoken English. But the norms of spoken and written language are not the same; people don't talk like books even in the most formal of situations or contexts. If you can't refer to a written norm to describe spoken language, then, as we have seen, you base your judgements on the speech of the 'best people', the 'educated' or higher social classes.

But basing your judgements on the usage of the educated is not without its difficulties. Speakers, even educated ones, use a variety of different forms. Quirk and Stein (1990: 117) give the following as examples of **variation** within spoken standard English:

1(a) Who/whom did they elect to speak for them?
1(b) His sister is younger than him/he
1(c) The data is/are just not available
1(d) Neither of them were/was present

So which of each pair is correct? Quirk and Stein suggest that the assessment of correctness in English can depend on 'style and personal judgement', saying that, although in each of these examples the second alternatives are:

preferable in certain circumstances (such as formal writing), all of these are used freely by educated people and must be regarded as acceptable within Standard English. But we should be prepared for honest disagreement in such matters...

(1990: 117)

So it seems that variation is acceptable within standard English, but only on the authority of educated speakers (although they might disagree).

However, another, perhaps more controversial, example comes from Cheshire *et al.* (1993) who investigated the use of *sat* in expressions such as *she was sat there*, where the standard English of the grammar books would have *she was sitting there*. The feature *was sat* is now widespread in English English and Cheshire *et al.* report that it also appears in educated spoken and written English. The fact that educated speakers are using this construction should make it standard English, but purists, who Milroy and Milroy (1985) call language 'guardians',[4] would not regard *was sat* as a standard form of English, even if it is used by educated speakers. Such guardians might even claim, along with John Honey, that 'misuse of the language was so prevalent that even "educated" people were unable to speak correctly'(*The Observer*, 3 August, 1997). So the authority of educated speakers is not total it seems. In which case, you might be tempted to ask the unanswerable question 'whose is?'.

The notion of 'educated speakers' is, in any case, a problematic one. The people who make up this group will be different in different countries and produce different norms. So standard Englishes in different parts of the world may have differences from one another. Trudgill and Hannah (1994: 77) give details of the differences between different standard Englishes around the world, including such examples as:

2(a) I haven't bought one yet.
2(b) I didn't buy one yet.

3(a) Have you read it already?
3(b) Did you read it already?

where the second sentence of each pair would be acceptable to speakers of standard US English, but not to speakers of standard English English. Whilst many such differences may seem trivial, and standard Englishes may have more similarities than they have differences, it does present a difficulty in deciding precisely which constructions should be accepted as 'correct' and which should not, and such examples are liable to cause controversy and debate.

It should also be pointed out that standard and non-standard varieties of English are not separate linguistic systems either. There are large areas of overlap between standard and non-standard grammars, although linguists descri-bing different varieties of English, and prescriptivists complaining about usage, concentrate on the differences, which may give them a greater emphasis than they deserve. Speakers use features of the systems (standard and non-standard) to a greater or lesser degree, but not exclusively. It is a question of choice, although not necessarily a conscious choice. Speakers and listeners are not typically aware of the variation that takes place in their spontaneous spoken language, but will choose forms that are appropriate to the contexts they are in. Variation is not random, but is subject to a variety of different factors, some of them related to linguistic contexts and some of them related to real world contexts; it is a normal part of everyday language use.

ACTIVITY 10.3

3   The **pronouns** *who* and *whom* exhibit variation in their use and it is not difficult to find examples of confusion over their use in educated speech and writing. Check your own intuitions about usage on the following examples:

> The girl who he met
> The girl whom he met
> The girl who spoke to him
> The girl who he spoke to
> The girl whom he spoke to
> The girl to whom he spoke
> The girl whom he thought was speaking to him

Check with your friends or family and see whether their answers are the same as yours, then check in a reference grammar. According to *Fowler's Modern English Usage*, *whom* is regarded by some as 'moribund' or as 'something frozen, archaic, stifling, or artificial' (Burchfield, 1996). Do you agree?

10.3.2 Logic and correctness

As we have seen, one of the claims which is made for standard English is that it is 'correct'. Other varieties are therefore by definition 'incorrect'. Sometimes the basis for the notion of correctness is that the standard variety is 'logical', or that it is systematic and rule-governed (i.e. it has grammatical rules), whereas non-standard varieties are not. Linguists resist these notions, arguing instead that standard English is no more 'correct' or systematic than any other dialect. It may be desirable to know and be able to use standard English when necessary and especially in writing, but this does not make standard English 'better' or more 'correct'. So let's have a closer look at the basis for these arguments.

We saw in the example of multiple negation (see section 10.2.1) that applying logic to English is not always successful, but this doesn't stop people from trying. In an article in the *Evening Standard* on 17 November, 1988, John Rae[5] criticised linguists and educationists who argue that the form *we was* is a dialect form and therefore not incorrect:

> You could have fooled me. I thought it was correct to write 'we were' and incorrect to write 'we was'. I did not realise it was just a question of dialect; I thought it was a question of grammar or, if you do not like that word, of logic. You cannot use the singular form of the verb with a **plural pronoun**.

I don't think many (or any) linguists or educationists would support the use of *we was* in formal writing; neither did the report which this article criticises (the Cox report). The point that the report was trying to make was that, although the standard English form *we were* is appropriate for writing, this doesn't make the corresponding non-standard form *we was* incorrect, just not appropriate. The same argument would apply to spoken English; spoken standard English is more appropriate in some contexts than non-standard English. But (putting the reasons for why one is more 'appropriate' than the other aside) can the claim for 'correctness' and 'logic' be upheld? To answer this question we need to look at the way verbs in English work, and to do this we need to look at what is called a 'paradigm'. A paradigm is a set of things which belong together and a verb paradigm shows how bits of a verb work in relation to each other. A typical past **tense** standard English verb pattern looks like that of the following verbs:

Singular	Plural
I loved	we loved
you loved	you loved
s/he loved	they loved
I walked	we walked
you walked	you walked
s/he walked	they walked

These verbs show us the standard English pattern for the past tense forms of most verbs; they are called regular verbs and they end in -*ed*. There are also irregular verbs and they behave in different ways, for example:

Singular	Plural
I saw	we saw
you saw	you saw
s/he saw	they saw
I went	we went
you went	you went
s/he went	they went

In both sets of verbs, regular and irregular, you can see that the form doesn't change between singular and plural; in fact it doesn't change at all throughout the paradigm. The verb *be*, however, behaves in a different fashion from other verbs:

Singular	Plural
I was	we were
you were	you were
s/he was	they were

Looking at the different patterns which standard English verbs have, it's difficult to apply the notion of 'logic' to one which behaves in a totally idiosyncratic manner. The verb *be* is alone in its distinction between singular and plural and could be considered quite 'illogical'. For many non-standard varieties of English, however, this illogical distinction doesn't exist; they simply have *be* with one past tense form, like all the other verbs, to give:

Singular	Plural
I was	we was
you was	you was
s/he was	they was

This is no less systematic than the standard and seems more logical.

Rae's point about using singular forms of the verb with plural pronouns doesn't even stand much scrutiny within the standard itself. You can see that there is no distinction in standard English between the form of *be* with singular *you* (*you were*) and plural *you* (*you were*), although there is a distinction between the forms used with the other singular and plural pronouns. This doesn't seem 'logical' either.

The use of *we was* is every bit as systematic and rule-governed as the standard, and there are many other examples of non-standard forms for which the same claim can be made; it's just that the systems and rules are different (for examples see: Trudgill and Chambers, 1991; Milroy and Milroy, 1993; Thomas, 1996).

10.3.3 So what is standard English?

We have shown that historically the standard dialect of English is based on linguistic forms that were selected from among many competing forms that were in general use. It is bound up politically with notions of national identity and it is connected socially with the middle and upper classes and consequently with education, correctness, and prestige. As a linguistic system, the grammar of standard English has similarities with and differences from the grammars of other varieties of English.

ACTIVITY 10.4

4   The following appeared in a column in a British newspaper:

THEY SAID IT

"I'm talking to you slightly differently than I would if I was buying tomatoes" – Two solecisms in one sentence addressed to Melvyn Bragg by Jean Aitchison, Rupert Murdoch Professor of Language and Communication at Oxford.

'solecism – 1a) the non-standard use of a grammatical construction; 1b) any mistake, incongruity, absurdity. 2. a violation of good manners' (*Collins Dictionary*).

What is the nature of the journalist's objection? Use a reference grammar to check, then try this exercise on your friends. Consider whether you think the objection is justified and why (not).

10.4 Standard English and education

10.4.1 Standard English in the school

The debate about standard English in England often centres on education and education standards. This brings us to a problem with terminology. The word 'standard' has at least two meanings. It can mean a 'unified form' or 'consistency' (as in 'standard' measures) and this is probably what the term is meant to convey in relation to 'standard' English. But the term 'standard' also refers to levels of attainment, as in 'standards of excellence' or 'falling standards' and it is easy to confuse the two meanings. Once standard English is the 'standard of excellence' rather than the 'unified form', 'non-standard' is reinforced as synonymous with 'sub-standard'.

In the discussion about education we have, once again, to separate ideas about written and spoken language. Teaching literacy, and therefore written standard English, is one of the main functions of the school, but the State-imposed national curriculum in England and Wales also made it a requirement that children should be taught to speak in standard English when appropriate. 'Appropriate' contexts tend to be both public and towards the formal end of the spectrum; in other words, prestigious contexts, although why standard English is appropriate in these contexts is not examined. At the same time, the same orders try to support dialects other than the standard, the dialects that most children coming into school will speak, by talking of the 'richness' and 'integrity' of non-standard varieties. Teachers are encouraged to aim for the 'high standards of excellence' in spoken language that only standard English is said to bring, without undermining the validity of the non-standard varieties spoken by the children in their classes. Similar sentiments are uttered in the US. In her discussion of English in the education system, Lippi-Green notes a statement by the National Council of Teachers of English which claims to 'respect diversity in spoken and written English' whilst arguing for the imposition of a standard form (1997: 109). It is difficult to see how teachers might maintain the validity of non-standard varieties, or respect for diversity, given the status and prestige of the standard, the constant confusion of 'non-standard' with 'sub-standard' and the explicit message that nothing else counts, both inside and outside the school. As we saw above, *we was* is not recognised as a different form of English with different appropriate occasions for usage, but as an incorrect form, not to be used at all.

A look at Quirk and Stein's prose also illustrates the difficulty of both promoting the standard and accepting the non-standard. On the one hand they say

What pupils bring to school is their language and it is a very precious part of that identity which...is essential to their personal, family, and community pride.... If the English teacher is going to challenge this, she or he had better look out.

(1990: 97)

On the other hand, they repeatedly refer to non-standard forms as 'errors', 'wrong', or 'bad grammar' and talk about 'correcting', rather than 'changing', from one (non-standard) grammatical system to another (standard) one. Value judgements such as 'correct' or 'bad' only serve to reinforce judgements about the validity of standard and non-standard forms.

The motivation for making children speak standard English in school is explicitly given as the need to communicate effectively. Apparently, those who don't speak the standard (and that constitutes the majority of the population of Britain) can't communicate effectively. Whilst there are undoubtedly contexts where standard English is designated as appropriate, does this really mean that non-standard Englishes don't work as forms of communication? It would appear that for some people in Britain and the US the answer to this question is 'yes'. In 1995 the then UK government launched the 'Better English Campaign'. The aim of this campaign was to improve standards of spoken English around the country; in other words to encourage spoken standard English. The committee included prominent educated speakers and its mission was to 'declare war on communication by grunt'. The Secretary of State for Education, Gillian Shephard, in promoting the campaign, claimed that 'grunts and slack language were impoverishing children'. By 'grunts and slack language' she meant non-standard English. Compare this with a statement made in the early part of the twentieth century:

> Come into a London elementary school and see what it is that the children need most. You will notice, first of all, that in a human sense, our boys and girls are almost inarticulate. They can make noises, but they cannot speak.
>
> (quoted in Crowley, 1989: 242)

Crowley comments that what it is these children lack is the ability to speak standard English, not the ability to speak. Lippi-Green records a similar comment about non-standard speakers from a teacher in the US in the late twentieth century:

> These poor kids come to school speaking a hodge podge. They are all mixed up and don't know any language well. As a result, they can't even think clearly. That's why they don't learn. It's our job to make up for their deficiency.
>
> (1997: 111)

It seems there is a long and varied history equating non-standard English with having no language at all, or being unable to communicate.

In a report in the *Daily Mail* on 14 October, 1994, Gillian Shephard openly equated 'grunt English' with 'local dialects' and is quoted as urging parents to 'correct' children who say *we was* to say *we were*. We saw above that non-standard *we was* is as systematic as standard *we were*, and in any case the suggestion that *we was* doesn't communicate anything more intelligible than a grunt is patently untrue. The exhortation to parents also ignores the fact that *we was* is a feature of the parents' own dialect. Children grow up speaking the dialect of the home and the neighbourhood they come from. The forms that they use are not plucked randomly out of space, either through ignorance or in defiance of the 'rules'. They form part of a grammatical system.

ACTIVITY 10.5

5   The following are all recorded utterances from the non-standard speech of British schoolchildren[6]. Which features seem non-standard to you? Check in a reference grammar and see if you agree with its judgement.

> I think they've threw it in the house
> It could have came in the window
> She probably come out the TV
> There's hundreds of people on the waiting list
> See them paperclips?
> I can always do lids up quick
> There's a bit of glass what you step on
> It's not getting no water inside it
> They climbed to the top and was amazed at the sight
> Me and Ryan thought that
> Give us a kiss
> I wasn't just sat at a desk, doing nothing
> He needs it to dry hisself
> It don't work
> We ain't got enough

10.4.2 Standard English and social equality

The debate about standard English tends not to centre on written but on spoken English; who should speak it, where and when. Those who view standard English as the only really 'correct' form of English argue that speaking it brings increased personal power and social equality for everyone. John Honey (1997) for example argues that to encourage the maintenance of non-standard varieties is to deny social equality to the speakers of those varieties. In this argument, non-standard speakers are trapped by their language in the lower social orders. Others agree. John Rae, for example, says:

> And nothing more effectively condemns an individual to his class or ethnic ghetto than an inability to communicate clearly and logically in English. It is not a question of teaching children to 'talk posh'. It is just a question of giving them the essential tool for survival in our society.
>
> (*Evening Standard*, 17 November, 1988)

Notice again the reference to 'logic' and the suggestion that non-standard English speakers cannot communicate clearly, a similar idea to that of 'grunt' English. Rae's suggestion that standard English is essential for survival is a reference to economic survival; in other words, getting a job.

Again, there is a comparison to be made with the situation in the US where speakers of a non-standard variety of English known as African American Vernacular English (AAVE) (see also Chapter 6) may suffer discrimination at the hands of teachers and employers. Although it is politic in the US to make statements to the effect that standard and non-standard varieties are equally valid, AAVE is seen as sub-standard and the onus is firmly placed on its speakers to change. The argument for this is summarised as follows:

> FACT: Language A [standard] and Language B [non-standard] are equal in linguistic and cultural terms.
>
> ⇓
>
> FACT: Language B is rejected by teachers and employers.
>
> ⇓
>
> FACT: Rejection has a negative effect on the speakers of Language B.
>
> ⇓
>
> CONCLUSION: Language B must be discarded in favour of Language A.
>
> The teachers writing this essay never even discuss an alternate conclusion: *Teachers and employers must learn to accept Language B*.
>
> (Lippi-Green, 1997: 113)

Standard English is therefore seen as the appropriate dialect in the job market and indeed the former Secretary of State for Education in the UK, Gillian Shephard, went so far as to suggest that: 'those who have not mastered "our marvellous language" should not expect to be able to get a job' (*Daily Mail*, 14 October, 1994). By this she means speaking standard English, and again there is a clear onus on non-standard speakers to change if they wish to keep their rights as citizens to take up employment.

Many employers set great store by their employees' ability to speak standard English when appropriate in the work environment, and they have a reasonable expectation that their employees should be literate in standard English. It is misleading, however, to suggest that the only bar to full employment is lack of ability to speak standard English; that if everyone spoke standard English, everyone would have a job. Equality or inequality of opportunity may be linked to language, but language is not the sole contributor.

The linking of standard English with employment and on employers' expectations seldom focuses explicitly on why standard English is so important. As we saw, appeals to logic and correctness cannot be sustained as non-standard dialects have equally systematic and rule governed systems. But we also saw how standard English is related to education and, in an extension of that debate, standard English is also equated with society's rules. In Britain there is a link between standard English, or what is seen as correct grammar, and the morality of a well-ordered world. This link tends to be made in the context of education and English teaching, and again it's not new. Deborah Cameron (1995: 94–96) explores the links between standards of 'good' English (i.e. standard English) and high standards of moral behaviour which are made explicit in the language of prominent public figures at both ends of the twentieth century:

> The great difficulty of teachers in Elementary schools in many districts is that they have to fight against the powerful influences of evil habits of speech contracted in home and street. The teachers' struggle is thus not with ignorance but with a perverted power.
>
> (Newbolt Report, 1921)[7]

> If you allow standards to slip to the stage where good English is no better than bad English, where people turn up filthy at school ... all these things tend to cause people to have no standards at all, and once you lose standards then there's no imperative to stay out of crime.
>
> (Norman Tebbitt, MP, 1985)

> Attention to the rules of grammar and care in the choice of words encourages punctiliousness in other matters.... As nice points of grammar were mockingly dismissed as pedantic and irrelevant, so was punctiliousness in such matters as honesty, responsibility, property, gratitude, apology and so on.
>
> (John Rae, *The Observer*, 7 February, 1982)

Thus we have a 'perverted power' working against authority and morality and causing the social order to break down. Cameron explains how this link between 'correct' grammar and order comes about. On the surface, she suggests, it is baffling to see how grammar can be equated with moral behaviour. But, she goes on, grammar is a **metaphor** for morality and related ideas such as order and authority; the conditions for an ordered society. The opposites are disorder and lawlessness and 'a panic about grammar is therefore interpretable as the metaphorical expression of persistent conservative fears that we are losing the values that underpin civilisation and sliding into chaos' (1995: 95).

Thus, standard English is equated with authority, discipline and a traditional social and moral order and its speakers are consequently seen as both educated and as having respect for society's standards or norms; as having status and respectability. Those who do not conform, or who conform to a different set of rules, are, we saw, attributed with a kind of 'perverted power'. Perverted power undermines the authority of those who seek to impose their rules, the socially powerful people. Standard English on the other hand supports that power and is promoted as being able to give access to it. This is because the contexts in which standard English is used are institutional ones such as education, law, government; public arenas where large-scale social decisions are taken. Its use in these prestige contexts means that its status is reinforced. It also means that to take part in the higher order functions, you must use standard English. The link between standard English and power is well recognised. Honey's book, for example, equates language with power in its title (*Language is Power: The story of standard English and its enemies*) and Trevor Macdonald, the chair of the Better English Campaign, also expressed his wish, 'I want every young person in the country to understand that language is a source of power' (quoted in *The Sunday Times*, 21 April, 1996). In both cases 'language' means standard English. Speaking standard English should then in theory enable us all to become part of the socially powerful group. It is, however, doubtful to suppose that if everyone really did speak standard English, then the class barriers would automatically be removed and we would achieve the social equality which those such as Honey and Rae suggest is denied us simply because of a dialect of English. In any case, even if we could all become members and adopt the norms of high status social groups, it's unlikely that we would all want to.

Rather than impose standard English, there are those who support the genuine acceptance of non-standard dialects of English and who maintain that it is possible to have the best of both worlds. Access to the standard should not come at the expense of a home dialect, which is neither illogical nor incomprehensible, but as an addition to it. Accepting the usefulness of standard English, or society's general high regard for it, should not invalidate other varieties, nor promote intolerance of them. There are many complex social reasons for the dominance of standard English and its use in the important public and institutional arenas of social and political life and we should be aware of these, rather than simply accepting the notion that standard English is inherently a linguistically superior form.

10.5 Summary

In this chapter we have considered the difficulties in defining standard English and have looked at its historical, social and linguistic foundations. We have seen how notions of 'logic' and 'correctness' cannot be applied linguistically to standard English, but how these ideas are connected with social and political values, and with the maintenance of moral, social and institutional order. We have discussed the fundamental role of standard English in education as giving access to literacy and to wider communication, but we have argued that promotion of the standard should not invalidate non-standard varieties, and that access to, and acquisition of, the standard does not have to be at the expense of a home dialect.

Notes

1   The south-east Midlands is the area in central to south-east England which includes the capital, London, and the cities of Oxford and Cambridge, the homes of England's two oldest and most prestigious universities.

2   There are occasions when written language is less formal, such as when you write a note to a friend. There are also occasions when non-standard English is deliberately used in print, for example in magazines which are aimed at younger audiences and try for an air of informality and intimacy, or novels. It isn't possible to define language use by strict categories as people are very creative and varied in the way they use it. So ideas about contexts which relate to formality and planning and their corresponding linguistic forms are referring to tendencies rather than absolutes.

3   Mackinnon gives an example of a change in accepted use by comparing the entry on *due to* in Fowler's 1926 *Dictionary of Modern English Usage* with that of the 1983 *Oxford Guide to English Usage*. Fowler claimed that *due to* was 'impossible' in sentences like 'The old trade union movement is a dead horse, largely due to the incompetency of the leaders' whilst the *Oxford Guide* puts the same construction among its accepted usages.

4   In Britain it is common for individual people take it upon themselves to comment on English usage by way of letters to newspapers or complaints to broadcasters, setting out to prescribe what everyone else should do with their language. The people who make such comments act as 'guardians' of the language and are part of what Milroy and Milroy (1985) call the 'complaint tradition' serving an unofficial but nonetheless prescriptive function.

5   John Rae is the former head of Westminster School, one of England's leading public schools. In England the term 'public school' is used to refer to a small number of high status private schools. Schools maintained from the public purse, and which the majority of children go to, are referred to as state schools.

6   Examples taken from 'Children's use of spoken standard English', SCAA Discussion Papers: No. 1, February 1995.
7   A government report on the teaching of English.

Suggestions for further reading

Cameron, Deborah (1995) *Verbal Hygiene*, London: Routledge.
   Chapter 3 presents an interesting discussion of the issues involved in the standard English debate in Britain.
Leith, Dick (1992) *A Social History of English*, 2nd edn, London: Routledge.
   A comprehensive and comprehensible account of the history of English, including coverage of standardisation processes.
Milroy, James and Milroy, Lesley (1985) *Authority in Language: investigating language prescription and standardisation*, London: Routledge & Kegan Paul.
   Examines notions of 'correctness' and issues of prescriptivism.

Chapter 11

Attitudes to language

Linda Thomas

11.1 Introduction

Attitudes towards language(s) and language use are commonplace throughout the world. People assign various attributes to language forms; they may feel that a language or **variety** of a language is 'elegant', 'expressive', 'vulgar', 'guttural', 'musical' or that one language form is 'more polite' or more 'aesthetically pleasing/displeasing' than another one. All levels of language use are subject to such notions and we invest some language forms with prestige whilst others are stigmatised. Prestige and stigma are connected with speakers of languages and have to do with social class and social or national identity, and with ideas about status, solidarity and unity. Popular evidence from the media and academic surveys of language attitudes reveal the same underlying and recurrent patterns of values and value judgements within a community about the languages and varieties of language within it, and such judgements affect our social and cultural lives in important and influential ways.

11.2 The evidence

Throughout this book we have shown that issues to do with language are far from peripheral, but are central to people's daily lives. Similarly opinions about or attitudes to language, whilst common, are not trivial; people hold their opinions very seriously. We can find evidence of positive and negative attitudes in relation to a wide range of linguistic issues, such as whole languages, varieties of a language, words and **discourse** practices, pronunciation and **accent**, or anything perceived as different, new or changing. Such attitudes are not themselves necessarily new, nor are they restricted to English, although it is English we will be concentrating on here and attitudes to English in the UK and the US.

11.2.1 Whole languages

Fasold (1984) gives a summary of the academic research into people's language attitudes around the world, showing, for example, how bi- or multilingual speakers may regard one language as more suitable to a particular topic than another,

ACTIVITY 11.1

1   Before we begin to consider the broad picture, jot down the kinds of features that you like and/or dislike in other people's (or your own) speech. These might include someone's accent, the words or expressions they use, the quality of their voice, and so on. Try to figure out why you like or dislike the features you've noted and then check your opinions with your family or friends to see how much agreement exists between you.

or may regard one language as aesthetically more pleasing than another, or have clearly expressed feelings about their languages in relation to their social and cultural identities. In the UK, although many languages are in daily use, only English has official recognition. For the English especially, multilingualism is viewed with suspicion and as a threat to national unity. In a speech to a meeting at the Conservative Party Conference in October 1997, Lord Tebbitt, a prominent Conservative, called for national unity saying 'we need common values, a common culture and a single language'. A similar kind of idea is expressed by Beryl Goldsmith in *The Sunday Telegraph* (26 January, 1997). She describes her irritation with the 'enterprising Asian[1] couple' who own her local newsagents when they speak to each other in their native tongue, rather than in the 'fluent English' that they use for their customers. Goldsmith regards this use of another language, and one which she doesn't understand, with suspicion: 'I am not comfortable with this [use of their native tongue]; are they making personal remarks?' She also see it as evidence of lack of unity. 'Why', she asks, 'are they determined to establish a permanent kind of "separatism" from their fellow Brits?' She goes on to say:

> Asian Britons no doubt do respect the country chosen by their parents or grandparents in which to settle, and to rear their families. But they should show it – by using English, even at home.

So for this writer, use of a language other than English is threatening and indicates lack of respect, not the valid maintenance of part of someone's cultural and personal identity (see also Chapters 6 and 9). Older indigenous languages don't escape this negativity either, and are seen not only as threatening but as inferior, as Jan Morris writing about Welsh (*Cymraeg*) in *The Times Weekend* (28 February, 1998) illustrates:

> The English have always resented the very existence of *Cymraeg* – think of it, an apparently inextinguishable foreign language within the limits of

their own island. They have always laughed at its spelling and jeered at its pronunciation...

The writer then goes on to explain that the English have traditionally regarded the Welsh language as *gibberish*, a claim borne out by the letter to *The Guardian* which we saw in Chapter 1 (p. 10).

Attitudes towards English in the US have an association with national unity similar to that found in the UK. Dennis Baron (1990) describes the 'English-only' movement which seeks to establish English as the official language of the US, and corresponding attitudes to minority languages. He suggests that 'many Americans continue to regard speakers of languages other than English as suspicious if not un-American' (1990: xiii) and he uses ideas about language and worldview, such as those outlined in Chapter 2, to explain the connection between English and Americanism:

> Extrapolating from the notion that language both reflects and influences worldview, it naively assumes that English is the language of liberty because British and American society are democratic in structure and because the United States was founded on principles of individual liberty. Furthermore, it supposes that immigrants to America who learn English thereby demonstrate their understanding and endorsement of the principles upon which the nation was founded, while those who decline to learn English, or who are unable to master it, pose a threat of subversion to the American system of government.
>
> (1990: 28)

Again, multilingualism is seen as threatening and subversive and opposed to images of the ideal society as a homogenous one; homogeneity and national unity, therefore, mean getting rid of linguistic differences, as Rosina Lippi-Green points out:

> English, held up as the symbol of the successfully assimilated immigrant, is promoted as the one and only possible language of a unified and healthy nation.
>
> (1997: 217)

The promotion of English, both in the UK and in the US, leads to the marginalisation of the other languages which exist there. Popular attitudes towards them may on the surface see them as less useful or expressive than English, even as unintelligible, as the Welsh example illustrates. On another level, minority languages and their speakers may be seen as divisive, even dangerous, and a threat to political, social or economic stability.

11.2.2 Varieties of a language

Attitudes towards languages and language use also focus on varieties of the same language. For example, Fasold (1984) describes how the French spoken in Europe is seen to be more prestigious than that spoken in Canada, even by native Canadian French speakers. Mackinnon (1996) reproduces letters of complaint about English usage in the Englishes of New Zealand and Singapore, and we saw in Chapters 6, 8 and 10 the negative attitudes toward non-standard varieties of English in the UK, or towards American varieties such as African American Vernacular English (AAVE) in the US.

Although there may be discrimination against anything other than the status (i.e. standard) variety of American English in the US, in the UK standard American English itself is a favourite for complaint and stigmatisation. Media style guides warn against the use of 'Americanisms', meaning any usage which is typical of the English of the US, but not of varieties of British standard English. The American Bill Bryson recalls working for *The Times* in London when the editor would criticise him for using Americanisms:

> He would say something to me along the lines of: "Mr Bryson, I'm not sure what patois you spoke in Idaho or Ohio or wherever it was your misfortune to be born, but here at *The Times* we rather like to stay with the English."
>
> (reported in *The Sunday Times*, 22 May 1994)

Deborah Cameron (1995: 240) reports that *The Times* traditionally distinguished between 'English' and 'American' as two separate languages. The 1992 *Times* style guide similarly warns not to use Americanisms 'as alternatives to an English phrase'.

Both Baron and Bryson (1994) point to the long history of derision of American English by the British, although Bryson also points out that many Americanisms have passed into common usage in British English without British speakers being aware of them. For example, words like *reliable* and *influential* were originally Americanisms, as was the phrase *to keep a stiff upper lip*, traditionally regarded in the UK as a very British activity. He also explains how American English has preserved English words and phrases which have died out, or all but died out, in Britain. Perhaps the most well known example is the word *fall*, in its meaning of a season.

Given that many Americanisms are no longer recognised as such on the British side of the Atlantic, it is not clear how to define an 'Americanism'. Current criticisms may be directed at usages which haven't made the transition (such as *visit with someone* for British English *visit someone*); at less well known older British forms, such as *gotten*[2,] which are still in use in the US and which show evidence of 're-invading'; or at innovations, such as turning **nouns** into **verbs**. This method of making new words is one that is popularly criticised, as in this letter to *The Times*:

> could we stop assuming that any noun can automatically be turned into a verb? "To access" may be a battle already lost but I draw the line at "to impact", heard last week. As for "to outsource", words fail me.
>
> (*The Times*, 1 January, 1994)

The creation of verbs from nouns tends to feature more in American English than in varieties of British English (see Figure 11.1) and it receives positive acclaim from Bryson:

> We turn nouns into verbs to give them inventiveness not seen in English since the Elizabethan age. The list of American verb formations is all but endless: to interview, to highlight, to package, to curb, to demean, to corner, to endorse, to engineer, to notice, to advocate. I could go on.
>
> (*The Sunday Times*, 22 May, 1994)

Again, these examples would no longer be recognised as Americanisms by most people, so the definition remains unclear. It seems, then, that charges of 'Americanism' are reserved for newer usages that are somehow seen as a threat to standards of British English, but which are equally likely to be absorbed into it.

Figure 11.1 Turning nouns into verbs
Source: Calvin and Hobbes: Universal Press Syndicate, 1993

What does seem clear is that the influential attitudes towards language varieties in both societies are determined by powerful groups (such as those who control newspapers or have access to them) or those in authority (such as those responsible for education). Mainstream US attitudes serve to marginalise and stigmatise non-mainstream varieties. Similar mainstream attitudes prevail in the

UK towards its own non-standard varieties, and, in a hopeless attempt to preserve some kind of ideal embodied in the 'Queen's English', towards other varieties of English abroad.

11.2.3 Words and interaction

Words, the meanings ascribed to words, their usage and who gets to use them, are also the subject of comment and debate. We saw in Chapter 1 how Ofsted's decision to use the word *attainment* rather than *ability* in respect of pupils' assessment caused comment via a letter to *The Daily Telegraph*. Examples of such decisions on usage can also be found elsewhere. In 1997 the British Psychological Society decided to prohibit the use of the word *subjects* in its publications to refer to those taking part in psychological experiments. Such participants were to be referred to as *individuals*, *people*, *students*, and so on. The letters to October 1997's edition of *The Psychologist* describe this decision as 'tosh' or 'trivial', and one which leaves the eminent writers of these letters 'baffled'. Most of the letter writers use 'political correctness' as a generally disparaging term for the Society's decision and to convey their dislike of what they see as interference with, or policing of, their use of language (see Chapters 1 and 3 for more on 'political correctness'). At a more general level, discussion of the use of the word *gay* to mean 'homosexual' still continues in the national press in the UK, with letters to *The Daily Telegraph* recording readers' attitudes as 'deploring the loss of that useful word', as being 'in mourning for dear old *gay*' or accusing those who use it of 'mis-use', 'destruction of the word' or 'misappropriation of the English language'. Arguments over meaning and who has the right to dictate or control it often centres on individual words.

Attitudes to words may be so negative that the words may be considered not suitable for use at all. We often invent **euphemisms** to cover such words so that, for example, instead of 'death' and 'dying' we might talk about 'passing away'. Some words are considered so unsuitable that they become totally taboo. In a discussion of four-letter or offensive words entitled 'The big C', *The Guardian* (3 March, 1998) discusses a forthcoming television play in which 'the most reviled single utterance in the English language' is to be used. The 'little four-letter word' is so taboo that, as *The Guardian* writer points out, many people feel incapable of writing it, let alone uttering it (see Figure 11.2). Taboo words of this kind are 'immensely powerful', as the scriptwriter says, and have the power to shock. The fact that its use on television warrants serious newspaper discussion is indicative of social attitudes towards such words and their public expression. When looking at taboo words we can see how our dislike (for whatever reason) of the thing a word refers to gets transferred to the word itself.

Figure 11.2 The power of taboo words
Source: Ros Asquith, *The Guardian*, 3 March, 1998

Those who continue to use the word then take on the same stigma. The complex link between attitudes to words and attitudes to their users is a difficult one to unravel.

Other expressions, such as *right*, *like*, *you know*, *see you later*, also come in for negative treatment. Some of these expressions may be associated with certain groups and may function as identity markers, such as those discussed in Chapter 9. For example, *see you later*, meaning 'goodbye' first came to my immediate attention in the part of Surrey where I live as an expression used by young adults, such as my grown-up children and their friends. A friend of mine complained long and hard about this innovation, the focus of her complaint being that the expression didn't mean anything; those uttering it were not necessarily going to see either her, or each other, later. Her objection, of course, ignored the fact that more acceptable expressions like 'Good morning' or 'How do you do?' don't mean what they seem to on the surface either. The morning could be anything but good and you don't really want to know how someone 'does'. In reality her complaint was only superficially about *see you later*; her real complaint was about the linguistic behaviour of the young, which, like other aspects of youth behaviour, is different from, and challenging to, the **norms** of the older generation. As *see you later* is now widespread, it would appear that her battle has in any case, predictably, been lost.

It's not only in the UK that negative attitudes to such terms are expressed. An investigation by Stubbe and Holmes (1995) into the use of phrases like *you know* in New Zealand, opens with a quote from the *New Zealand Listener*:

The phrase 'you know' is used with monotonous regularity when a person is being interviewed on TV or radio – to commence a sentence, be interspersed throughout, and even to conclude the same sentence. Let's hope 'you know' will soon die a natural death, although another exasperating expression will probably replace it – to ruin my listening enjoyment.

(*New Zealand Listener*, 16–22 April, 1994)

You know is a stigmatised form, as the quote suggests, considered to be a 'marker of imprecise, uncertain or uneducated "lower class" speech'. Although its use was found in this survey to be frequent in both middle and working class groups, it is used more frequently by working class speakers and this accounts for the stigma attached to it.

Linguistic features (such as *you know* or *see you later*) may be preferred, then, by different groups. People might also have opinions about preferred linguistic behaviour for different groups. It might be considered appropriate, for instance for children 'to be seen but not heard'. Silence has also been seen as appropriate behaviour for women. When women do speak, attitudes towards their talk are often negative; women's talk is labelled as 'chatter' or 'gossip' about 'inconsequential' or 'trivial' topics (see also Chapter 5; for a summary of attitudes to women's language see Coates (1993)).

Attitudes to linguistic behaviour can also vary cross culturally. At the height of his career, the African-American boxer, Muhammad Ali, was noted for his brand of self-promotion which consisted of boasting at length about his abilities. His bragging style alienated many people, although European-Americans typically had a more negative attitude towards it than African-Americans. In a test to determine why this might be, Holtgraves and Dulin concluded that European-Americans and African-Americans may have different conversational rules:

> For European Americans, positive self-statements seem to violate a rule prescribing modesty, and this results in an overall negative evaluation of someone who brags.... African American rules regarding positive self-statements are more complex.... Boasts and truthful bragging are relatively acceptable and this results in a less overall negative evaluation of someone who brags truthfully.
>
> (Holtgraves and Dulin, 1994: 282)

Cultural differences in attitudes towards linguistic behaviour like this one can therefore contribute to cross cultural misunderstanding or even communication breakdown.

The attitudes we have explored in this section can relate to the power to ascribe meanings to words and to the power we invest in words themselves. Our attitudes can also be a reflection of the social groups we associate particular words or kinds of linguistic behaviour with; negative evaluations are often associated with stigmatised or less powerful groups.

11.2.4 Pronunciation and accent

The way in which something is said is often at least as influential for the message as what is said. The British press happily prints the numerous complaints from its readership on pronunciation and accent. These, and the many articles and comments on this issue journalists themselves write, give ample illustration of the British obsession with the way people talk.

It also seems that we commonly have stereotypical ideas about people on the basis of their accents. Advertisers draw on these ideas in the UK, using country accents to indicate the wholesome nature of food products, or more prestigious accents such as **RP** (see Chapter 8) to promote financial services. Country accents can also used to denote lack of intelligence with the stereotypical image of the 'country bumpkin'. The connection between gender and lack of intelligence is signified not only by accent but also by patterns of stress and intonation, as illustrated by the silly and high pitched voice of the character, Marilyn, from the Australian soap *Home and Away*. Negative attitudes to female voices are so strong that the former British Prime Minister, Margaret Thatcher, took great pains to change her own voice:

> making it lower in pitch, less 'swoopy' in range and slower in rate. This collection of deliberate modifications can best be understood as a response to the perceived disadvantages suffered by the unreconstructed female speaker, who is stigmatised as 'shrill' (high pitch), 'emotional' (broad intonational range) and 'lacking in authority'.
>
> (Cameron, 1995: 170)

In the US lack of intelligence is associated with women with southern accents who may be perceived as 'sweet, pretty and not very bright' (Lippi-Green, 1997: 215). Lippi-Green also suggests that southern accents in general are associated with native wit rather than educated intelligence and with images of dimwittedness or villainy. In the UK, however, villainy may be associated with a Birmingham[3] accent. The *Daily Mail* (1 October, 1997) reports that 'crime suspects with a Birmingham accent are twice as likely to be considered guilty'. The fact that these two different and distant accents (southern-states American and Birmingham, England) can both have overtones of criminality suggests that this is an attribute which resides in the minds of those who judge, rather than being inherent in the accents or their speakers.

Urban accents in the UK tend to have low status in the eyes of British speakers, coming at the bottom of a hierarchical pecking order with speakers with urban accents judged low on intelligence and competence. As one elocution teacher put it: 'people still think that if you have a London accent then you're common' (quoted in *The Observer Review*, 24 March, 1996). In Chapter 8 we saw that the New York accent, 'Noo Yawkese', is similarly stigmatised and its speakers regarded as less trustworthy than those using the more standard American accent of the mid-west.

Criticism of New York accents includes an objection to the loss of 'r' in words like *sugar* (*shuguh*) or *never* (*nevuh*). This objection provides a contrast with British English accents, where 'r' has largely disappeared from words like *sugar* and *never* and its pronunciation tends to be stigmatised. This was not always the case. Lynda Mugglestone (1995) describes the loss of 'r' in England and attitudes towards its loss during the nineteenth century. Speakers without 'r' were variously described as 'vulgar', 'illiterate' and 'lower-class' whereas those with 'r' were 'elegant', 'polished' and 'educated'. The poet Keats was apparently criticised as illiterate and ignorant for creating rhymes such as *thorns* and *fawns*, or *thoughts* and *sorts* by those who refused to acknowledge that the sound pattern was changing. Now the change is virtually complete, at least for accents in England, with 'r' pronunciation seen as belonging to the stereotypical, rural 'country bumpkin' accent. Thus, one small unit of sound can provoke different responses according to time and place. Such questions of salience (what is regarded as important and who it is important to) are part of what we all learn when we learn our native language.

To find out what kind of attitudes to language and its speakers are generally shared by members of a particular **speech community**, researchers have devised a method of testing called '**matched guise**'. Matched guise tests may follow different formats according to the subject of the experiment, but they aim to get people to make evaluations of different groups of speakers based on the different languages or language varieties they use. Researchers using matched guise techniques in experiments get their **informants** to judge speakers' characteristics based on what they hear. Measures are taken to control other factors that might influence the judgement, such as the age, gender, or voice quality of the speakers, so that the judges are reacting only to the language variety or varieties under consideration. They will then respond with the attributes that are typically ascribed to the users of those varieties. Tests carried out in the UK reveal attitudes which consistently attribute speakers with RP accents with qualities such as intelligence and confidence, while speakers with regional accents are attributed with qualities such as sincerity or friendliness. The difference in perception is one of status versus solidarity. Speakers who score high on the status scale, tend to score low on the solidarity scale; that is, they are not seen as being particularly friendly or sincere. Speakers who score high on the solidarity scale tend to score low on the status scale; that is, they are not seen as being particularly intelligent or confident. Attitudes which rate speakers on the status and solidarity scales also exist in the US. Giles and Coupland (1991) report a 1990 study in Kentucky where Kentucky students were asked to evaluate standard American and Kentucky accented speakers. The Kentucky speakers scored high on solidarity, low on status; standard American speakers scored low on solidarity, high on status.

It seems then that attitudes are consistently held and widely spread within various communities and that attitudes to languages or language forms are inextricably linked to attitudes to the speakers. The article in *The Times Weekend*, quoted above, which talks about English attitudes to the Welsh language also talks about the attitudes of the English to the Welsh people:

> English denigration of things Welsh is almost as old as history.... Just the word "Welsh" has all too often been a term of abuse, implying thievery, trickery, lasciviousness, mendacity and a tendency to run away from debts.

Attitudes to the Welsh language (the resentment and mistrust) are tied up with these attitudes to the people themselves and we talk about the language as a cover for talking about the people. Lippi-Green explains this relationship with reference to stereotypes associated with southern accents in the US:

> we use accent to talk about bundles of properties which we would rather not mention directly. When a northerner appropriates a pan-southern accent to make a joke or a point, he or she is drawing on a strategy of condescension and trivialisation that cues into those stereotypes so carefully structured and nurtured: southerners who do not assimilate to northern norms are backward but friendly, racist but polite, obsessed with the past and unenamored of the finer points of higher education.[4]
>
> (1997: 215)

It's important to remember that people who are unfamiliar with the language variety in question may find it difficult, if not impossible, to make the kinds of evaluations which appear in the research and in popular opinion as expressed in the press. Aesthetic qualities such as 'elegance' or 'vulgarity' are not ones that necessarily travel beyond the confines of the speech community but seem to reside within the socially conditioned ear of the hearer, not in the language form itself.

ACTIVITY 11.2

2   Broadcast media such as TV, film, and radio use different accents to portray different characteristics or personality traits. During your regular viewing or listening, note which accents are used in connection with which kind of character portrayal and check whether there are any regular patterns in such portrayals.

11.3 The effects

We have seen that attitudes to languages and language varieties can be related to social and cultural identity, to power and control, to notions of prestige and solidarity, and that our attitudes are often influenced by conventionally held stereotypes of language forms and their speakers. Our ability to respond to different types of language are not always negative. Giles and Coupland also talk about our perceptions being related to 'uncertainty reduction'. When you meet someone for the first time, you try to work out what the other person is like so that you know how to respond to them and how to behave appropriately. Listening to the way they talk is one of the factors you can use in forming an impression about them and the formality of the social situation, and you can adapt your behaviour, including your linguistic behaviour (your speech style) to match theirs. It's also useful to be able to manipulate your speech styles in other situations; for example you may want to give an impression of status by adopting a more prestigious style when you want to make a complaint about goods or services. Hopefully, the person you're making the complaint to will then attribute you with the qualities that are conventionally associated with prestige accents and see you as intelligent, capable, confident and so on. This in turn will influence their behaviour and bring about a speedy and satisfactory resolution to your problem. In this latter example, the impression of status will be based on the stereotypes that the hearer has learnt to associate with different forms of language as they relate to different groups of people. We need, then, to be aware of how our attitudes are linked to stereotypes, and what role they may play in our analysis and expectations of other people.

There may be occasions when our perceptions of a speaker's personal attributes are considered welcome. A survey quoted in the *Glasgow Herald* (28 October, 1997) reports that, in the UK, speakers with Scottish accents are rated the highest on sex appeal. In other cases, an attributed character trait might look superficial. A report in *The Guardian* (26 October, 1991) about a court case against a doctor states 'in court she admitted her temper matched her red hair and Belfast/Glasgow accent'. This association between (uncontrolled) temper and accent seems fairly trivial until you remember that this is a court case for slander, where someone's ability to control their temper might be an important consideration. At perhaps a more serious level, we saw earlier how a Birmingham accent or a southern states accent is linked with criminality. In the US, negative and criminal stereotypes are also associated with Spanish-accented speakers; the more negative the stereotype, the more heavy the accent. This stereotype is reinforced in the media, where Mexican-Americans are portrayed negatively:

recent stereotypes in film and television...have one thing in common: Mexican Americans are almost always portrayed as violent: they are drug-pushers, gang-members, pimps.

(Lippi-Green, 1997: 236)

As with many stereotypes, such perceptions can have far reaching effects. Lippi-Green records the evidence of a research student who was discussing language styles with a businessman whose job was to hire sales personnel. The businessman was positive that he wouldn't hire anyone with a Mexican accent. His reason for this was that he 'wouldn't buy anything from a guy with a Mexican accent' and therefore assumed that his customers wouldn't either. Job prospects can also be considered in relation to other speakers. Speakers with a southern accent with its **connotations** of dimwittedness have reported discrimination in employment contexts, and speakers of 'Noo Yawkese' find their accents a liability: in the words of *The Washington Post* (16 December, 1997) 'natives of New York can get rich faster if they sound like they are from someplace else'. In the UK, reports in the press indicate that the way people speak also affects their job prospects. *The Daily Telegraph* (12 March, 1994) covers the story of a Birmingham employee of a Birmingham company who was fired for having a Birmingham accent, and a survey by the Institute of Personnel and Development confirms that 'employers tend to look down their noses at those who speak in the accents of Liverpool, Glasgow and Birmingham' (*The Guardian*, 3 January, 1993) . However, there are occasions when issues of solidarity are more important than issues of status, and less prestigious accents are sought. The same *Guardian* report suggests:

in some other trades, standard English is a disadvantage. The disc jockey John Peel, a profile reveals, is the son of a middle class Cheshire cotton broker who sent him to public school. He upgraded to Scouse only later, when he got into turntables.[5]

British Telecom was also reported as locating new telephone sales jobs in the north of England because of a 'belief that regional accents exude honesty' (*The Guardian*, 8 April, 1997). Politicians are not immune from prevailing attitudes to accents either. Those who traditionally appeal to lower status groups may emphasise their non-prestige accents if they have them, or adopt features from them if they haven't, while politicians who traditionally appeal to high-status groups may adapt their language to prestige norms. People can, then, manipulate norms for their own ends. Those who are less fortunate, however, may find themselves in a double bind. Giles and Coupland record that research in Canada, the US and Britain indicates that people with low-status accents are regarded negatively for employment in high-status jobs, but positively for employment in low-status jobs. They are therefore doubly likely to be kept at the bottom of the job market.

Another major area of social life where language attitudes can be important is that of education. Lippi-Green (1997), commenting on attitudes to Hawaiian **Creole** English (HCE) in the US, illustrates how this variety has been described as a 'speech defect' or classed as a **pidgin**. Negative attitudes have resulted in calls for an educational ban, not only in the classroom but anywhere within the school environment, an attitude which stigmatises both the language and its speakers. And such effects can be far-reaching. Teachers' perceptions of pupils' language can influence their assessment of pupils' ability:

> Overall, research indicates that the perception of children's so-called 'poor' speech characteristic leads teachers to make negative inferences about their personalities, social background and academic abilities.
>
> (Giles and Coupland, 1991: 45)

Negative inferences in turn may influence attainment. On the other side of the coin, attitudes can affect students' perceptions of teachers. Lippi-Green (1997) outlines a study in which undergraduate students were divided into two groups and asked to listen to a recording of introductory lectures. With the recording one group was shown a picture of an Asian woman lecturer and the other group was shown a picture of a Caucasian woman lecturer. Both pictures were evaluated equally in terms of physical attractiveness. The recordings were however the same, both made by a native American English speaker; only the pictures differed. In their evaluations of the lectures, the students rated the lecture with the picture of the Asian woman as being more foreign accented than that with the picture of the Caucasian woman. Not only that, the students also scored lower on a comprehension test where they believed the lecturer was Asian. Remember that the recordings were identical, so the students couldn't actually have heard any difference at all; they only thought they did. And their lower expectation of an Asian lecturer was enough to interfere with their comprehension and learning. So it seems that complaints about accent and pronunciation have more to do with the complainant's perception of the speaker, than the utterance itself.

11.4 Summary

In this chapter we have looked at the way our attitudes to language can be focused on any level of language use. As we said at the beginning of the chapter, our attitudes to language are far from trivial and we have seen how they may be influential in our assessments of the characteristics of individuals and social groups. These assessments can then be carried over into the decisions that are

made in important areas of our lives such as law and order, employment, education and equality of opportunity. Awareness of how attitudes might be formed or
manipulated may not make us immune to them, but it may help us to evaluate
their influence on our own practices.

Notes

1 In the UK the term 'Asian' is used to refer to people whose ethnic background is
from the Indian subcontinent: e.g. India, Bangladesh, Pakistan. In the US this term
is used more extensively to include people whose ethnic background is from a
wider geographical area incorporating, for example, China, Indonesia, Japan, Korea,
Vietnam.
2 As, for example, in a discussion on English usage on **BBC** Radio 4's *Today*, 19
March, 1997. Incidentally, *gotten* still exists in some traditional British English
dialects, where it is also stigmatised.
3 Birmingham is a large industrial city in the British Midlands.
4 Lippi-Green points out that stereotypes of southern African-Americans are different
from these.
5 Public schools in England are in effect private schools; they charge fees and have
high status. 'Scouse' is the term for the Liverpool accent and dialect. It has low
status in mainstream society but has, or had, high credibility in the popular music
industry.

Suggestions for further reading

Cameron, Deborah (1995) *Verbal Hygiene*, London: Routledge.
    A thorough, interestingly presented and easy to read look at attitudes to language
    and those who seek to regulate it.
Lippi-Green, Rosina (1997) *English with an Accent: language, ideology and discrimination in the United States*, London: Routledge.
    An absorbing coverage of the far-reaching effects of language attitudes and repre-
sentation of language varieties in the US.
Giles, Howard and Coupland, Nikolas (1991) *Language: contexts and consequences*,
Milton Keynes: Open University Press.
    Chapter 2 covers a wide range of academic research on language attitudes around
the world and the methodologies used to discover them. For the more technically
minded.

Glossary

accent features of a speaker's pronunciation that can signal their regional or social background.

active active and **passive** are terms which refer to the **voice** of the **verb**. In the active voice the sentence has a structure where the 'doer' (**agent**) of the action is in the subject position and the 'done-to' (affected) is in the object position. This contrasts with the passive where the 'done-to' is in subject position and the agent becomes optional.

active: *Tom hit Bob;*
passive: *Bob was hit by Tom* or *Bob was hit*

address forms expressions used to refer to a person when you are talking to them directly. Address forms can vary according to the context of use and the relationship between the speaker and hearer. Variation can involve the use of 'titles' like *Ms*, *Dr* or *Reverend*; whether or not a person is called by their first name; and in some languages, the form of the **second person pronoun** as in the *tu/vous* distinction in French. (See also **honorific**.)

adjective a class of words which is generally used to describe or modify a **noun**. The adjectives in the following examples are in small capitals:

The LUCKY cat ran away   The PERSIAN cat ate my trout
That cat is BIG

agent see **active**.

Amerindian a general name for the languages spoken by the native peoples of North and South America.

arbitrariness of the sign Saussure argued that there was no inherent connection between combinations of sounds/letters and the concepts which they refer to. The fact that different languages label concepts differently, for example French speakers using *arbre* for what the English speakers call *tree*, supports this.

asymmetry/asymmetrical see **symmetry**.

audience design the notion that speakers will take into account who they are addressing and alter their speech style accordingly.

auxiliary verb see **modal auxiliary verb**.

back channel support the feedback that listeners give to speakers, by verbal expressions like *mmm*, *uhuh*, *yeah*, and by nodding, frowning or other facial and body gestures.

BBC The British Broadcasting Corporation (BBC) is the oldest and most prominent television and radio broadcasting company in the UK with two national television and five national radio channels. Supported by public funds, it has a reputation for good quality programming which reflects established norms and values.

code a term sometimes used instead of language or **dialect** to refer to a linguistic system of communication. There are also non-linguistic communication codes such as dress codes or gesture codes.

codification a process where scholars analyse and record the vocabulary and grammatical patterns of a language. For English, much of this codification took place in the eighteenth century. The vocabulary and grammatical patterns that were written down in dictionaries and grammar books then became 'rules'.

commonsense/common sense discourse see **discourse**.

connotation the personal associations conjured up by a word, although they are not strictly part of its definition. For example, a *spinster* is an adult female human who has never been married, but for many people this word also carries connotations of 'old', 'unattractive' and 'not sexually active'.

consonant a speech sound made by partially or completely obstructing the airflow from the lungs. The bold letters in the following examples represent some of the consonant sounds in English:

   s**at**, **b**e**l**ieve, **m**a**n**.

convergence a process where speakers change their speech to make it more similar to that of their hearer, or to that of other people in their social group.

covert prestige covert means 'hidden or non-obvious'. Sometimes speakers use a seemingly less prestigious or non-standard **language variety** to identify with a group that uses that variety. Thus, the language variety of that group can have a covert prestige.

creole see **pidgin**.

crossing a process where speakers of one group will occasionally use the speech patterns of another group as means of identifying with some aspect of that group (see also **covert prestige**).

dialect a **variety** of a language that can signal the speaker's regional or social background. Unlike **accents** which differ only in pronunciation, dialects differ in their grammatical structure: *Do you have…?* (US) versus *Have you got…?* (UK), and in their vocabulary: *sidewalk* (US) versus *pavement* (UK).

disambiguate to indicate more exactly what a term refers to in a particular context (see also **topical ambiguity**).

discourse as used in linguistics, it has a range of meanings. It can refer to any piece of connected language which contains more than one sentence. It is also sometimes used to refer specifically to conversations. In sociology, it can be used to refer to the way belief systems and values are talked about, as in 'the discourse of capitalism'. The prevailing way that a culture talks about or **represents** something is called the **dominant discourse**. That is, the '**common sense**' or 'normal' representation.

divergence a process where speakers choose to move away from the **linguistic norms** of their hearer or social group. This can involve using a style or **language variety** not normally used by the group or even speaking an entirely different language.

dominant discourse see **discourse**.

epistemic modal forms see **modal auxiliary verb**.

euphemism the use of an inoffensive or more 'pleasant' term to substitute for one which might be unpleasant or taboo. For example, *passed away* is a euphemism for *died*. Euphemism can also be used to promote a more positive image, for example, *air support* for *bombing* or *pre-owned* for *second hand*.

field see **register**.

first person pronoun see **pronoun**.

generic generally, an expression which is used to refer to a class of things. For example, a distinction is drawn between the generic use of *man* in *Man has walked the earth for millions of years* where this term refers to humans in general and *I now pronounce you man and wife* where this term refers only to male humans.

genre a 'kind' or 'type'. As used in discourse analysis it can refer, for example, to writing genres such as thrillers, scientific writing or recipes. It can also refer to other media genres such as talk show, documentary and soap opera.

glottal stop a **consonant** made by a tight closure of the vocal chords followed by an audible release of air. It can be heard in several British **accents** where this consonant replaces the /t/ in a word like *butter* pronounced *buh-uh*. The phonetic symbol for a glottal stop is /ʔ/.

hedges linguistic devices such as *sort of* and *I think* which 'dilute' an assertion. Compare *He's dishonest* and *He's sort of dishonest. She lost it* and *I think she lost it.*

honorific in general it refers to the use of language to express respect or politeness. More specifically it can refer to certain **address forms** which express respect such as *Sir/Madam, Your Highness, Reverend*, and the 'formal' version of *you* in languages which make that distinction.

ideology a set or pattern of beliefs.

implicature a meaning which can be extracted but is implicit rather than explicit. For example, 'A dog is for life, not just for Christmas' implies that some people regard dogs as a short-term rather than a long-term responsibility.

informant someone who acts as source of linguistic data or information.

ingroup a social group to which the speaker belongs. The **outgroup** are people who do not belong to that group. For example, gang members may use certain expressions with each other that mark them as members of a particular gang or ingroup. At the same time, the use of these expressions can differentiate them from members of other gangs, the outgroups in that situation.

language norm see **linguistic norm**.

language variation/variety see **linguistic variation**.

language variety see **linguistic variety**.

langue this is Saussure's term for the perfect knowledge of a language that he believed we all have in our heads, in contrast to what he thought of as the corrupt versions of language we actually produce, which he called *parole*.

lexical item a term used by linguists for one of the senses of 'word'. This term is useful because while *loves* and *loved* are two different words in terms of their form, they still represent the same lexical item, the **verb** *to love*. Notice that we can also have two words with the same form but which represent two different lexical items. An example is: *bow* as in 'the bow of ship' and *bow* as in 'to bow one's head'.

lexis vocabulary.

linguistic norm generally, a norm refers to 'standard practice'. **Speech communities** can differ with respect to the linguistic norms being followed. These norms can involve grammar (e.g. whether or not *I don't know nothing* is acceptable); pronunciation (e.g. whether or not *pie* is pronounced as 'pah'); vocabulary (e.g. whether the pedestrian walkway is called the *sidewalk* or the *pavement*); and the appropriate social use of language (e.g. whether or not you should address your parents as *Sir* and *Ma'am*).

linguistic variation refers to the many ways that language systems can change or vary with respect to their grammar, pronunciation, and vocabulary.

Language systems change over time. They also change or vary according to the geographical or social identity of their users and according to the situations in which they are used. (See also **linguistic variety**.)

linguistic variety this has several meanings, but generally refers to an identifiable language system which is used in particular geographic or social situations and has its own **linguistic norms**. For example, the variety of English spoken in Birmingham, Alabama will differ from that spoken in Birmingham, England. Within a geographic region there may also be varieties based on social class or occupation. Similarly, the variety of English used in casual conversations will differ from that used in academic writing.

marked generally speaking, 'marked' means noticeably unusual. More specifically, marked terms refer to anything which deviates from the norm and this deviation is signalled by additional information. **Unmarked** linguistic forms are neutral in so far as they **represent** the 'norm', and carry no additional information. For example, the unmarked form *nurse* is often assumed to refer to a woman. To refer to a nurse who is a man, the additional term *male* is often added: *male nurse* (the marked form). The notion of markedness has also been applied to pairs of opposites like *tall/short*, where *tall* is considered to be the unmarked term. We can see this in certain constructions where the use of the unmarked term seems more 'natural'. Compare: *How tall are you?* to *How short are you?* and *She's five feet tall* to *She's five feet short*.

matched guise experiment a method of investigating people's attitudes to different languages. It involves **informants** listening to several recordings of the same 'script' spoken by the same speaker (or by other speakers matched for voice quality) but using a different language for each recording. The informants are then asked to judge each speaker's personal characteristics based on what they hear. Matched guise experiments can also be adjusted to elicit people's attitudes to different voice qualities, **accents** or **dialects**.

metaphor/metaphorical a figurative expression where a word or phrase from one area of meaning (semantic field) is used to refer to something from a different semantic field. Metaphorical expressions transfer some features from the first semantic field to the second. For example, *Her uncle is a snake* transfers features associated with snakes such as stealth, danger, evil, to a person. Rather than asserting that her uncle actually is a snake, it implies that he is like a snake in some respects. This contrasts with **simile** where the comparison is made explicit rather than implied: *Her uncle is LIKE a snake*.

modal auxiliary verb the modal auxiliary verbs of English are *will, shall, would, should, can, could, must, may, might*. Modal auxiliaries have several meaning functions. One important meaning function is **epistemic**. That is, speakers use modals to express their attitude towards the 'certainty' of what they are saying. Note the meaning difference between *That is a bird* and *That could be a bird*.

mode see **register**.

multiple negation see **negation**.

negation sentences can be negated in English by using *not*: *I knew* versus *I did not (didn't) know*. They can also be negated by the use of other negative words like *nothing, never, nowhere*: *I knew nothing*. The grammar of standard American and British English does not allow a sentence like *I didn't know nothing* because it contains **multiple negation**, the use of *not* plus the negative word *nothing*. However, the grammatical rules of other **dialects** of English as well as other languages like Italian and Spanish require the use of multiple negation.

Newspeak a term coined by George Orwell in his novel, *Ninteen Eighty-Four*, where it referred to a special vocabulary invented by a totalitarian regime to manipulate people's thinking. This term has now passed into common usage to mean loosely, new words or uses of words, but more specifically new words or uses of words in political jargon or propaganda.

norm see **linguistic norm**.

noun a class of words which, generally speaking, name people or things, but more importantly share certain grammatical characteristics. For example, in English nouns (in small capitals) can be preceded by *the*: *the* MUSIC. They can be marked for plural: CAT/CATS. They can be modified by **adjectives**: *the big* BRIDGE.

noun phrase a phrase with a **noun** or **pronoun** as its 'head'. A noun phrase can consist of a single noun or pronoun or a noun which has been pre-modified and/or post-modified by other words or phrases. The following are examples of noun phrases (the 'head' is in small capitals): FIDO, HE, *the* DOG, *my big* DOG, *that expensive* DOG *from the pet shop*.

orthography refers to the writing system of a language and how words are spelled. For example, in English orthography both *so* and *sew* have different spellings even though they sound the same when spoken.

outgroup see **ingroup**.

parole this is Saussure's term for the language we actually produce, which may not match the system of *langue* in our brains because, Saussure believed, of errors we make in the actual production of speech.

passive see **active**.

phoneme the smallest significant sound unit in a language. For example *bat*, *sat*, and *pat* are different words in English because they differ in their first sound unit. The sounds /b/, /s/ and /p/ are three of the phonemes of English. English has approximately 44 phonemes, although this number varies slightly between **accents**.

phonetics/phonetic refers to the study of speech sounds, especially how they are made by speakers and perceived by hearers. Analysing the phonetics and **phonology** of a language generally involves looking at speakers' pronunciations.

phonology/phonological refers to the study of the sound systems of languages. It looks at what sounds are significant for a language (its **phonemes**) and the permissible ways that sounds can be combined in words. For example the phonology of English would permit a word like *tump* but not *mptu*. Analysing the **phonetics** and phonology of a language generally involves looking at speakers' pronunciations.

pidgin a simplified form of language (both in terms of vocabulary and grammar) which arises when speakers of different languages need a common means of communication, usually for trading purposes. Pidgins are not fully fledged languages and have no native speakers. A **Creole**, while it may have developed from a pidgin, is a fully fledged language with native speakers. In its most 'standard' or **prestige variety**, a Creole will closely resemble one of the original languages from which it came.

plural pronoun see **pronoun**.

post-vocalic 'r' post-vocalic means 'after a **vowel**'. A speaker whose **accent** does not have post-vocalic 'r' will only pronounce the 'r' when it occurs before a vowel as in *arise*, *trap* or *rip*. However, speakers whose accents contain a post-vocalic 'r' will also pronounce the 'r' in words where it occurs after a vowel at the end of a word, as in *floor*, and in words where it occurs after a vowel and before another **consonant**, as in *smart*.

prestige variety when used with respect to language it refers to a variety which society associates with education and high social status.

pronoun a class of words which can replace a **noun/noun phrase** in a sentence. This is an example from the English pronoun system:

	Singular	Plural
first person	I/me	we/us
second person	you	you
third person	he/him, she/her, it	they/them

received pronunciation/RP the **accent** which is generally used by news readers on national television in the UK. Sometimes called a '**BBC** accent' or an 'educated British accent'. An RP accent is not marked for a particular region of Britain, but is marked for relatively 'high' social class. It is thought that only about three per cent of the British population normally use RP.

register refers to the way that language can systematically vary according to the situation in which it is used. Different registers can be characterised by their sentence structure, pronunciation, and vocabulary. Three factors that determine variation in register have been proposed: **field** which refers to the subject matter of the **discourse**; **tenor** which refers to the role being played by the speaker and the resulting level of formality in the situation; **mode** which usually refers to the medium of communication, e.g. speech or writing.

represent/representation as used in discourse analysis, it is basically how the speaker chooses to refer to something or someone. For example the same act could be represented as *terminating a pregnancy* or *killing an unborn baby* depending on the worldview of the speaker. Similarly, the same person could be represented as either a *terrorist* or a *freedom fighter*. (See also **euphemism**.)

rhetoric/rhetorical refers to the use of language to persuade or convince the hearer.

RP see **received pronunciation**.

second person pronoun see **pronoun**.

semantic derogation refers to a process where a word can take on a second meaning and/or **connotations** which are negative or demeaning. Examples in English are the words *mistress*, *madam*, and *spinster*. Compare these to their masculine counterparts *master*, *sir*, *bachelor*.

sign the **arbitrary** combination of concept and label which exists in the minds of members of a **speech community**. Saussure called the 'concept' half of the sign the **signified**, while he referred to the 'label' half as the **signifier**.

signified see **sign**.

signifier see **sign**.

simile an expression where something is figuratively compared to something else. Unlike a **metaphor** where the comparison is implied, the comparison in a simile is made explicit by the use of expressions like *as, as if, like*. For example: *You're as red as a beet. He's working as if there's no tomorrow. She's like a tiger defending her young.*

speech community a human group, defined either geographically or socially, whose members share a common **language variety** and set of **linguistic norms**.

speech event a specific unit or exchange of speech which has a well-defined structure. For example: a greeting or a sermon.

stratified/stratification division into layers, where a layer can be 'above' or 'below' another layer. In terms of social stratification, people in any one layer share certain social characteristics and are 'equals' but differ from and are not 'equal' to people in other layers. One example of social stratification by class is: upper, middle, and lower or 'working' class.

style-shifting people do not always talk in the same way. They can shift their speech styles and this can involve using different words, pronunciations, or even grammatical forms. Notice the style differences between: *singin'* and *singing*; *verdant* and *green*; *So I says*.. and *So I said*.. (See also **audience design** and **register**.)

symmetry as used in linguistics, symmetry refers to an equal balance between expressions, while **asymmetry** refers to an imbalance between expressions. For example, standard English shows symmetry between the **first person** singular and plural **pronouns** *I/me* versus *we/us* (two forms for each). However, it shows asymmetry between the first and **second person pronouns**. There are four forms for the first person pronouns: *I/me* and *we/us* but only one form for the second person pronouns: *you*. Asymmetry can also be seen in some **address forms**: only *Mr* for men but *Mrs*, *Miss*, and *Ms* for women. Symmetry and asymmetry can also refer to the distribution of speakers' rights to talk in given situations. In a trial, speakers' rights are asymmetrical. Lawyers have more rights to ask questions than the witnesses.

syntactic/syntax refers to the grammatical rules which determine how words can be combined into phrases and sentences. For example, the syntactic rules of English permit the phrase *the nice book* but not **book the nice* and the sentences *Jane is happy* and *Is Jane happy*? but not **Is happy Jane*.

tenor see **register**.

tense refers to the way that grammatical information about time can be marked on **verbs**. In English there are two tenses, present: *I leave* and past: *I left*. Future time is not expressed by tense marking but by other constructions like *I will leave* or *I am going to leave*.

thesaurus a book of words arranged by meaning categories.

third person pronoun see **pronoun**.

topical ambiguity refers to a situation where the hearer needs to know the topic of the discussion in order to correctly interpret a word. For example, *a hit* means one thing in the context of talking about pop songs, another when talking about baseball, and yet another when talking about the Internet.

transitive/intransitive refers to the kind of verb used in a clause. A transitive verb requires a direct object in order to make sense, whereas an intransitive verb does not. For example, in *Lucy loves Fred*, 'Fred' is the direct object of the verb 'love'. 'Love' is a transitive verb and would be incomplete without its direct object, as you can see from *Lucy loves....* On the other hand, in *Fred snores*, 'snores' is an intransitive verb; there is no direct object and the verb is complete on its own.

unmarked see **marked**.

variation see **linguistic variation**.

variety see **linguistic variety**.

verb a grammatical class of words, which commonly refer to 'acting' or 'doing', although many verbs like *to seem* or *to know* do not quite fit into this meaning category. More importantly, verbs take characteristic forms or endings like those marking **tense** and **voice** and they perform a specific function in a sentence. The verbs in the following sentences are in small capitals: *She WAS ELECTED president. I AM WALKING quickly. He LAUGHED a lot. They MIGHT WANT some. I HAVE SEEN her. Bob SEEMS nice. SIT there.* (See also **modal auxiliary verb**.)

vernacular this word comes from the Latin meaning 'of the home'. It refers to the indigenous language or **dialect** of a **speech community**, for example, the 'vernacular of Liverpool' (UK), or 'Black English vernacular' (US). It is often used in contrast to the standard or **prestige variety** of a language.

voice see **active**.

vowel a speech sound made with no obstruction to the air flow from the lungs. The bold letters in the following examples represent some of the vowel sounds in English *sat, top, health, silly.*

References

Alladina, Safder and Edwards, Viv (1991) *Multilingualism in the British Isles*, London: Longman.

Allport, G. (1990) 'The Language of Prejudice', in P. Escholz, A. Rosa and V. Clark, (eds) *Language Awareness*, New York: St. Martins Press.

Andersen, Roger (1988) *The Power and The Word*, London: Paladin.

Andersson, Lars-Gunnar and Trudgill, Peter (1992) *Bad Language*, Harmondsworth: Penguin.

Atkinson, K. and Coupland, N. (1988) 'Accommodation as ideology', *Language and Communication*, 8.

Baron, Dennis (1990) *The English-Only Question*, New Haven, CT: Yale University Press.

Becker, J. (1988) 'The success of parents' indirect techniques for teaching their preschoolers pragmatic skills', *First Language*, 8: 173–182.

Bell, Allan (1984) 'Language style as audience design', *Language in Society*, 13: 145–204.

Bolinger, Dwight (1980) *Language – The Loaded Weapon*, London: Longman.

Breines, W. (1997) 'Combatting Middle-Ageism', *Radcliffe Quarterly*, 83(2).

Bryson, Bill (1994) *Made in America*, London: Secker & Warburg.

Burchfield, R.W. (1996) *The New Fowler's Modern English Usage*, 3rd edn, Oxford: Clarendon Press.

Cameron, Deborah (1992) *Feminism and Linguistic Theory*, 2nd edn, London: Macmillan.

Cameron, Deborah (1994) '"Words, words, words": the power of language', in Sarah Dunant (ed.) *The War of the Words*, London: Virago.

Cameron, Deborah (1995) *Verbal Hygiene*, London: Routledge.

Cameron, Deborah (1998) *The Feminist Critique of Language*, 2nd edn, London: Routledge.

Carroll, J. B. (ed.) (1956) *Language, Thought and Reality*, Massachusetts: MIT Press.

Casagrande, J. (1948) 'Comanche Baby Language', reprinted in Hymes, D. (ed.) (1964) *Language in Culture and Society*, New York: Harper & Row.

Chambers, J. and Trudgill, P. (1980) *Modern Dialectology*, Cambridge: Cambridge University Press.

Cheshire, Jenny (1982) *Variation in an English Dialect*, Cambridge: Cambridge University Press.

Cheshire, Jenny, Edwards, Viv and Whittle, Pamela (1993) 'Non-standard English and dialect levelling', in James Milroy and Lesley Milroy (eds) *Real English: the grammar of English dialects in the British Isles*, London: Longman.

Cheshire, Jenny and Milroy, James (1993) 'Syntactic variation in non-standard dialects: background issues', in James Milroy and Lesley Milroy (eds) *Real English: the grammar of English dialects in the British Isles*, London: Longman.

Coates, Jennifer (1989) 'Gossip revisited: language in all-female groups', in Jennifer Coates and Deborah Cameron (eds) *Women in their Speech Communities*, Longman: London.

Coates, Jennifer (1993) *Women Men and Language*, 2nd edn, London: Longman.

Coates, Jennifer (1996) *Women Talk*, Oxford: Blackwell.

Cockcroft, Robert and Cockcroft, Susan M. (1992) *Persuading People: an introduction to rhetoric*, London: Macmillan.

Coupland, N., Coupland, J. and Giles, H. (eds) (1991) *Language, Society, and the Elderly: Discourse, Identity, and Ageing*, Oxford: Blackwell.

Coupland, J., Nussbaum, J. and Coupland, N. (1991) 'The Reproduction of Aging and Agism in Intergenerational Talk', in N. Coupland, H. Giles and J. Wiemann (eds), *Miscommunication and Problematic Talk*, London: Sage.

Coupland, N. and Nussbaum, J. (1993) *Discourse and Lifespan Identity*, London: Sage.

Cox Report: see DES (1989).

Cromer, R. (1991) *Language and Thought in Normal and Handicapped Children*, Oxford: Blackwell.

Crowley, Tony (1989) *The Politics of Discourse: the standard language question in British cultural debates*, London: Macmillan.

Crystal, David (1987) *The Cambridge Encyclopedia of Language*, Cambridge: Cambridge University Press.

DeFrancisco, Victoria (1991) 'The sounds of silence: how men silence women in marital relations', *Discourse and Society* 2(4): 413–24.

DES (1989) *English for ages 5–16* [the Cox report], London: DES.

Dunant, Sarah (ed.) (1994) *The War of the Words*, London:Virago.

Eckert, Penelope (1997) 'Gender and sociolinguistic variation', in Jennifer Coates (ed.) *Language and Gender: A Reader*, Oxford: Blackwell.

Edwards, Viv (1986) *Language in a Black Community*, Clevedon: Multilingual Matters.

Edwards, Viv (1997) 'Patois and the Politics of Protest: Black English in British Classrooms', in Nikolas Coupland and Adam Jaworski (eds) *Sociolinguistics: A Reader and Coursebook*, London: Macmillan.

Ervin-Tripp, Susan (1979) 'Children's Verbal Turntaking', in E. Ochs and B. Schieffelin (eds) *Developmental Pragmatics*, New York: Academic Press.

Ervin-Tripp, Susan (1980) 'Sociolinguistic rules of address' in John Pride and Janet Holmes (eds) *Sociolinguistics*, Harmondsworth: Penguin.

Fairclough, Norman (1989) *Language and Power*, London: Longman.

Fairclough, Norman (1995) *Media Discourse*, London: Edward Arnold.

Fasold, Ralph (1984) *The Sociolinguistics of Society*, Oxford: Blackwell.

Fishman, Pamela (1980) 'Conversational insecurity', in Howard Giles, Peter W. Robinson, and Philip M. Smith (eds), *Language: Social Psychological Perspectives*, Pergamon Press: Oxford.

Fishman, Pamela (1983) 'Interaction: the work women do', in Barrie Thorne, Cheris Kramerae and Nancy Henley (eds), *Language and Sex: Difference and Dominance*, Rowley, Massachusetts: Newbury House.

Fletcher, P. (1988) *A Child's Learning of English*, Oxford: Blackwell.

Franklin, B. (ed.) (1995) *The Handbook of Children's Rights*, London: Routledge.

Gal, Susan (1998) 'Cultural bases of language-use among German-speakers in Hungary', in Peter Trudgill and Jenny Cheshire (eds), *The Sociolinguistics Reader*, Vol. 1, London: Arnold.

Giles, Howard and Coupland, Nikolas (1991) *Language: contexts and consequences*, Milton Keynes: Open University Press.

Giles, Howard and Powesland, Peter (1975) *Speech Style and Social Evaluation*, London: Academic Press.

Giles, Howard and Sinclair, Robert (1979) *Language and Social Psychology*, Oxford: Blackwell.

Gleason, J. (ed.) (1997) *The Development of Language (4th edn)*, Boston, MA: Allyn & Bacon.

Graddol, David and Boyd-Barrett, Oliver (eds) (1994) *Media Texts: Authors and Readers*, Clevedon: Multilingual Matters.

Gullette, Margaret (1997) *Declining to Decline: Cultural Combat and the Politics of Midlife*, Charlottesville: University Press of Virginia.

Gumperz, John (1982a) *Discourse Strategies*, Cambridge: Cambridge University Press.

Gumperz, John (1982b) (ed.) *Language and Social Identity*, Cambridge: Cambridge University Press.

Halliday, M.A.K. (1972) *Language as a Social Semiotic*, London: Edward Arnold.

Harris, M. and Coltheart, M. (1986) *Language Processing in Children and Adults*, London: Routledge.

Harris, Roy (1988) *Language, Saussure and Wittgenstein*, London: Routledge.

Heller, Monica (1982) 'Negotiations of language choice in Montreal', in John Gumperz (ed.) *Language and Social Identity*, Cambridge: Cambridge University Press.

Hewitt, Roger (1986) *White Talk, Black Talk*, Cambridge: Cambridge University Press.

Hoeg, Peter (1996) *Miss Smilla's Feeling for Snow*, London: The Harvill Press.

Holtgraves, Thomas and Dulin, Jeffrey (1994) 'The Muhammad Ali effect: differences between African Americans and European Americans in their perceptions of a truthful bragger', *Language and Communication*, 14(3): 275–85.

Honey, John (1997) *Language is Power: the story of standard English and its enemies*, London: Faber and Faber.

Hudson, R. (1980) *Sociolinguistics*, Cambridge: Cambridge University Press.

Hutchby, Ian (1996) 'Power in discourse: the case of arguments on a British talk radio show', *Discourse and Society*, 7(4): 481–97.

James, Deborah and Clarke, Sandra (1993) 'Women, men, and interruptions: a critical review', in Deborah, Tannen (ed.) *Gender and Conversational Interaction*, Oxford: Oxford University Press.

James, N. (ed.) (1998) 'The mouth and the method', *Sight and Sound*, 8(3).

Jenkins, Nancy and Cheshire, Jenny (1990) 'Gender issues in the GCSE oral English examination: part 1', *Language and Education* 4: 261–92.

Labov, William (1966) *The Social Stratification of English in New York City*, Washington, DC: Centre for Applied Linguistics.

Labov, William (1972a) *Sociolinguistic Patterns*, Philadelphia: University of Pennsylvania Press.

Labov, William (1972b) 'The social stratification of (r) in New York City department stores', in *Sociolinguistic Patterns*, Philadelphia: University of Pennsylvania Press.

Labov, William (1972c) 'The linguistic consequences of being a lame', in *Language in the Inner City*, Philadelphia: University of Pennsylvania Press.

Labov, William (1972d) 'The social motivation of a sound change', in *Sociolinguistic Patterns*, Oxford: Blackwell.

Labov, William (1994) *Principles of Linguistic Change*, Oxford: Blackwell.

Lakoff, Robin (1975) *Language and Woman's Place*, New York: Harper & Row.

Lawrence, D.H. ([1928] 1961) *Lady Chatterley's Lover*, Harmondsworth: Penguin.

Lee, David (1992) *Competing Discourses: Perspective and Ideology in Language*, London: Longman.

Leith, Dick (1992) *A Social History of English*, 2nd edn, London: Routledge.

Lippi-Green, Rosina (1997) *English with an Accent: language, ideology and discrimination in the United States*, London: Routledge.

Livingstone, Peter and Lunt, Sonia (1994) *Talk on Television: Audience Participation and Public Debate*, London: Routledge.

Lucy, J.A. (1992) *Language Diversity and Thought: A Reformulation of the Linguistic Relativity Hypothesis*, Cambridge: Cambridge University Press.

Mackinnon, Donald (1996) 'Good and bad English', in David Graddol, Dick Leith and Joan Swann (eds) *English: history diversity and change*, London: Routledge.

Maxim, J. and Bryan, K. (1994) *Language of the Elderly*, London: Whurr.

Mills, Sara (1995) *Feminist Stylistics*, London: Routledge.

Milroy, James and Milroy, Lesley (1985) *Authority in Language: investigating language prescription and standardisation*, London: Routledge & Kegan Paul.

Milroy, James and Milroy, Lesley (eds) (1993) *Real English: the grammar of English dialects in the British Isles*, London: Longman.

Milroy, James and Milroy, Lesley (1998) 'Mechanisms of change in urban dialects: the role of class, social network and gender', in Peter Trudgill and Jenny Cheshire (eds) *The Sociolinguistics Reader*, Vol. 1, London: Arnold.

Milroy, Lesley (1987) *Language and Social Networks*, 2nd edn, Oxford: Blackwell.

Montgomery, Martin (1996) *An Introduction to Language and Society*, 2nd edn, London: Routledge.

Moore, Stephen and Hendry, Barry (1982) *Sociology*, Sevenoaks: Hodder & Stoughton.

Moores, Shaun (1993) *Interpreting Audiences: the Ethnography of Media Consumption*, London: Sage.

Morley, David (1980) *The 'Nationwide' Audience*, London: British Film Institute.

Morley, David (1992) *Television, Audiences and Cultural Studies*, London: Routledge.

Mugglestone, Lynda (1995) *Talking Proper: the rise of accent as social symbol*, Oxford: Clarendon Press.

Mühlhäusler, Peter and Harré, Rom (1990) *Pronouns and People: the Linguistic Construction of Social and Personal Identity*, Oxford: Blackwell.

Naipaul, S. (1976) *The Adventures of Gurdeva and other Stories*, London: André Deutsch.

Nkweto Simmonds, Felly (1998) 'Naming and identity', in Deborah Cameron (ed.) *The Feminist Critique of Language*, 2nd edn, London: Routledge.

Ochs, E. (1991) 'Misunderstanding Children', in N. Coupland, H. Giles and J. Wiemann (eds) *Miscommunication and Problematic Talk*, London: Sage.

Ochs, Elinor (1993) 'Constructing social identity: a language socialisation perspective', *Research on Language and Social Interaction*, 26(3): 287–306.

Orwell, George ([1946] 1962) 'Politics and the English Language', in *Inside the Whale and Other Essays*, Harmondsworth: Penguin.

Orwell, George ([1949] 1984) *Nineteen Eighty-Four*, London: Secker & Warburg.

Parmar, Pratiba (1982) 'Gender, race and class: Asian women in resistance', in Centre for Contemporary Cultural Studies, *The Empire Strikes Back*, London: Hutchinson.

Quirk, Randolph and Stein, Gabriel (1990) *Language in Use*, London: Longman.

Rampton, Ben (1995) *Crossing: Language and Ethnicity among Adolescents*, Harlow: Longman.

Richardson, Kay and Corner, John (1986) 'Reading reception: mediation and transparency in viewers' accounts of a TV programme', *Media, Culture and Society* 8: 485–508.

Sacks, Harvey (1995) *Lectures on Conversation*, Oxford: Blackwell.

Scannell, Paddy (1988) 'The communicative ethos of broadcasting'. Paper presented to the *International Television Studies Conference*, July 1988.

Shuy, Roger, Wolfram, Walt and Riley, William (1968) *Field Techniques in an Urban Language Study*, Washington DC: Centre for Applied Linguistics.

Simpson, Paul (1993) *Language, Ideology and Point of View*, London: Routledge.

Spender, Dale (1980) 'Talking in class', in Dale Spender and Elizabeth Sarah (eds) *Learning to Lose*, London: Women's Press.

Spender Dale ([1980] 1990) *Man Made Language*, London: Pandora.

Stubbe, Maria and Holmes, Janet (1995) '*You know, eh* and other "exasperating expressions": an analysis of social and stylistic variation in the use of pragmatic devices in a sample of New Zealand English', *Language and Communication*, 15(1): 63–88.

Stubbs, Michael (ed.) (1985) *The Other Languages of England*, London: Linguistic Minorities Project.

Swann, Joan (1989) 'Talk control: an illustration from the classroom of problems in analysing male dominance in education', in Jennifer Coates and Deborah Cameron (eds) *Women in their Speech Communities*, Longman: London.

Swift, J. ([1726] 1994) *Gulliver's Travels*, Harmondsworth: Penguin.

Tannen, Deborah (1990) 'Gender differences in topical coherence: creating involvement in best friends' talk', in Bruce Dorval (ed.) *Conversational Organisation and its Development*, Norwood, NJ: Ablex.

Tannen, Deborah (1991) *You Just Don't Understand: Women and Men in Conversation*, Virago: London.

Thomas, Beth (1988) 'Differences of sex and sects: linguistic variation and social networks in a Welsh mining village', in Jennifer Coates and Deborah Cameron (eds) *Women in their Speech Communities*, London: Longman.

Thomas, Linda (1996) 'Variation in English grammar', in David Graddol, Dick Leith and Joan Swann (eds) *English: history, diversity and change*, London: Routledge.

Thornborrow, Joanna (1997) 'Having their say: the function of stories in talk show discourse', *TEXT* 17(2): 241–62.

Thornborrow, Joanna and Wareing, Shân (1998) *Patterns in Language: An Introduction to Language and Literary Style*, London: Routledge.

Thorsheim, H. and Roberts, B. (1990) 'Empowerment through story-sharing: communication and reciprocal social support among older persons' in H. Giles, N. Coupland and J. Wieman (eds), *Communication, Health and the Elderly*, Manchester: Manchester University Press.

The Times (1992) *The Times English Style and Usage Guide*, London: Times Newspapers.

Tout, K. (ed.) (1993) *Elderly Care: A World Perspective*, London: Chapman & Hall.

Trudgill, Peter (1972) 'Sex, covert prestige and linguistic change in the urban British English of Norwich', *Language in Society* 1, 179–95.

Trudgill, Peter (1974) *The Social Differentiation of English in Norwich*, Cambridge: Cambridge University Press.

Trudgill, Peter (1983a) *Sociolinguistics: An Introduction to Language and Society*, Harmondsworth: Penguin.

Trudgill, Peter (1983b) 'Acts of conflicting identity: the sociolinguistics of British pop-song pronunciation', in *On Dialect: Social and Geographical Perspectives*, Oxford: Blackwell.

Trudgill, Peter (1990) *The Dialects of England*, Oxford: Blackwell.

Trudgill, Peter and Chambers, J. K. (eds) (1991) *Dialects of English: studies in grammatical variation*, London: Longman.

Trudgill, Peter and Hannah, Jean (1994) *International English: a guide to the varieties of standard English*, 3rd edn, London: Edward Arnold.

Turner, G. (1973) *Stylistics*, Harmondsworth: Penguin.

van Dijk, Teun A. (1987) *Communicating Racism: Ethnic Prejudice in Talk and Thought*, London: Sage.

van Dijk, Teun A. (1991) *Racism and the Press*, London: Routledge.

van Dijk, Teun A. (1993) *Elite Discourse and Racism*, London: Sage.

Wardhaugh, Ronald (1992) *An Introduction to Sociolinguistics*, 2nd edition, Oxford: Blackwell.

Watts, D. (1987) *The West Indies: patterns of development, culture and environmental change since 1492*, Cambridge: Cambridge University Press.

Whorf, B.L. (1939) 'The Relation of Habitual Thought and Behaviour to Language', in J. B. Carroll, (1956) (ed.) *Language Thought and Reality*, Massachusetts: MIT Press.

Wolfram, Walt and Schilling-Estes, Natalie (1998) *American English*, Oxford: Blackwell.

Zimmerman, Dan and West, Candace (1975) 'Sex roles, interruptions and silences in conversation', in Barrie Thorne, Cheris Kramerae and Nancy Henley (eds) *Language and Sex: Difference and Dominance*, Rowley, Massachusetts: Newbury House.

Index

205